THE TOLLS OF UNCERTAINTY

The Tolls of Uncertainty

HOW PRIVILEGE AND THE GUILT GAP SHAPE UNEMPLOYMENT IN AMERICA

SARAH DAMASKE

PRINCETON UNIVERSITY PRESS

PRINCETON & OXFORD

Published by Princeton University Press
41 William Street, Princeton, New Jersey 08540
6 Oxford Street, Woodstock, Oxfordshire OX20 1TR

press.princeton.edu

Library of Congress Cataloging-in-Publication Data

Names: Damaske, Sarah, author.
Title: The tolls of uncertainty : how privilege and the guilt gap shape
    unemployment in America / Sarah Damaske.
Description: Princeton : Princeton University Press, [2021] |
    Includes bibliographical references and index.
Identifiers: LCCN 2020046926 (print) | LCCN 2020046927 (ebook) |
    ISBN 9780691200149 (hardback) | ISBN 9780691219318 (e-book)
Subjects: LCSH: Unemployment—United States. | Discrimination in
    employment—United States. | Unemployed—Mental health—United States.
Classification: LCC HD5724 .D323 2021 (print) | LCC HD5724 (ebook) |
    DDC 331.13/70973—dc23
LC record available at https://lccn.loc.gov/2020046926
LC ebook record available at https://lccn.loc.gov/2020046927

British Library Cataloging-in-Publication Data is available

Editorial: Meagan Levinson, Jacqueline Delaney
Production Editorial: Elizabeth Byrd
Jacket Design: Karl Spurzem
Production: Erin Suydam
Publicity: Maria Whelan, Kathryn Stevens

Jacket image by Aleksandr Davydov / Alamy Stock Photo

This book has been composed in Arno

Printed on acid-free paper. ∞

Printed in the United States of America

10 9 8 7 6 5 4 3 2 1

For Stephen Knapp, who taught me "The Definition of Possible,"
and
to Paul Damaske, who still makes me mix tapes

CONTENTS

PREFACE

MY FIRST semester of college was my introduction to Dorothea Lange's photographs of the unemployed and their families during the Great Depression. In many ways, I could not have been further removed from the people in her photographs, sitting, as I was, in a small class of twenty students in an old stone building on a picturesque campus set on top of a hill. In this class, an introduction to the liberal arts, we listened to Mozart, read about Lincoln at Gettysburg, considered philosophical debates about knowledge, and examined a book of Dorothea Lange's photographs.[1] The contrast felt stark to me as we sat in those elite halls, where I did not feel quite at home, examining her portraits of people living in poverty nearly a century before.

Lange is probably best known for a portrait called *Migrant Mother* that appeared in the book. In Lange's time, migrant referred to someone who had moved across the United States to find work and earn money; it was not an immigrant from another country, as we might think today. A woman with furrowed brow, lines etched into the corners around her mouth and eyes, has one hand cupping her face, as if she were about to rest her chin on it; her eyes look bleakly out into the distance. She has a baby in her arms and a child on either side, snuggled into her. We cannot see their faces, only the dirt and grime that cover their clothes. Lange's notes on the photographs of the mother and her children explain that the family is destitute and living in a squatter's camp, having sold their car tires to pay for food that morning.

Lange understood the power of her photographs. She wanted her work to effect change, particularly after her marriage to social scientist Paul Taylor, who shared her passion for documenting American society and for bringing attention to those without a voice. I did not need to read about their shared commitment to social change in the historical essays to have known this as her truth; it is vividly evident in her work.

Other photographs moved me. The picture of the men lined up at the "White Angel Breadline" in San Francisco, tightly crowded next to one another, waiting for someone to dole out the desperately needed food. Yet one man had turned away, his hat falling forward to cover his eyes and his hands clasped, perhaps in prayer, as he leaned against a wooden fence. The photograph, "A Sign of the Times," depicts a woman's legs below the knees with tired-looking shoes and nylons worn beyond repair. The nylons have tears that have been mended, but they also have newer rips that have not been fixed.

I yearned to better understand the experiences of precarity faced by so many not so long ago. I was also moved by Lange's call for social justice. Her call has guided my research interests in college, graduate school, and today. After I graduated, I set the book aside while I moved to first Boston, then New York, then Houston, then central Pennsylvania, working for a time and then earning first my master's, then my doctorate, and holding first a postdoctoral fellowship and then finally a position on the faculty at Penn State. Yet Lange's images always stayed with me. And I still have the book, nearly twenty-five years after I first sat with it in that class in a college on a hill.

When writing my first book, *For the Family? How Class and Gender Shape Women's Work*, I discovered a pattern of women's employment that had previously been ignored—a pattern that involved women's repeated experience of unemployment—and I knew it was time to rediscover Lange's photographs. After that book's publication, I began the research that would comprise this one, and I examined the photograph of the Migrant Mother again. This time, I saw that picture with new eyes, wondering who the mother was, who all of the unemployed were, what had brought them to that place, and what happened next. While I could not ask those questions of Lange's subjects, I could ask them of the people I set out to meet for this project.

By the time this book is published, I will have spent nearly ten years researching and writing on this topic, in addition to the time I spent studying unemployed women for my first book. I have done so almost a century after Lange started her photographic career and about eighty years after her Farm Security Administration photographs were completed. In the passing years, a lot has changed about unemployment. Yet Lange's work still calls out to us from across time. She reminds us that we have an obligation to look and to see the unemployed and to take up her call to action.

THE TOLLS OF UNCERTAINTY

Introduction

NEARLY A HUNDRED years after the Great Depression, I set out to meet people who had recently lost their jobs. One of the people I met was Tracy. In the small rural town in Pennsylvania where Tracy grew up and lives today, jobs have been steadily leaving since before she was born.[1] The first time her dad lost his job was before she could walk; the second was when her youngest sister was born. The last big factory closed when she was in high school; her dad lost his job again then and was unemployed for over a year.

Although the town is surrounded by wide open spaces, the small row houses are tightly nestled against each other, as if huddled against the cold winters and tight times to come. Tracy's house was tidy but dimly lit. We sat in the kitchen, which was the warmest room, thanks to the pilot light in the oven. Unlike the other sparer rooms, the kitchen had stockpiles of canned foods, dried goods, and snacks found on sale before Tracy lost her job. A longtime "hoarder" of preserved food products, Tracy had raided her pantry in recent weeks. There hadn't been money for fresh food in months, and Tracy worried about the weight she was gaining from eating junk food.

A hundred miles away, Neil grew up in wealthy suburbs largely protected from the job losses that shaped Tracy's youth. Neil's dad was the general manager of a Pennsylvania steel production company, and although this industry was not known for job stability, the company had a specialized niche and Neil's father had great job security. The public high school Neil attended had over a dozen advanced placement classes, elite athletics programs, and during the 1990s and 2000s received both state and national awards for its educational programs.

Neil didn't live in the house he grew up in but in a relatively new and spacious two-story house that he and his wife had bought a couple of years before our meeting. Neil's most recent job had brought them to the area, and he was excited for "change and for something smaller and quieter." Their house sat on three acres of land, but it was an easy commute to their professional jobs in the small city nearby. Yet Neil's job had ended abruptly, and life in their new town wasn't going as Neil had hoped. His wife had made great friends at her new job, but Neil spent too much time working to get to know anyone well. His job loss, they hoped, might give him a fresh start; Neil and his wife had bought bikes and were starting Saturday bike rides together now that he had more time on his hands.

Anthony grew up in a family that was not as poor as Tracy's, but he did not have the financial security of Neil's childhood. Even though they didn't have a lot of money, Anthony's family seemed a lot like the "Leave It to Beaver" ideal: working father, stay-at-home mother, two kids. At least, they did at first glance. Like Neil's dad, Anthony's father never experienced job loss. For over thirty years, he worked as a computer service technician for the same company in a college town. But Anthony's mother had lost her job when he was still in day care because "she was a mom." Anthony's father felt that Anthony's mom should have welcomed the chance to be back at home taking care of him and his siblings. But his mom missed working and felt that she'd been pushed out of her job by men who believed women belonged at home. So, in spite of the traditional family veneer, there was a lot of unhappiness at home. Looking back, Anthony remembers his mother's desire to go back to work unfavorably. "I hold a little resentment toward my mom," he said.

Now older than his parents when his mother lost her job, Anthony married six years ago, just after his wife and her two children (whom Anthony considers his own) moved into his house. Anthony's sporadic work history, coupled with the house's temperamental appliances and old age, made their home challenging to maintain at times, although his wife diligently worked at it, cleaning the old wood floors routinely with water and vinegar. The battle to save the dishwasher had been lost before I met them, and they had reluctantly sent it to salvage and taken to doing the dishes by hand. After Anthony lost his most recent job, hand-washing the dishes was even more necessary during the brief period they spent without electricity because of unpaid bills.

Growing up in a different part of that same college town that Anthony grew up in—the part of town with cookie-cutter two-story houses with white picket fences—Joan remembered quite a bit of instability during her elementary school years. Her dad, a PhD who worked in the mining industry, lost his job when she was quite young, and there were several bumpy years as he searched for work and ultimately started his own business. The college town was big enough to support this new venture; the family weathered the tough times with help from her grandparents, and eventually his business took off. By the time Joan went to high school, her family was prosperous; even so, her mom found a part-time job as an administrative assistant. Joan was an excellent student in high school, and she longed to follow her dad into the sciences.

The day I met Joan, the sun shone brightly down, cheering up an otherwise cold winter day. Her home—a white ranch with neat exterior landscaping and a combination of tidiness and toddler whirlwind on the inside—seemed warm and cozy, located not so far from where she grew up. Her husband's family lived within easy driving distance, making it possible to see them often on weekends. Since her job loss, Joan noted that the family budget felt "tight," but they had not made any changes to their purchasing habits, although she was now regularly cutting coupons for cleaning and household supplies, buying "cheaper bulk items," and stocking up when toilet paper was "incredibly cheap."

In the weeks before I met them, Tracy, Neil, Anthony, and Joan all experienced job losses that sent them to the unemployment line. But what would this job loss and their subsequent unemployment mean to them and their families? Tracy lived in a community that had been wracked by devastating job losses for decades—what kinds of jobs were left to lose or to find in her small hometown? Like father, like son for

Neil and Anthony, as Neil had become a manager and Anthony had followed his dad into electronic repairs, but both had done so during changing economic times. Joan, too, had followed in her father's footsteps, although she stopped at a master's degree rather than a PhD, becoming a scientist in someone else's lab rather than the one running it. How would their occupational choices shape the tolls that unemployment would bring? And what about the story of Anthony's mom; nearly thirty years later, would the women—like Joan and Tracy—face different challenges at home and searching for work than the men?

Dorothea Lange's indelible photographs of unemployment and the Great Depression remain vivid in our collective memory. Her portraits show down-and-out men waiting in breadlines and the desperation of families living through the trauma of being unemployed, unsupported by the government, and unable to find work. Though evocative, these pictures don't look much like today's unemployed, as represented by Tracy, Neil, Anthony, and Joan. Instead of male laborers or women in relief camps, today we see men *and* women in equal numbers, blue-collar workers *and* high-flying executives, high school graduates *alongside* those with college degrees. A truth about unemployment is the anxiety and disquiet that Lange captioned the "Toll of Uncertainty." To understand the many tolls of unemployment today, I will examine how Tracy, Neil, Joan, and Anthony, and people like them, lost jobs and experienced unemployment and how that affected them, their families, and their search for future work. As we learn their stories and those of others, we will see that the tolls of unemployment are both more numerous than we previously imagined and not evenly shared by the unemployed.

———

I became consumed with the need to know more about how men and women, whether college graduates or high school dropouts, experienced unemployment while researching my first book, *For the Family? How Class and Gender Shape Women's Work*.[2] For that project, I investigated how women make decisions about whether to work or stay at home. In the course of my research, I discovered something earlier research had overlooked. Most research on women had asked why women chose to work or not work. But I found a third group, a small group of women whose multiple job losses moved them involuntarily from paid work to home. These unexpected transitions took their "choice" of paid work or staying at home away from them. I called this group the "interrupted" workers. After I finished that book project, I wanted to know more about women who lost jobs and how they compared to men. But as I looked at the existing research, I discovered very little had been written comparing men's and women's experiences with job loss and unemployment, and almost nothing compared these experiences across class.[3]

In order to learn more, I needed to talk to men and women, from the middle and working classes, who were unemployed. From 2013 to 2015, fifty-one men and forty-nine women who had lost a full-time job and received unemployment from the state of Pennsylvania sat down and spoke with me and my research team.[4] I wanted to learn about diversity in unemployment experiences, so I recruited people from a range of areas including a midsize rust-belt city, small cities (one with low unemployment rates and one with high unemployment rates), and rural areas, including some high-poverty areas in the upper regions of Appalachia. Even though my team and I remained in one state, we encountered a wide range of labor market experiences.

Because men and women typically have very different work and family responsibilities, I wanted to interview people who would be in the thick of forming families, making decisions about childcare, career building, and possibly changing occupations, so I only talked to people between the ages of 28 and 52. Most people my team and I interviewed had either a spouse or a partner, although twenty were single, about half of whom were single moms, like Tracy, and a few single dads. The vast majority of people we talked to had kids who relied on their income, which meant the whole family took a hit when they lost their job, but sixteen of the interviewees didn't have kids, like Neil.[5]

Just over half were "working class," meaning they held jobs for which they didn't need a college degree, while the "middle class" held professional jobs requiring college degrees.[6] The men and women had been unemployed, on average, eleven weeks when we met.[7]

One of the drawbacks of interviewing people in the places where I did is that the sample was whiter than it would be in many parts of the United States. Eighty-nine people were white, seven were Black, three were Latino, and one was Asian. But that does not mean that race isn't an important part of this story. It is. Neil, Joan, Anthony, and Tracy all experienced a buffer from the worst of the labor market simply because of their race; they were white. There is a substantial body of academic work that finds race plays a fundamental role in organizing most areas of life, including an outsize role in unemployment, even as whites remain largely unaware of the advantage of their race.[8] These advantages come in many forms that have important implications for how job loss and unemployment play out in this book. For one, none of the whites experienced racial discrimination (although few realized their privilege in the absence of such constraint). Even among my small sample of people of color, Black and Latina participants experienced discrimination at work; a few were fired because of their race (some even won complaints against their employers). Nationally, there is evidence Black and Latino people face discriminatory firings at work.[9] Moreover, when companies have to downsize middle management, people of color are fired first.[10] Some of the middle-class white men I met benefited from such policies when their companies downsized, and they were among the last to be let go; some white women were also among the last to be fired. As we'll see, this allowed white middle-class men to feel differently about their job losses. White Americans are also more likely to own their own homes, which gives them greater financial stability than Black Americans have, something historians, economists, and sociologists agree is attributable to the lasting legacy of racial discrimination, redlining practices, and differential lending practices in the United States.[11] In practice, this meant that Tracy and her kids owned the roof over their heads (the house was her parents' before it was hers), while a Black single mom I met, Samantha, rented and faced greater precarity as a result. Finally, racial advantages also play out in hiring networks, as whites tend to have a broader range of social networks to help them find work after they've lost a job (in fact, as we'll see, networks would come to the rescue of Joan's and Anthony's job searches, and Neil used his networks, too).[12] Black job seekers are less likely to have the same access to networks and, among the Black poor, may be less willing to use them.[13]

I had many questions to ask Tracy, Neil, and the others I met, and I did my best to let people answer questions in their own way, asking for details when they gave unclear responses or inviting them to provide examples when their first response was either brief or vague. The stories the unemployed told were often tough to hear. There were many stories of hunger, of heat being turned off in the winter, and even of homelessness. Some people, like Tracy, cried. Sometimes, when I got home, I did, too.

From 2015 to 2016, my research team contacted respondents to see where people stood about a year after we first met. We couldn't reach about a third of the original participants—mail was returned to sender and phone numbers were out of service. Some e-mails bounced back with a message reading "mailbox full." It's hard to say what happened to those we could not contact, but it seems likely many had to relocate. The working-class men were hardest to reconnect with for a follow-up interview. One year later, the majority of those I met had fallen far behind where they had been before they lost their jobs, a small few were almost back to maintaining their previous lives, and some, particularly the white middle-class men, had managed to move ahead.

———

Job loss and unemployment both reproduce existing inequalities and generate new inequalities during the time people spend unemployed, meaning that those who had more before their job loss had a greater buffer from the strains of unemployment and that some of these preexisting differences become greater over the unemployment period because of the way unemployment is experienced. Men and women did not go through the same experiences. Neither did the middle class and the working class. Neither did their families. Nearly thirty years after Anthony's mother lost her job (a time period that included the rapid expansion of women's employment as well as large cultural shifts in our national understanding of women's opportunities at work and at home), I met women whose families told them that they should be pleased to have lost a job. One working-class woman told me her husband was happy about her job loss, explaining, "Now I could stay at home and he made a huge garden for me to have to work on, so that's what I'm supposed to do." Yet she wanted to return to work, not tend a garden.

For their part, not all men wanted to rush back to work, particularly not the middle-class men. Some, like Neil, were excited by the idea of some time off. As Neil told me, "I've been enjoying the past few weeks of not having much responsibility because it's been 25 years of more than most normal people would work, and the stresses. So, I'm like gosh, darn, it's my time." He relished the time spent not working because he had felt burdened by the years of overwork.

There were many ways in which the men and women, the college and high school educated, I talked to differed in their experiences. The following pages reveal the myriad ways in which job loss and unemployment shape both the American work experience and American lives outside of work.

Unemployment is an institution—like workplaces, families, or schools— that both generates and reproduces inequalities. Let's consider, first, what scholars mean when they say something is an institution. If unemployment is an institution, it would suggest that it is like other fundamental parts of American society that are central to adult life, that are governed by state and federal laws and bureaucracies, that are hierarchical and shaped by the resources that the unemployed bring to the experience, that provide resources and serve as resource brokers to other institutions, and that have far-reaching consequences for outside realms.[14] Let's consider these points in turn: First, unemployment plays an outsize (and not well understood) role in adult life. Although the unemployment rate has averaged around 6 percent annually for the past thirty years (with large swings during recessionary periods), this relatively low number conceals that evidence suggests between 65 to 70 percent of Americans will experience at least one bout of unemployment, and some will experience many more.[15] Second, as we will learn over the course of the book, both the state and the federal government wield enormous influence over the process, from determining whether people are considered unemployed or eligible for unemployment insurance to how much support they will receive and for how long. Third, as we will see, the way people access the unemployment system is dependent on their own social location (e.g., their class privilege, their gender, their race) prior to coming into the unemployment system, and their experience throughout their unemployment journey is shaped by the resources the unemployed have available when they lose their jobs. Fourth, the state unemployment system provides both direct benefits (via unemployment insurance) and acts as a broker to additional resources (through career center services). Finally, like other institutions, we know from prior research that unemployment shapes not just the time a person may spend out of work, but many areas of life, and it does so over a long period of time, having what is known as a "scarring effect." Just one unemployment spell diminishes a person's future job prospects, lowers future wages, hurts families, decreases satisfaction with life, and even harms health.[16] Over the course of the book, we will learn how fundamental—even all-consuming—the unemployment period is for a person's life. We will see how the rules of the unemployment system and the resources that people bring to the table shape their experience of unemployment, and how unemployment does not only shape their next job and their finances, but also extends to their household chores and childcare tasks and even their health with consequences that reverberate far beyond these spheres.

Unemployment not only generates and reproduces inequalities between the employed and the unemployed, but also among the unemployed. Now, let's consider how unemployment generates and reproduces inequality. As I describe above, prior research has documented that unemployment has effects in areas of life—health and family, for instance—well outside the world of work, thus generating inequality. We also know that some people are more at risk of experiencing unemployment—people of color, people with a high school education or less, immigrants—thus reproducing inequality. But what about inequality *among the unemployed*? In this book, I look only at those who have lost jobs and are unemployed and find vast inequalities emerge among them. I further find that these inequalities widen over the period of unemployment and expand beyond the world of work, as a difference in one realm bleeds into and then becomes magnified in another. We will see how differences in the path one takes to a job loss shape the job loss experience itself, which shapes access to severances, which shapes differences in financial stability that further shape both decisions about health and decisions about searching for work. In this way, unemployment does not simply distinguish those who lose jobs and must search for work from those who don't, but also generates new differences among those who lose jobs, creating winners and losers among the unemployed.

There was a clear "guilt gap" between men and women. Scholars have long emphasized the particularly bad impact unemployment has on men.[17] Our culture holds that a man who cannot provide for his family is a failure—less than a man.[18] Yet the women I spoke with took on greater levels of self-blame for their job loss than the men did. They felt they owed their families an apology for their job loss. Women gave this apology in two primary ways. First, many women literally sacrificed their health. After losing health insurance, they acquired it for spouses or children but not themselves. They stopped taking their medicines, going to their doctors, or taking care of themselves in the ways they knew they should. Women also apologized at home by doing more of the daily household and childcare chores. While both men and women increased these tasks when they became unemployed, women were much more likely to take on all of the chores—many women said they felt too guilty not to. Most men reported no such guilt.

Men and women even looked for work in different ways, and these gender differences were further cross-cut by class. I was surprised by Neil's slow start in searching for a job, but in fact many middle-class men decided to take some time off before they started searching in earnest. In contrast, most of the middle-class women were like Joan, who started looking for work right away. These searches were careful and deliberate, with clear goals and timetables; many of the women even clocked in and out as if they were still at work. Working-class men like Anthony also started looking right away, but their searches were desperate scrambles to find any job they could, regardless of whether the work was similar to what they had done before. Tracy, and many other working-class women like her, found themselves unable to search for work. In fact, at the very start of the unemployment period, they were immediately bogged down by the challenges of daily poverty or by family pressures to increase their work in the home, diverting their job searches before they could begin.

Finally, middle-class men had advantages that cumulated during their time spent unemployed that were less available to everyone else and left the men advantaged in their job search. The middle-class men started the process in a better financial position, as they were much more likely to receive a severance package. They then received a higher unemployment insurance benefit due to higher wages at their previous jobs (wages that typically meant they had more money set aside in savings to help stem the tide). They were more likely to retain access to good health insurance and more likely to feel entitled to use it and were more successful at deflecting demands that they do household work. Their resources allowed them to enjoy the period of unemployment as a respite and to avoid their legal obligation to search for work by working the system to buy time. They also had the security of knowing that there were good jobs to return to—something that was not readily available for many of the middle-class women or the working-class participants in the study. Being white also gave Neil and other middle-class white men like him advantages in the labor market—perhaps even advantages that they would not recognize but that labor scholars have documented give white middle-class men a step up in the world of work.[19] Lauren Rivera's research on law firms, banks, and the consulting industry demonstrates that a preference for "fit," to hire people who are like them, gives white men a significant advantage in accessing elite professions.[20] Social networks, an important source for finding a job, were often key to the success of white middle-class men's job searches, yet prior research has shown that men and women of color do not have this same access to job-seeking networks.[21] Despite all of the ways that their privilege shaped their unemployment experience, most middle-class men remained unaware of their advantages.[22]

This book is about unemployment, but it's also about American workplaces, American families, and American values. In the pages that follow, I will explore how we came to have the unemployment system that we do, who it helps, who it hurts, and what, if anything, we can do about it. This book is set in America's heartland just before an election that rocked the nation, and we will see many of the divides that have since become so familiar to us surfacing in these people's stories. We will follow Tracy and Neil, Anthony and Joan, and dozens of others through their struggles and their triumphs, see many fall behind while a small few rise. And I will suggest we must take a new way forward in order to reduce the inequalities that are maintained and created by our unemployment system.

PART I

Losing a Job

1

Job Loss in the Twenty-First Century

WHEN I STARTED work on this project in 2012, the Great Recession was only recently in our rearview mirror, and I had no idea that the decade that lay ahead would be one of unprecedented economic growth. The stock market recorded Wall Street's longest-ever winning streak on Wednesday, August 22, 2018.[1] By December 2019, the unemployment rate was down to 3.5 percent, a level not seen in decades.[2] But it was also a decade in which, even as corporate profits boomed, millions of Americans lost their jobs, struggled with long-term unemployment, worked part-time because they couldn't find full-time work, and gave up searching for work.[3] Now, as I sit down to revise the final draft of this book, at the start of a new decade, we have entered into the midst of the worst economic crisis since the Great Depression.

What, then, does losing a job during good economic times have to teach us about unemployment at any time? As it turns out, quite a lot, because even during good economic times, our support systems were inadequate and the tolls of job loss and unemployment were both numerous and unequally shared. We need, now more than ever, to understand how our unemployment system shaped these experiences if we are to respond to the challenges that lie ahead.

Despite the large-scale closures during the Great Recession at the end of the first decade and the coronavirus pandemic at the start of the third decade, job loss during much of the twenty-first century looked different than it had in America in past generations. During Ronald Reagan's presidency, job losses were glaring and made the national news. They were sudden large-scale events that seemed like natural disasters— auto factories closed down, telecommunications giants merged, jobs went overseas. Today, layoffs have been built into most companies' everyday practices.[4] Instead of mass layoffs, we see smaller layoffs that respond to bad quarterly or annual reports rather than sustained downturns in the economy. Although recessions garner the most media coverage of job loss and unemployment, companies don't wait for bad economic times to cut jobs or restructure their workforce. Instead, it has become commonplace to lay off portions of the workforce when the company needs to produce a short-term profit report.[5] While recessions can cause a flood of layoffs, they are not needed for job loss to happen. In 2014 to 2016, when these interviews took place, job cuts were simply part of doing business in Pennsylvania.

―――――

By 2014, Tracy had become a single mom of two kids and had worked at the same local restaurant waitressing for most of her life. She enjoyed the work more than the job she'd had at a local deli back in high school or the one she'd had after that as a cashier at a local market; she was sociable and liked chatting with customers. She laughed easily when we met, and I could see how she would have charmed both the locals in her small town and the truck drivers grabbing a bite as they passed through. Although Tracy had worked at the restaurant a long time and earned seniority there, management had cut her hours, which made it tough to support her family. In town, there had been many layoffs, and lately the truckers had also had lean years. It was a tough time to work at a job so dependent on the generosity of others. As a tipped wage worker, Tracy was paid a starting hourly wage below the federal minimum, and while management was legally obligated to match the difference if the tips didn't, no one was around to enforce that law. Tracy had left her kids' father because he was abusive, her dad had been ill and died shortly before we met, and her mom was barely getting by, so Tracy didn't have anyone to rely on other than herself. But Tracy had expected to work when she was growing up and "always knew I had to take care of myself and my kids."

When a manufacturing company came to town promising stable hours and an increase in pay, Tracy decided to make the change. She didn't love her new job cutting speaker wires on the factory line. It was mundane, and the sociable Tracy found it boring to be doing "the same thing all day, every day." She did appreciate the regular nine-to-five hours and Monday-to-Friday schedule. She also liked the money. She made $8.25 at the factory; she was thirty-seven years old, and it was the highest wage she'd ever earned—a full dollar higher than Pennsylvania's state minimum wage.

She worked for seven months before the company went through a layoff. Work had been busy when she started, but then "it slowed down, and I knew I was one of the new people. So, I kind of felt it coming but I was still shocked. And nobody wants to be told [they are fired]. It's one thing when you make that choice [to leave]." Tracy and ten others lost their jobs that day; she said she "cried like a baby." Her family experienced financial hardship almost immediately. While Tracy's kids were fed, she often went hungry because "we don't have food in the house like we used to." There wasn't enough money left for new school clothes, either; when I met her kids, their pants hung above their ankles, and their shirts stretched in the shoulders.

Tracy had done everything right; she seized a manageable opportunity to make life better for herself and her kids. For a short period, she seemed to have achieved the American dream, but less than a year later, she was much worse off than she'd been before she left the restaurant to work at the factory. She couldn't go back to the restaurant; they had already found another waitress. As we spoke for hours that day, Tracy cried yet again; what was she going to do?

As Tracy discovered, employees of some industries, like manufacturing, were at higher risk of unemployment than others. Neil also discovered that the hotel industry had more risk of unemployment than he had anticipated. Although he wanted to follow his father into management, he credits a family vacation to Canada during his late teens for his decision to go into hotel management. Sitting in the bar of an upscale hotel, he thought to himself, "Boy, this is the life." Neil earned his BA and then his MA degree in hotel management. He moved away from Pennsylvania for a while, living in states along the East Coast and in the South, where he met his wife. They eventually decided to return to Pennsylvania, where he worked for several years as the director of banquet services for a resort. Then the opportunity to become a general manager of a hotel in a small city opened up. A gregarious guy with a wide smile, Neil jumped at the opportunity—it would be a promotion with better hours (banquets meant weddings, which could run until 2 A.M. or later). While Neil and his wife couldn't have children, they were looking into fostering or adoption, and switching to a job with better hours might make them better candidates. His wife also worked full-time as a graphic designer. Married for over fifteen years, Neil spoke very fondly of his wife, often going off topic to tell stories of her volunteering work or her outdoorsy nature.

But Neil's new job proved difficult; the hotel had been in the red for several years, and he had been hired to help turn things around. During the year he worked there, Neil worked long hours and increased revenues, getting the hotel in better financial shape than his predecessor had. But about a year after he was hired, his boss invited him to lunch, bought an expensive bottle of wine, and told him the company was letting him go. Neil recalls, "It was frustrating because when you're let go, you kind of have this expectation that you've done something wrong." But Neil felt he wasn't to blame for the hotel's continued financial troubles; in fact, he thought they were headed in the right direction and that his bosses had hampered his ability to do more. Had some of the cost-saving measures he suggested been implemented, he thought, it could have moved the hotel out of the red.

When I asked if he felt the financial pinch of his job loss, he replied, "It's been two months." He further clarified that he certainly had not been out of work long enough to experience any financial repercussions. Neil had a spouse with a high income, no children, and he described a "nice unemployment" benefit from the state.

Instead, Neil was most concerned about his next career move. After two decades in the hotel industry, Neil was burned out by the long hours and bruised by the casual way he was tossed aside. Neil and his wife sat down and assessed his next steps; she suggested he take additional time off and look at the job loss as an opportunity to think about a new career. His job loss also coincided with the start of fly-fishing season, and Neil decided to take some time to enjoy his favorite hobby. While Neil's loss stung, it was a chance to try something new, and it was nothing like the devastation experienced by Tracy.

———

Social class matters a lot for how people experience their job loss. While the media often claim that everyone thinks they are middle class these days,[6] scholars argue that Americans have a much more nuanced understanding of how they compare to others.[7] In recent years, more Americans have come to identify themselves as working class instead of middle class; this is particularly true of Black Americans.[8]

Part of why Tracy and Neil experienced their job losses differently was that their different education levels gave them different levels of protection against the effects of job loss. At Penn State, where I am a professor, my students sometimes say that relatives have needled them about how college is a waste of money. I understand this accusation: colleges are expensive—too expensive, in my opinion. But a college degree remains one of the best buffers against the effects of job loss and unemployment. And the biggest gains from college go to those whose parents didn't attend college—in other words, you get the most from college if you are the first in your family to graduate.[9]

People with a college degree have many advantages over those without a degree. Overall, they are much less likely to lose a job when a recession hits—in the Great Recession, the college-educated were not immune from job losses, but their chances of losing their jobs were much lower than those who had only a high school degree.[10] People with college degrees also generally get better jobs, partly because of those degrees and partly because they meet people in college who can introduce them to people who can hire them. Researchers have found that people with college degrees are healthier and happier, too.[11]

Having a college degree even changes who you are likely to marry.[12] My mother's parents met at a cotillion for nurses and sailors during World War II. My grandmother earned her nursing degree through a war program designed to train more women as nurses. My grandfather did not have a high school diploma. After the war ended, they married, he went to work as a mechanic, and she stayed home and raised their two girls. It wasn't unusual back then for married couples to have different levels of education. Today, it is increasingly likely that people will marry those with similar education levels.[13] Take me and my husband, for example. We met in college, started dating at the end of our first year, finished college, got married, and now both have advanced degrees. Today, people are increasingly likely to marry people who are like them, increasing inequality in America, because it allows people to keep important resources for themselves (like access to education and to better jobs) and to pass those resources down to their children.[14]

The change between then and now in who we marry is important because people with college educations are likely to have spouses with good jobs that they are less likely to lose. Conversely, people with a high school education not only tend to marry people with fewer resources, but they are more likely to divorce or not marry at all.[15] Thus, there are a lot of resources—gaining a college degree, using that degree to get a good job, using that job to purchase a house in a good school district, using that good school district education to help your children go to a good college—that end up creating a pretty wide gap between people like Tracy and people like Neil.[16]

Tracy made a lot less money than Neil, and she also had fewer resources on which to draw after she lost her job—she wasn't married, and her extended family didn't have the resources to help her out. She was also raising two children on this smaller income. In contrast, Neil was married to someone who earned a stable middle-class income, and while they were hoping to adopt, they didn't have kids yet. As we will see in future chapters, when the consequences of the job loss started to play out in Neil's and Tracy's lives, there were buffers in place to protect Neil from some of the worst of it, but Tracy and her kids were relatively unprotected. I want to be clear: I don't mean we should root against Neil. I am glad he didn't face more hardship than he did, and he struggled as well. But it is important for us to think about why Tracy had it quite as hard as she did, and as we'll see, things got worse for Tracy before they got better.

Part of the reason behind Tracy's and Neil's differing unemployment experience is alluded to in Neil's earlier quote about his unemployment benefit, which he described as "nice." Tracy described her unemployment benefit quite differently; she said, "Honestly, it's not enough." To understand their different views of their unemployment benefits, we need to understand how unemployment insurance works in the United States. We have a somewhat complicated system because the federal government has guidelines, funds administrative costs, and oversees the programs, yet each state pays for and runs its own program. But most states have the same basic model. In the state of Pennsylvania, where everyone I met lived, eligibility for unemployment was based on some common rules (rules that are generally followed throughout the United States): domestic workers, farm workers, and the self-employed were excluded from coverage; workers had to have involuntarily lost the job through "no fault" of their own (in other words, they could not have quit or been fired for something like insulting their boss); workers had to have worked at least eighteen of the last fifty-two weeks (one-third of the year), and to have earned a minimum of $116 in each week worked. Arindrajit Dube, professor of economics at the University of Massachusetts-Amherst, estimates that these restrictions mean that nationally only 25 percent of the unemployed are eligible for unemployment insurance.[17]

Once individuals are determined eligible for unemployment, they apply for benefits from the state and are required to attend a meeting at the Pennsylvania CareerLink Center, the clearinghouse for job seekers. At this meeting, the unemployed do not actually learn about their benefits or how to maintain their eligibility. For that information, the state provides a twenty-page handbook with the rules of unemployment that the unemployed are supposed to read and review. During the course of my interviews, I learned many people had not read the handbook, or, if they had read it, they did not understand the rules.

I understood why participants didn't read the handbook; it is filled with technical language and graphs that somehow manage to make the rules even more confusing. Many people were overwhelmed when they lost their jobs and didn't have the energy to decipher the manual. Additionally, some had lost jobs before and thought they understood the rules (even though the rules are constantly changing). As a result, many of the people I met weren't sure how long they would receive unemployment, whether they could receive an extension, or even how much money they should be receiving. The unemployed did expect to receive unemployment benefits, but they were woefully uninformed about how their years of paying into the unemployment system would now yield benefits.

Instead of discussing rules or eligibility, the meeting at CareerLink focused on the nuts and bolts of finding a job. This was a tough task for the CareerLink staff, as they faced a group of people with a wide range of education and work experiences. Most sessions included people who had never lost a job before and were attending their first meeting; at the other end of the spectrum, some people knew the CareerLink staff so well they greeted them by name when they entered the room. It is nearly impossible to pitch an informational meeting for such a varied group, but the unemployed were surprisingly uncritical of the meetings and of the fairly low levels of help provided by the state. If the state helped with their search at all, they were grateful; almost no one had any expectation that meaningful assistance could or should be provided.

In fact, in addition to no guarantee of services, the minimum benefit for unemployment insurance can be as low as $5 a week—a weekly rate that is considerably less than both the minimum wage and the poverty line.[18] Tracy received $154 a week.[19] This left Tracy and her family well below the poverty line. Neil, on the other hand, received the maximum allowed: $572 a week. In Pennsylvania, as in many states, the weekly benefit amounts to roughly half of the individual's weekly earnings, up to the maximum; in some states, weekly benefits are set lower, at only one-third of weekly earnings.[20] Since Tracy and Neil had worked full-time for the prior two quarters, they were both eligible for twenty-six weeks of unemployment benefits. But there would be no possibility of an extension of unemployment for either of them—the temporary extensions that had served to keep many out of poverty during and following the Great Recession no longer existed, despite the fact that long-term unemployment remained a problem both nationally and in Pennsylvania.[21]

There are some additional requirements for those wishing to receive unemployment. In addition to attending the CareerLink meeting, the unemployed person must check in weekly with the unemployment service (this now can be done online rather than in person), the person must actively search for work during each week that they receive benefits, and, very crucially, if offered a job, they are obligated to take it under most circumstances.[22] These rules are important, as they guide many of the decisions we will see people take over the course of the book. And we will also see how people navigate them.

———

Joan's job loss loomed over her life for years before it actually happened. A scientist with a master's degree, Joan worked on a series of federally funded grants at a large research university, but she couldn't secure a permanent position within the university. She depended on other people to find grants to fund her job. Sometimes they found a grant and sometimes they couldn't, so she moved from team to team depending on where the funding was. This meant her office physically moved and sometimes she was even told that "we don't have any space in the building." Before her last year she was "shipped out" to a new office space that she and her new office mates called "the land of the misfit toys." She spent a dozen years working in this fairly unstable environment, watching as the federal money for the type of grants she worked on became harder and harder to get. Six months before her last day, her boss gave her the bad news that her job was going to end and that they weren't going to be able to find another extension or a different team for her.

She explained, "Well, that's when my acid reflux started. It started soon after that. I was depressed. Yeah. And I was scrambling [to find work], you know?" By the time we met, Joan had started treatments for both her stomach and the depression, and she was relaxed, wearing her shoulder-length brown hair loose and dressed in jeans and a T-shirt. She was preparing to pick up her preschool-aged son from childcare after our meeting. Her son had remained in day care despite her job loss, so she could continue to search for work and so he would not lose his coveted spot there.

Joan and her husband met in college and had been together almost twenty years. She referred to herself as a "trailing spouse"; when she and her husband first started dating, she said, "we made the decision early on that whoever got the solid job, we would follow that person. And so [my husband] had the solid job and so we stayed within [this area]." Even though Joan and her husband had similar levels of education and she had the higher income, they had decided to prioritize his job.[23] They never reconsidered that decision, despite Joan's difficulties securing a permanent position within the university. After Joan's grants finally dried up, it was unlikely another position would become available in the area (or even the state). There were, she knew, other departments in other universities with funded lines for her research area that could hire her. In fact, some had tried to recruit her to move out of state. But Joan and her husband never considered changing their commitment to prioritizing her husband's job. They might have been better off financially if they had moved to a new area where they could both find jobs similar to the ones they currently had; if they stayed put and she changed fields, she was unlikely to earn as much as she had at the university, and maintaining her income was important to their middle-class lifestyle. But the notion of moving was never even discussed, she told me, because they never revisited that long-ago decision to prioritize his work over hers.

Unlike Neil, Joan didn't see the change as a chance for something new; she loved her job so much that losing it literally made her sick to her stomach. Her acid reflux had been so bad at first that she found it difficult to eat many of her favorite foods. She also had difficulty sleeping at night. Like Neil, she had a spouse who worked full-time, so she didn't experience the financial worry that plagued Tracy. But Joan didn't want to take time to think about her options; she wanted to find a job as soon as possible. She explained, "I'm not a stay-at-home mom. It's not in me to do that. I need to be out contributing to society. I think that's just how I am."

Among some of those I met (mostly working-class men), job loss and unemployment had become such a part of their lives that they did not feel nearly as worried as Joan, even though they were in far more precarious circumstances. Anthony was someone far too familiar with job loss. He had tried college for a semester, but it didn't work out. He didn't like living so far from home, and he found his classes overwhelming. His parents had wanted him to try college even though neither of them had gone, but in the end, they were happy for him to be back home. His dad used his connections to find Anthony work as a computer technician in town. Over the years, Anthony worked in computer and electronic repairs for a diverse range of companies, which meant that he often learned skill sets on the fly. Once he "took the job" and was told, "Nobody really knows [how to do] this. It's something you're trained to do." Sometimes his job title was service technician, sometimes electronics repairman, and still other times he was called a computer technician. Anthony met and married his first wife during those early years and adopted her two children. That marriage didn't work out, but he remained close with his adopted children. His second long-term relationship also soured, but his third wife stuck, and Anthony adored her elementary-school-age children and considered them his own. I also met Anthony's wife and family during our interview.

I asked Anthony where he would like to meet, as I did with everyone I interviewed, suggesting that I could take him out for coffee or even lunch, if he would prefer not to meet at his home. Anthony had not eaten out in months, nor did he feel comfortable (I later learned) having me come to his home; they were keeping the heat down very low because of the cost, and he felt they would have little to offer me to eat. So, we met at a sandwich shop, and while we ate sandwiches and soup, he told me about his ten job losses.

I initially had taken Anthony to be in his early fifties, but I learned he was only forty-four. A life of uncertainty about where his next paycheck would come from had aged him. Anthony had worked in different jobs and was experienced in electronic, computer, and technical repair work. But every time he felt settled in a position, the company would downsize, or management would change, and he would be back looking for work again. Sometimes, Anthony found work quickly, but sometimes it took weeks or even months. After so many periods of unemployment, Anthony and his family had used up their savings, and they had mounting credit card debt that went unpaid.

When we met, Anthony had not worked for over six months. His last job was "the best pay I've [ever] had," and even better, he liked the work. But that seemed like the distant past now. Anthony's wife didn't work, they had two children in elementary school, and the job loss tipped them into poverty. His church helped out with food sometimes, so his family didn't miss meals, eating mostly tomato soup and grilled cheese sandwiches or ramen noodles.

Unlike Tracy, Anthony didn't cry when he lost his job—in fact, when his company let him go, he felt "pretty numb." It happened too frequently for him to feel much, he explained. Anthony and his wife talked about her looking for a job, but, he said, "it's tough to transition from raising the children and not having a job." So, they decided she would continue to stay home with the kids and Anthony would continue his search for work. Like Joan, Anthony was determined to find a job as soon as possible.

Neil and Joan, both middle class, and Anthony and Tracy, both working class, all had fairly different job loss experiences. While certain differences can be traced to class, some of these differences stem from how gender shapes someone's job-loss experience. Academics use the word *gender* to mean the differences between men and women that we think of as being natural but that are actually learned behaviors: for example, the way that women and men typically dress differently, wear their hair in distinct styles, or sit on a bus with their legs crossed or spread wide.[24] We also know that these physical ways we differentiate ourselves from each other are just the tip of the iceberg when it comes to how gender frames our everyday interactions.[25] Starting at a young age, often girls are given dolls to care for and boys receive tools and trucks; as we move into adulthood, these early learned differences are nurtured by our broader cultural ideas about how people differ by gender.[26] Girls and women learn that mothers are expected to be child focused (work is fine, but only if kids come first), but boys and men learn that fathers are expected to have external pursuits and that the best way of being a good dad is to earn a good living to provide for your family.[27] Now, not all men and women agree with these ideas—what the sociologists Cecilia Ridgeway and Shelley Correll call our shared gender beliefs—but even those who don't share these beliefs feel societal pressure to conform to them.[28] Thus, regardless of our own ideals, job loss and unemployment might be experienced quite differently depending on whether the broader social norms value our commitment to family or to work. Perhaps women may turn toward home or may feel shut out from work after a job loss in a culture where women's commitment to family is emphasized over their commitment to work. Or maybe men find that when they lose their jobs, they aren't doing what it means to be a man in America.

————

Although the media dubbed the Great Recession of 2007 to 2009 a "man-cession" because men's job losses were double women's at first, women experienced greater job loss *after* the so-called conclusion of the recession *and* recovered jobs at a slower rate than men. Women also appeared to face greater economic consequences of job loss: they were more likely than men to experience hunger and deprivation. These trends bring us to one of the puzzles at the heart of this book: Do women and men experience job loss and its effects in different ways?

We often don't think of women when we think of the unemployed. But since the 1950s, women and men have experienced fairly similar annual rates of unemployment, although men remain, on average, at greater risk of job loss and unemployment.[29] Even so, we still don't know enough about how men's and women's experiences of unemployment compare.[30]

There are good reasons to think men and women may experience job loss and unemployment differently, because men and women experience work and home very differently. Men and women typically work in different sectors of the labor market, which means men are more likely to be police officers or construction workers while women are more likely to be elementary schoolteachers or nurses (something we will explore more in chapter 2).[31] Men have historically had higher levels of labor force participation than women, although the majority of American women now work full-time and steadily throughout their adulthood, just like Tracy and Joan.[32] Men also continue to earn more than women even when they work in the same occupations and even when they have a similar amount of experience and work similar hours.[33]

Men and women have different responsibilities at home. Women continue to do more of the household chores and more of the routine caregiving for children, even though men have increased their participation over the years.[34] When women become pregnant, they are often asked if they are going to "choose" to stay at home or stay at work.[35] Yet for many heterosexual women, these "choices" are complicated by inflexible work demands (long hours and little flexibility), a lack of accessible and affordable quality childcare, and/or not enough help at home from spouses and partners—a combination that too often propels a large minority (although certainly not all) of women out of the labor market either entirely or for periods of time.[36] Thus, we see the lack of choice play out because of workplaces that continue to function as if families still had a stay-at-home spouse to take care of the kids (even though those days are long gone) and because of the lack of state-sponsored, affordable, quality childcare in the United States (even though other countries have long since adopted such models). While modest progress has been made on the home front, where men have increased chores and assumed more childcare duties, it is not enough to move us toward true equality.[37]

In my own work, I've found that women are more likely to stay employed steadily during the years when their children are young, if they find work rewarding and when they have opportunities for advancement at work. They are also more likely to stay employed when the family agrees that their work is worth supporting, which is more common among well-paid jobs with benefits. Finally, finding reliable childcare (either paid or unpaid) is a crucial component of continued employment.[38] Many of the reasons women stay, then, are beyond their control, making the "choice" a very constrained one. This is also shaped by race, as women of color have had fewer opportunities to withdraw from the labor market because of the racial earning gaps of their husbands, while also finding themselves stuck in "devalued work."[39]

These differences in expectations about work and family can have lasting implications for job loss. The sociologist Noelle Chesley found that men who lose jobs and are out of work for years are quick to tell people that they are between jobs rather than saying that they are taking care of their kids, even though most had stopped looking for work and had become full-time caretakers for their children.[40] In contrast, in my own work, I have found that women who lose jobs are quick to say they are spending time with their kids rather than admitting they had been fired.[41] Moreover, in their book, *Opting Back In*, family experts Pamela Stone and Meg Lovejoy found women who leave the workforce to take care of children—even for relatively short durations—strongly identify as stay-at-home mothers rather than as in-between jobs, as men do.[42] The question of whether to leave work or remain employed after having children is also one that is highly gendered. Men rarely make such choices; in my first book, I interviewed a few women who substantially outearned their husbands when their children were born, but gender sometimes trumped earning potential for women, leading them to leave high-paying jobs to stay at home with their children.

This might lead us to expect that Tracy's and Joan's experiences of job loss and unemployment will look different from Neil's and Anthony's.

Others might argue that the gender differences may not matter nearly as much as class differences. In other words, we might expect that Neil and Joan, because of their professional jobs, better educations, and working spouses, may end up more alike than Tracy and Anthony, who only have high school educations and are the sole providers for their families.

This is where our second puzzle comes into play. The second puzzle emerged out of the wreckage of the Great Recession when some communities appeared to have recovered financially from the recession while others did not. This puzzle crystallized during the surprising results of the 2016 presidential election and the news media coverage that followed. The media focused its attention on the rural, white working-class communities in Pennsylvania, Michigan, and Wisconsin that turned away from Democrats and gave Donald Trump his electoral college victory. Many in the media speculated that "economic anxiety" lay behind these working-class communities' response to Trump's fiery rhetoric (although Trump support was notably absent in poor and working-class Black communities, which had struggled even more).[43] Nonetheless, the unevenness of the recovery was apparent. Some groups of people appeared to be able to lose work and find new jobs while others had no such luck. If high-flying executives now sit next to manual laborers on the unemployment line, are they equally likely to find work the next day? This second puzzle intersects with the first, as we must also ask, What happens when the manual laborer or the executive is a woman?

Solving puzzles about how gender and class shape employment and family transitions has been at the heart of my research agenda since I first entered graduate school. My first book looked into why we persist in thinking that working-class women are the ones who work full-time, and that they have to because of their financial circumstances—a popular misconception. National data shows the exact opposite—women with more education and better occupations are more likely to be employed full-time and to stay that way compared to women who are less well educated and who hold jobs that aren't as good.[44] My research suggested there were a couple of things going on. First, women say that they need to work or that they need to stay at home for their families' sake, because it helps them deflect criticism about their choices. One of the women I met while researching my first book, Paula, said something that illumines the criticism women anticipate facing surrounding work and motherhood. Paula explained to me, "People look down on you if you do work, people look down upon you if you don't work."[45] Regardless of whether or not a woman works for pay, Paula felt, other people were going to judge her for it. I found women say that they are doing something because it's "for the family" in order to account for their actions with a rationale that they believe will be seen as socially acceptable—as we saw in the earlier paragraphs, women learn early on that society sees family as women's primary duty. The other thing I discovered is that for women to stay employed full-time over a long period, particularly once they start having children, it takes resources (i.e., money) to afford good-quality childcare (or family members to help if affordable care is not available) and household help, a supportive spouse, and a job that everyone in the family agrees is worth the effort of supporting.

Women with college educations or advanced degrees like Joan usually find themselves employed in "good jobs"—positions that come with opportunities for advancement, with benefits, with access to paid leave, with higher job status—all of which can help them stay employed over the long term.[46] They can afford to put their kids in really good childcare like the one Joan had arranged for her son or to outsource some of the mundane household labor that can burden women's workloads when done on top of their paid labor with little or no help from a spouse.[47] Holding a good job may make middle-class women reluctant to leave work. But working-class women like Tracy may not have these same opportunities. Their job options may be poorer overall, and they may be less able to afford childcare or to receive help from family members (who may deem their paid work as less deserving of support because it does not come with good pay or with benefits). It might be harder to stay employed in these circumstances.

The picture is also murky for the men. Since the 1970s, the labor market has become divided into two segments. One segment is full of dead-end jobs with low pay and few benefits; the other features good pay, opportunities for advancement, and many benefits.[48] Working-class men like Anthony end up stuck in the same bad jobs that working-class women do, but they rarely leave the workforce to care for children in the way women do. Men continue to have high levels of labor force attachment over their prime working years.[49]

Since men's full-time employment is taken for granted, unemployment may be one of the few times in a man's life in which he does not work for pay. Over the past century, much of the policy debate economists have had about the generosity of unemployment benefits has stemmed from the assumption that men, particularly working-class men, would withdraw from the labor force if benefits were generous enough to give them the opportunity to do so.[50] This question certainly was at the heart of the political debate surrounding a provision in the 2020 CARES Act that extended an extra $600 a week to those receiving unemployment. GOP senators claimed that too generous benefits acted to discourage employment, making it impossible for small business owners to "rehire workers," according to Texas Senator John Cornyn.[51] This kind of worry that generous unemployment benefits induce the unemployed to remain at home has been at the heart of economic debate since the turn of the twentieth century. Back then, famed economist William H. Beveridge wrote that the best policy solution for unemployment would be to "abolish industrial and social conditions which induce or pander to the vices of idleness, slovenliness, and irresponsibility."[52] This debate continues today, as some of the most notable economists of our time weigh in on whether greater unemployment benefits induce men to return to work slowly, although many now suggest more generous benefits are beneficial and do not discourage a return to employment.[53] Yet most of the discussion about generous benefits only focuses on the economics of returning or not returning to work for men and not on the other factors—social and psychological— that we know also shape these decisions.

The devastation of the Great Recession appeared to remove some of the stigma of not working for working-class men.[54] When job loss seems commonplace, as it can be for working-class men, the shame fades and the rush to return to work might fade. Yet there is little evidence to suggest working-class men are content not to work; most working-class men face both financial and social pressure to return to work even if their wives work and even if they are doing a lot of the caregiving at home.[55] Some scholars have found that the reason working-class men take longer to find jobs is because they have to find jobs that let them help shoulder the burden at home while their wives are at work. This means that working-class men sometimes can't take a job if the schedule conflicts with when their wives are working already.[56]

In contrast, middle-class men have fairly good jobs to go back to and relatively more to lose financially (because of their greater incomes) if they stay at home. They also face increased marital distress when they are out of work a long time.[57] Aliya Rao, an assistant professor at the London School of Economics, finds that wives of unemployed middle-class men make their husbands' job search the family's top priority—even in households where the wives are working.[58] Psychiatrists warn that losing a job can be bad for men's mental health, and some have argued that when job loss is less common, the unemployed will feel greater shame.[59] But when all their peers still have nine-to-five jobs, middle-class men may feel like they have to rush back to work.[60]

There is evidence for both points of view: gender and class likely both matter. But exactly how each plays out over the arc of an unemployment experience is unclear. That is a question that this book addresses.

———

Through these in-depth interviews with 100 people from rural to urban counties in Pennsylvania, a picture began to emerge of unemployment in America. As I investigated their experiences, I saw that many of the ways we have thought about unemployment are either incomplete (like the breadline) or just plain wrong. Over the course of the book, we will follow Tracy, Neil, Joan, and Anthony through the loss of their jobs, see how their job losses impacted them and their families, and watch as they try to find work again. We'll get a close look at the lives of these four, but in each chapter, we will meet others, too, beginning with Heidi, Heather, and Dennis in the next chapter, and we'll learn about their unemployment experiences. If at any point readers wish to know some of the background details about Tracy, Neil, Joan, or Anthony, or about one of the other unemployed, they can refer to the appendix, which has some important information about all of the participants, including their gender, social class, marital status, number of children, and broad occupation category. I've also included a short index devoted to participants, so readers can easily find where anyone appears throughout the book.

Throughout the book, we will find many new truths about unemployment and job loss in the twenty-first century; these truths have been hidden from sight by political discourse that uses the unemployed as a straw man as we have allowed our unemployment support system to collapse. What we have been left with are myths that the stories in these pages may help to unravel. The unemployed are not lazy—the majority would work if they could find jobs. There are not clear distinctions between the unemployed and the not employed; the people we will meet will blur these boundaries on a regular basis. Despite men's assumed burden to provide, women appear to bear much higher levels of guilt and shame for losing their jobs than men do. The unemployment system's rules do not prevent people from taking time off, as Neil did to fly-fish. And those best at getting around the rules are white middle-class men. The experience of job loss is far more varied and complex than our Dorothea Lange, Great Depression–era imaginings suggest. Men and women, working-class and middle-class, have unequal experiences of job loss and unemployment. And people from groups that have historically been marginalized—white women, the working class, and people of color—are the ones whom we have left behind.

2

The Paths to Job Loss

HEATHER AND HER husband had moved into their new home, a beautiful old farmhouse, just before she and I met. The kitchen was white, gleaming, and well organized, looking like it could have been featured on one of the HGTV network shows. But the rest of the house was cluttered with unpacked boxes and kids' toys, full of the life that three young children and two hectic working parents bring to turn a new house into a home. As we drank tea and the children played, we chatted about the career trajectory Heather had taken since she had graduated college with a degree in ecology. In the years since her graduation, Heather had followed what is often thought of as a pretty typical path into adulthood. She got her first job, met her husband, married him, had children, and decided to stay working full-time. Unlike many of the others I met, her job loss was the first real stumbling point as she worked toward her career and family goals.

In this chapter, I take a close look at the paths people like Heather followed before their job loss. This is what scholars call a life course approach—looking at what happens over the course of someone's life.[1,2] As we saw in chapter 1, Tracy, Neil, Joan, and Anthony had lived pretty different lives up to the time when they lost their jobs. But were there broader patterns in these experiences? We know that Tracy had recently moved to the factory, that Neil had been at his job for only a year, that Joan had worked for her university for a long time, and that Anthony had had many job losses, but what else happened in between when they first entered the labor market and when I met them that could help us understand how they got here? Examining the many steps that led up to job loss—and how people may have taken different routes to get there—may help us understand how they make sense of their job loss *and* what kinds of resources are available to them after they've lost their job. While it is possible that the patterns I discovered in this small group of 100 people may not be representative of the country as a whole, I've been lucky to collaborate with noted life course scholar Dr. Adrianne Frech to examine some of these patterns at the national level, which I'll discuss throughout this chapter. We'll return to Tracy, Neil, Joan, and Anthony later in the chapter to see what twists and turns their work careers took; but first, we will take a closer look at Heather and meet two others, Heidi and Dennis, and examine the contours of their working lives.

Back to Heather's story. Overall, Heather had a very steady and unremarkable career path. There had been only one notable turn. After college graduation, Heather went to work with the state as an ecologist, but she didn't feel particularly passionate about the job. She explained, "It was kind of mindless. So, it wasn't anything that I wanted to keep doing." She laughingly recalled a time she set up a field-stream study, which meant she was in charge of putting out cages in a local stream. Nearby in the river, fly-fishermen teased her about her good fortune to have a full-time job that allowed her to wear knee-high waders and stand in the stream, asking her, "How do you get a job like this?" But they initiated this conversation over the summer, and once it was wintertime, the fly-fisherman were safely ensconced indoors while, she recalled with a smile, "I was still out there in my waders for a whole day in the stream, and it was snowing."

During this time period, Heather met the man who became her husband. They realized that two ecologists in the family might be tough if there was a government slowdown; how would they both find work? Heather also felt she had less passion for the work than her husband did. So, she went back to school, keeping her day job (she held it for over four years total) and earning a degree in accounting.

When she neared the end of her training, she looked for a full-time job that would be closer to her new area of expertise. She was hired as the accounting clerk for a small energy company. She stayed for four years and, after a round of particularly exemplary reviews, asked about the opportunity for advancement. She was told the company planned for her to take the comptroller's position when the comptroller retired . . . in fifteen years. After serious consideration, Heather decided to make a move to a new company. This company was also in natural resource extraction. Heather enjoyed the work at her new company, but, as with many companies in this industry in Pennsylvania, they eventually saw a shift in their financial fortunes. After this reversal, the company limped along for about a year, laying off a few people while maintaining most of the workforce, but eventually the owners sold the firm. It was after this sale that the series of mass layoffs began. Heather saw her coworkers and friends and eventually her own boss laid off before she, too, lost her position. It was the first time she'd ever lost a job and even the first time she'd had a period off in between jobs. Overall, Heather had held three jobs total before we met and lost a job only once.

Contrast Heather to Heidi, who was also married with two kids and with a full-time working husband. Like Heather, Heidi had earned a degree that she wasn't using: she had a bachelor's in education. But when she graduated, there were no teaching jobs in the area where she and her first husband lived. Her then-husband, whom she'd met in college, was able to find work locally. As Heidi explained, "I knew that his job was [easier to find with] more money. I knew he was going to be around that area, so I didn't want to go real far [to find a teaching job.]" Unsure of what to do for work, Heidi found a job as a nursing assistant, although it would be years before she formally returned to school to earn a certificate to become a certified nursing assistant (CNA). According to the National Center for Education Statistics, teachers in the United States remain predominantly female, and while their salaries have not kept up with inflation levels, in the 2018–2019 school year the average teaching salary was $59,100 (above the national median income).[3] But while teachers have relatively middle-class earnings, nursing assistants (also mostly women) often earn much less—the national average in 2019 was $29,640, according to the Bureau of Labor Statistics.[4]

Moreover, nationally, a majority of nursing assistants have received public assistance at some point,[5] suggesting that these jobs bring with them a level of insecurity not found in most teaching positions.

Unlike Heather, Heidi moved into a position that paid worse and had more volatility. And she held many more jobs than Heather had. Heidi had at least six jobs (she wasn't sure if she correctly remembered them all during her interview) and had experienced two job losses. She explained that several of her moves had been lateral because of either hospital closures or family changes. Heidi explained, "Then [my first husband and I] ended up getting divorced. I relocated and came here and that's when I went for my certificate for CNA," which she hoped would give her access to more stable (and better-paying) jobs. But it hadn't; the mergers and layoffs continued. So, after she married her second husband and was on more stable financial footing, Heidi went back to school yet again and earned her phlebotomy certificate. This training, she hoped, would stave off any future instability.

Yet her first position as a phlebotomist led Heidi back to the unemployment line. Discussing her most recent job loss, she said, "[Hospital A] and [Hospital B] merged. It was just they were cutting down. Like right now they're in a big hiring freeze." Unfortunately for Heidi, she hadn't been able to jump ship ahead of time, and she lost her job. Heidi explained that many of the local hospitals and nonprofits started merging over the past several years, which made it harder and harder to stay ahead of the curve when layoffs came.

It's important to pause here and to discuss the difference between a *job change* and a *job loss*—economists usually call this the distinction between voluntary and involuntary job loss. What I am calling a "job change" is what happens when people decide to switch jobs—either in search of better pay or more security or to accommodate a family move or simply because they want a change. So, when Heidi thought that a hospital might downsize and she decided to move ahead of it, this would be a job change (or what economists would consider a voluntary job loss, because she voluntarily left one job in order to take another). What I am calling a "job loss," on the other hand, is when someone is fired or laid off from a job—when an employer lets an employee go. So, someone can have a lot of job changes (leaving for a different job) without having many job losses. This is important, because both economists and sociologists tend to think that real job instability comes from job losses, not job changes. Job losses often (but not always) come with a period of unemployment.[6] This book focuses on when the two are entwined—unemployment following a job loss.

Finally, neither Heather's nor Heidi's path to job loss looked anything like Dennis's path. Dennis was also married with children, but he did not have a college degree. In fact, Dennis couldn't stand sitting inside all day long. He dropped out of high school his junior year when he found work on a nearby farm. While Dennis had disliked school, he enjoyed the "physical work" on the farm, where he could clean the barns and bail hay or even clean the chicken coops. Comparing the two, he explained, "I liked to work, I hated school." Chuckling he repeated, "I really hated school." But this decision would have far-reaching consequences. Men without a high school degree have some of the highest risk of unemployment. During the Great Recession, the unemployment rates of men without a high school diploma teetered over 20 percent—almost double the rate of high school graduates and four times the rate of college grads whose unemployment risk remained a relatively low 5 percent.[7]

Being a high school dropout also left Dennis with few good job options. Over the past several decades, the American job market has become increasingly divided into what sociologist Arne Kalleberg has called "good jobs and bad jobs."[8] For those who can get them, good jobs are still fairly desirable, providing more security (although still facing greater risk of job loss than in the past), health insurance, good pay, and a host of other benefits. For the rest—meaning for those like Dennis without a high school education—bad jobs often pay poorly and lack stable hours (meaning people do not get scheduled for a consistent number of hours in a week, so the time you work typically varies, week to week). Moreover, researchers have found that these types of "bad jobs" often have much more churning—people don't stay in them for very long. People get laid off, they leave for what they hope will be better-paying work, or their hours are cut so dramatically that they aren't able to cover their bills, which forces them to leave the company in search of other work.[9] Heidi also often found herself in these "bad jobs," despite her college degree, because she worked in a field that did not require a college degree.

Dennis worked at the farm for a year and a half but only earned minimum wage, so when the opportunity to earn more money laying cables came along, he left, excited for the new opportunity. He spent nine months in that job and then his uncle hired him to help him build cable TV systems. By this time, Dennis was earning much better money, and he worked for his uncle for two years. But then his uncle's business went under and with it went Dennis's job.

Dennis finally moved out of state to find work in a shipping and receiving job, where he worked for a little over a year. During that period, he met and married his son's mother back in Pennsylvania and decided to relocate back to the state. Once home, he found and lost another job and also experienced the end of both his first and his second marriage.

At this point, you may be wondering if the problem was Dennis—was he capable of holding down a job for a long period of time? Not long after the relocation to Pennsylvania (and subsequent job loss), Dennis experienced a couple of much longer job tenures that suggested that when he found a good-paying job, he was able to maintain stable employment. First, his uncle found him work for a larger cable company, and Dennis worked there for over five years until that company went bankrupt. He then found a similar job that he held for about eight years until, yet again, the company went bust. At this point, Dennis decided he needed a new line of work. He took a few courses and earned his GED. From there, he applied and got a coveted position in what at the time was the booming shale industry. Dennis hoped he had finally cracked the code and found work in an industry not bound for booms and busts. But only a year and a half later, he was out of work yet again. By the time of his interview, Dennis had lost four jobs and held at least ten.

Overall, the people I interviewed were similar in that they had recently lost a full-time job, but they varied considerably in how they had come to the place of losing that job. I observed clear patterns—across gender and class—in who was more likely to take a particular path. For nearly half of the middle-class women, like Heather, it was common to follow a *lockstep* path to this recent job loss, which I define here to mean that they had worked for one, two, or at most, three organizations for many years and that this was their first (or very rarely, their second) experience of job loss.[10] Lockstep paths were most common among middle-class women and followed less frequently by everyone else.[11] I borrow the lockstep term from sociologist Phyllis Moen and psychologist Patricia Roehling, who argue that "lockstep" workers—who were almost exclusively men during their heyday—were very common in America in the 1950s, 1960s, and even 1970s; like my lockstep workers, they spent their whole lives working for one or two companies, moving up the career ladder, and eventually retiring.

In contrast, folks like Heidi followed paths with many more job changes than I saw among the lockstep employees. This second path was actually the most common among those I met, and it was what I call the *transitory* work pathway.[12] Those who followed this path had changed jobs a fair number of times, working for a minimum of four different companies. Yet none of them had experienced more than two job losses, and most had experienced only this one most recent job loss. This meant that while *job changes* were fairly typical for this group, *job losses* were pretty unusual. This was the most common path for middle-class men (over half) and working-class women (nearly half), fairly typical for middle-class women (almost half), and not uncommon among working-class men (about a third) as well.[13]

Finally, Dennis and some others followed what I call the *chronic unemployment* path to job loss; for many more men than women, losing a job was just another part of having a job. In fact, men like Dennis were about twice as likely as women to follow a chronic unemployment pathway, and working-class men faced the greatest risk.[14] In a national study with Adrianne Frech, using data from the National Longitudinal Survey of Youth 1979 (NLSY79) that has tracked people's work experiences in great detail over time, we find similar evidence: Men, particularly working-class men, are significantly more at risk of chronic unemployment than are women.[15] All of the people in the chronic unemployment group experienced at least three job losses, with an average of about four. Unlike Heather in the lockstep group or even Heidi in the transitory group, they also had a lot more employers, averaging eight employers in their fifteen to twenty years of work. A long-term panel study examined by the sociologists Jennie Brand and Sarah Burgard found similar evidence that people who had experienced an involuntary job loss had more jobs overall than those who had not lost a job.[16] As I will argue in later chapters, there were lasting consequences of following each of these paths to job loss, but those working-class men who had been chronically unemployed often had low financial reserves for coping with the latest hit.

Lockstep Lives

Those who followed the *lockstep* path to unemployment were like Heather in many ways—they had long job tenures and usually no prior job losses. These working women (most often middle-class women) reported much longer average times on the job than their counterparts in the other groups. But this life course lens also tells us something fairly surprising: unlike the twentieth-century lockstep workers that Moen and Roehling discovered, the workers who follow this kind of linear path were most likely to be middle-class women. In my prior qualitative research on MBA graduates with sociologist Sarah Patterson and Penn State graduate Christen Sheroff, we also find that women were more likely than men to have a long tenure at a single company.[17]

While sticking with one company for a long period of time was once the hallmark of the "company man," are women now the more loyal employees? Research on women's organizational commitments suggests that when women and men hold similar positions and have similar family responsibilities, women report higher levels of commitment to their companies than men do.[18] But why might this happen? Researchers who specialize in management and human resources have investigated this question, and while they consistently find that women are more satisfied at work than are men, they have not found evidence that this translates to why women might stick around a job for longer periods of time.[19]

If we think about Heather's career paths, we can see another explanation for why the men and the women differed in their paths to job loss.
Heather prioritized her husband's career as an ecologist over her own
ecology job and switched to a career in accounting that would be more
compatible with his, allowing his job to drive their family decisions
(rather than have hers sometimes take the front seat). Prioritizing a
spouse's job ahead of their own meant women rarely made job transitions for themselves even when their careers stalled or their jobs were
at risk. Although prioritizing a spouse's job would not necessarily lead
to more job stability (in the next section, we will see how it sometimes
led to more moves for some women who "trailed" their spouses multiple times), it could if there were plentiful opportunities in the local area.
More important, it meant that the lockstep women rarely initiated
moves outside of their company, as they prized the stability they had
found.

And what about Tracy, Neil, Joan, and Anthony? How did they fit in?
Joan was the only one of the four to take this lockstep path to her job
loss. Like Heather, this was Joan's first job loss, and she had worked
primarily for one employer for most of her adult working years. Right
out of college, she and her husband had moved to a different state,
where she worked as an assistant for a research lab (enjoying the outdoor work, unlike Heather) until her husband found work nearer to
home and they returned to their roots. Once there, Joan found work at
the university, first teaching a few summer classes and then working for
one of the faculty. Her new boss convinced her to apply for a master's
degree (funded, in large part, by her employer). She would end up staying, working for the university or through grants related to that original
research, until I met her. The university was only her second employer.
Like Heather, Joan put her husband's job ahead of her own on multiple
occasions. This meant that even when Joan became the family breadwinner, she did not try to move the family when her career was threatened but stayed put instead.

We see family pressures leading to lockstep careers among women
who were trying to balance a demanding career with having kids. Consider Natalie's story. Early after having children, Natalie and her

husband agreed that her job would take a back seat to his, and she had repeatedly turned down promotions as a result of their bargain. Six weeks before she was laid off, she was given a clear choice by her manager that involved a location change. As she told me, "He said, 'As far as your next assignment goes, it's like, you have to decide whether you wanna stay at [the company] or whether you wanna stay in [town].' And when he told me that if I didn't take that opportunity, he was saying, I was gonna be laid off." Yet women very rarely took the opportunity to relocate their families, particularly when they were part of a dual-earner household. In fact, with the rise of dual-income households, both men and women have become increasingly reluctant to relocate their families.[20] But when families do decide to relocate (and 65 percent of relocating couples are dual-earner couples), women rarely lead the way on such a move.[21] Natalie decided not to relocate, although she did hope that her boss would change his mind. She'd worked there a long time, and she felt the kind of company loyalty she had shown deserved more than this flat ultimatum. It didn't. As these examples illustrate, I found that women on the lockstep path were unlikely to ask their spouses to follow them for work or to seek advancement externally.

There were few men on the lockstep path who made decisions about their jobs in order to prioritize their wives' careers or to minimize risk to their job stability. Frank was one of the only exceptions who prioritized his wife's career. Although he moved to follow his wife to a new town, he kept his old job. Frank had worked in marketing and sales for a large national corporation. He liked his job very much, and most of it was done online or over the phone with the occasional in-person meeting. When his wife, a surgeon, found a new job a couple of hours away from where they had been living, it was clear to them that they should move. Already this breaks the gender norms that we've seen in some of the other examples, as it was not always so clear-cut in other families that moves would happen if it were determined by the wife—even if the wife was the primary earner in the family. But unlike most of the women who moved for their husbands' careers (as we will see in the next section), Frank was able to keep his existing job and work remotely for a number of years, until the company was sold and new management did away with his position. Thus, Frank was mostly able to maintain his position in the company that he enjoyed working for while simultaneously prioritizing his wife's career; in other words, his career was, for a time at least, not impaired by his decision to prioritize his wife's career (unlike what most of the women experienced).

Tony also followed a lockstep path, but one that looked quite different. His wife had primarily stayed at home during the time he was working his way up in a branch of a national sports league. After over a decade with the league, he had reached a fairly high position within the local branch. But the league decided to cut the positions nationally, leaving Tony with a lengthy work history that was specific and hard to translate to another line of work. He cast a wide net in his search for new work and eventually received an offer out of state, doing similar work for a national chain, that would require the family to move to Pennsylvania. The pay was slightly lower but, overall, the job seemed comparable, so he decided to make the move. Importantly, almost all of Tony's decisions were about his relationship with his employer or what was best for his career; when relating his decisions about his career path and his move, he did not mention his wife. This stands in stark contrast to how most of the women in the lockstep group made decisions about their own careers. While a few had access to more promising jobs, most of the women stayed with their employers either out of convenience or because of family obligations that prevented them from searching farther afield.

Transitory Paths

Although we saw women outnumber men in the lockstep group (and we will see men outnumber women in the chronic unemployment group), men and women were pretty evenly distributed in the *transitory* group. A study done by faculty in a business school on white full-time workers in the United Kingdom had similar findings—men and women changed jobs at similar rates over a five-year period.[22] The same study also found that changing jobs fairly frequently was a common pattern among workers. A report from the U.S. Department of Labor similarly finds that by age 52, the average American has held about twelve jobs.[23] This supports what I found, as the transitory group was the largest of the three (and most common among the middle-class men and working-class women). This group was characterized by people who had numerous employers (at least four) but no more than two job losses. There was more variation in this group than in the lockstep group; some people had only four job changes while others had ten or twelve. One person even said he'd had so many he couldn't quite remember the count.

But while I found that men and women were distributed somewhat evenly in the transitory pathway group, I also discovered that what brought them along these paths actually looked different by gender. Just as we saw above in the lockstep group, women were more likely to see their careers shaped by their families' priorities. Additionally, women were more likely to leave a job, like Heidi from the beginning of this chapter, when they suspected that layoffs might be coming. The men, on the other hand, were more likely to leave jobs for what they hoped would be greener pastures, and they were more likely to make decisions either independently of wives or in ways that prioritized their careers while downplaying the importance of their wives' work (even when they lived in dual-earner households).

Heidi's family decided against prioritizing her work as a teacher, and instead she found work as a nursing assistant. In this sense, her experience was like Heather's. But unlike Heather, Heidi moved into an occupation that provided much less job stability. As a result, Heidi found herself having to job-hop when hospitals were about to merge. Unlike Heather, Heidi moved into an occupation—nursing assistant—that was less stable, *and* she had instability in her family life (she and her first husband divorced). With both job and family instability, Heidi experienced many more job changes (although only one more job loss) than Heather. None of Heidi's job transitions were in search of greener pastures—she was just hoping to maintain what she already had.

Of the four individuals we are following, Tracy was the only one who also had a transitory career, in which most of her job changes were driven by family responsibilities rather than a search for better work. During high school and then for two years after high school, Tracy worked in a small deli store, making minimum wage. She quit when she was in her third trimester with her son; since the store was a small business, she didn't qualify for unpaid leave benefits under the Family and Medical Leave Act (FMLA), and the store would not give her any leave or vacation before or after her son was born. (FMLA only protects workers who work at a company with fifty employees within seventy-five miles of each other.[24]) When her son was three months old, she found a "a better-paying job," making slightly above minimum wage, as a store clerk. She worked in that position for three years until her boss fired her when, she explained, "I found out I was pregnant with my daughter." In the United States, pregnancy is protected under the Pregnancy Discrimination Act, but research continues to find evidence that women lose jobs in this way.[25] Yet Tracy figured that her boss had unwittingly done her a favor by giving her some paid time to search for work while recovering from childbirth, explaining that in the end, the job loss "didn't really break my heart." Once her daughter was three months old, Tracy returned to work, this time as a waitress. She worked for that restaurant until it shuttered; then she worked for another restaurant for nearly eleven years before she moved to the better-paying factory job. Thus, Tracy had some periods of longer employment coupled with some periods where she was employed for shorter time periods—these shorter time periods were mostly tied to her pregnancies and the lack of available maternity leave. When she had the opportunity to do so, she stayed employed longer. Tracy only once made a job move that was not related to family reasons—when she took a chance on the new factory in town—and we know how that story ended. For the most part, Tracy's job changes were driven by her family responsibilities, which was quite common for women in this study.

I saw men make more upward transitions when they made a job change while women made more lateral moves.[26] Joel didn't have the education credentials that Heidi did, but he did gain valuable on-the-job skills as a mechanic early in his working career. Also, unlike Heidi,

Joel didn't move laterally between jobs; he almost always moved upward when he made a job change. He married young—right out of high school—and worked a few fairly short dead-end jobs, as a line cook, as a clerk at the mall, as an unskilled laborer in construction—jobs he described as "alright, but it wasn't my dream job." His first wife had connections to a local garage that worked on large diesel trucks and buses and she helped him "get [a] foot in the door." He spent eight years there, learning the trade and getting to know every engine and every part of every vehicle.

Three years before he left the local garage, he took a part-time job with an even bigger outfit that he knew offered more training opportunities and had a bigger career ladder within the organization. When a full-time position opened up within the organization, he took it. After he completed the trainings, he was offered a second-shift floor supervisor position in another organization. It was an opportunity he couldn't pass up. Unfortunately, it was also the job from which he was let go. Joel's moves were strategic, not made for family reasons, and they often moved him up the organization.

Derek also made strategic career (rather than family) job changes. He graduated college with a degree in music and had his own business for ten years. He enjoyed the work but felt his hours were too long for the relatively low salary he made. He went back to college and earned a second bachelor's degree, this time in information technology. When his daughter was six, he and his wife discussed the possibility of a move. Derek applied for and got what he considered a "fantastic" job in the area they wanted to live. His wife, a nurse, found a part-time job in the area. Derek's hours increased as his responsibilities grew, until he was regularly working fifty to sixty hours a week before his daughter ended elementary school. After several promotions, Derek also earned substantially more than he had when he owned his own business. Earlier research has suggested that men do prioritize their families, but how men make family a priority is different from how women do.[27] While women prioritize families with their time, men most often do it with their ability to earn money and provide financially for them, which usually demands long hours away from their families.[28]

Chronic Unemployment

There was a lot of variation among those who faced *chronic unemployment*; everyone had experienced at least three job losses and an average of over four, as Dennis had, but some people faced far more (as we learned was Anthony's experience in chapter 1). Those who experienced chronic unemployment had held an average of eight jobs, which could mean holding on to a job for two to three years, but sometimes it meant changing or losing a job within a couple of months of starting it. The people with chronic unemployment pathways had much less education overall than those in the other two groups. In fact, people on either the transitory or the lockstep path were about twice as likely to have graduated from college as were those who experienced chronic unemployment. And many more of those with chronic unemployment had not completed high school or had only a high school degree. This matches what we know about unemployment risks nationally; those with less education are at much higher risk.[29] Dennis fit into this group, as he had originally dropped out of high school and only recently earned a GED. While he had learned technical skills on the job, he found that this did not always translate easily to comparable new work when he lost the next job.

Both Neil and Anthony had faced chronic unemployment before I met them. Working in the hotel industry, Neil faced greater instability (three total job losses) as new ownership often brought changes in staff positions and hotels sometimes closed without warning. Describing one such incident, Neil remembered a tricky buyout where a father had been a minor partner in a group that owned the hotel where he worked as the manager. The father's son had worked at a different hotel in town, which closed, and in response, the father "bought out all the other partners. One big whoosh and a few of us were gone." Neil's position went to the son, and some of the other key managerial positions went to other family friends. But, as other research has found, middle-class men like Neil often landed on their feet after such incidents, as Neil had in the past.[30] This was less true for the working-class men for whom job loss was a bigger risk and happened more often. We remember Anthony, too, had faced chronic unemployment, but he had a far bumpier road than Neil. In fact, Anthony had lost so many jobs that he felt very discouraged about his prospects for retirement. He told me that "working thirty years and saving for retirement" was the "the light at the end of the tunnel," only he could no longer see that light because "it's been gone for a long time."

The men outnumbered the women at about twice the rate for risk of chronic unemployment, and working-class men faced the highest risk. This matches what Adrianne Frech and I have found using national data sets to track men's and women's unemployment patterns over time.[31] Nationally, looking only at men, we find that men have about an 8 percent likelihood of experiencing high risk of unemployment from age 29 to age 50. Men with lower levels of education face the greatest risk of being chronically unemployed. When we look at only women, we find that they have about a 4 percent likelihood of this high risk of unemployment when they are the same ages.[32]

Some of these gender differences are explained by the fact that the men and the women in the study typically worked in different occupations and industries. Now, men and women often end up in fairly different jobs—sociologists call this *occupational segregation*. Occupational segregation means that even when men and women work in a position with fairly similar tasks, they often are not working in the same job. For example, let's consider cleaning floors and emptying trash in a hotel. When the men hold such a position, they are most often called janitors, but when the women do, they are most often called maids. Very similar tasks, but the jobs aren't the same and neither is their pay (women are usually paid less).

When we look at what the men and women were doing before they lost their jobs, we see this play out in striking fashion. Men and women were rarely employed in similar jobs. To get a sense of how divided their jobs really were, I looked at the Bureau of Labor and Statistics list of major occupations and compared the occupations of the people I'd met to the list. I found men and women rarely overlapped. Certain occupations—management; computer and math; architecture and engineering; protective services; construction and extraction; installation, maintenance, and repairs; and production—were all dominated by men. Women outnumbered men in other occupations—life, physical, and social sciences; community and social services; education, training, and library; food preparation and service; and office and administrative support.[33]

When I looked at the last jobs of the people on the chronic unemployment paths, I found something striking: nearly three-quarters of the men *and* the women who frequently had lost jobs had come from a male-dominated occupational group while less than a quarter came from a female-dominated group. Prior research has similarly suggested that the industries men work in may put them at greater risk for experiencing layoffs.[34] While the loss of manufacturing jobs continues to play some role in today's job losses, it is not the outsize force that it used to be, because manufacturing is now such a smaller part of the overall labor force. Men also lost jobs in construction and extraction (the natural gas and shale boom in Pennsylvania fizzled during the time I conducted my interviews) and in more high-flying areas like computer and math or architecture and engineering.

Neil, Joan, Tracy, and Anthony all mostly had held jobs that fell into traditionally "male" or "female" occupational categories. Neil was in management, Anthony in computers, Joan in life sciences, and Tracy in the service industry for nearly her whole working career (until she took a chance and left waitressing for that factory position, when she became one of the women outliers in the production occupations). Neil and Anthony certainly experienced greater risk in their male-dominated occupations than Tracy and Joan had in their often female-dominated jobs. Working in hotel management, Neil experienced higher levels of unemployment than many of his middle-class peers, although there were similar levels of unemployment among those middle-class men employed in occupations known for booms and busts: IT, architecture, and hotel management were all fields in which middle-class men were at higher risk of job loss and unemployment.

Manufacturing jobs—once a hallmark of men's work—are increasingly unstable occupations, both during economic downturns and during periods of growth. Take, for instance, Lawrence's most recent job loss. Lawrence was a machinist who worked on the factory line making parts for railroad cars; he had left a very stable job (the first longer-tenured job he'd had in a while) for his most recent factory job. His previous position had been second shift and forty-five minutes away from where he lived, so when this new job opened, Lawrence thought it was an opportunity for something better. Working closer to where he lived would mean more time with his two children and with his long-time girlfriend. Instead, it meant merely a year and half of better employment until he received a phone call from his boss. No one flew in from corporate to fire Lawrence, as is common in mass factory layoffs. In fact, no one even told him face-to-face. He simply received a phone call asking him not to show up to work that day—or any day after that. When they called with the news, he asked, "Isn't there, you know, anything I can do?" His employers replied, "No." This kind of casual firing, when companies trim relatively new hires in order to cut costs, was common for those in chronic unemployment patterns, particularly those in traditionally male jobs. Both the worker and their employers took for granted that their employment was very tenuous.

One of the few white women to experience chronic unemployment had spent the majority of her working years in traditionally male jobs. Dana commented, "My most recent full-time job was running a bread route, believe it or not, delivering bread." Having worked in more male-dominated fields had often given Dana better pay than she thought she might have received otherwise. And both the public and scholars have wondered why more working-class women don't move toward the better-paying "blue-collar" industries.[35] But Dana's experience of losing job after job in these industries had convinced her that she might want to switch to an office job like those her girlfriends held, as she thought they had less experience with job loss than she had.

Just as occupation, gender, and education matter for chronic unemployment, race does, too. Victor Ray, a sociologist at Indiana University who specializes in studying race and organizations, notes that "whiteness is a credential" for employment, giving white job seekers (often unseen) advantages in the hiring process, demanding higher education levels from Black workers to achieve wage parity with less well-educated white workers, and protecting white workers from job loss (and subsequent unemployment) in the first place.[36] All of this leaves Black Americans at much greater risk of unemployment, often having double the unemployment rate of whites.[37] Using the longitudinal NLSY79 data, Adrianne Frech and I have found both Black men and women are at higher risk of chronic unemployment from their midtwenties until midlife than are whites. I also found evidence of this job instability among those I met. Tamara did not finish high school, but unlike many of the men in this group, she did go back to get her GED soon afterward. Like many without a high school degree, she started her work career with a series of dead-end fast-food restaurant jobs, which she quickly recognized weren't going to pay her enough to support herself, her son, and her son's father. Once she earned her GED, she began a program to become a licensed practical nurse (LPN). After successfully completing her first semester, she began her second semester, and then her son's father (who was also her son's primary caregiver at the time) left her. She couldn't find affordable childcare, and they were living in Pennsylvania at the time, away from her family and her hometown. She had to leave the program. She'd heard that doing medical records was a good backup plan, so she took and completed a certificate program on medical billing and coding. Since she'd already taken a number of LPN classes, she was familiar with the language, and it helped her find work relatively quickly.

But it became clear to Tamara that the certificate didn't bring her the types of jobs she had hoped to find. Even with a vocational certificate, she often earned little more than minimum wage, and she was on the front line of being cut whenever a hospital or medical office went through a retraction. She decided to try to take a paralegal course (luckily the employer she had at the time paid for the training), and while it was hard to juggle full-time work, full-time single-parenting, and part-time schooling, Tamara was hopeful this was the path out of the low-wage work. But her job was cut, yet again, and with it her benefits, including her access to the free tuition program.

Tamara most frequently lost jobs during "cost-saving measures," but more recently her single-parent responsibilities put a strain on her ability to meet job attendance requirements. In Pennsylvania, being fired for being absent too often is considered a "no-fault firing"—in other words, although it is not the same as a downsizing or a decision to shave costs by letting the last person hired go, being fired for being absent is also not considered to be the same thing as being "at fault" for losing one's job. It's a bit of a gray zone, where the employer has the right to fire someone for being absent but has to pay unemployment for this decision. In the case of Tamara's latest job loss, her son's school had called her; he had a medical emergency and she needed to go pick him up. He'd had a few of these emergencies in the past month (he had some health problems), and this most recent episode put her over the mandatory firing limit for her hospital (four absences in one month). Another job lost. Thus, Tamara faced both the challenges of frequent hospital mergers, in which she often was one of the first fired, as well as the responsibilities of being a single mother, increasing her risk for job loss.

Finally, differences in men's and women's aversion to risk seem to lead men to more chronic unemployment. The men took bigger risks than the women did when they decided to make a job change. This sometimes led to bigger rewards, but it also could mean that they took jobs that they weren't quite qualified for, which put them at greater risk of finding themselves on the unemployment rolls again. Sometimes the unemployment rules, which required workers to apply for all available jobs, could encourage workers to apply for positions for which they weren't particularly qualified. Men were particularly likely to apply for jobs they were underqualified for in these circumstances. Brent described applying for a job for which he had little experience: "I applied for a manager job. They said 'We like your history. We want to try out this other position that we think you may be fit for,' and being that I was collecting unemployment, I was like, 'Oh yeah, I can do it.' But I'm not a salesperson and it doesn't make sense for me to even try out for a sales job because that's not my personality." Despite his lack of history in sales, Brent went ahead and applied for the position, and he got it. Unfortunately, he only lasted in the position about nine months. Sometimes the men lost jobs so quickly that in between the time they were recruited for this study and the time I actually met with them, they had found and lost another job. This is not to say that women took no risks. Just think of Tracy leaving her stable restaurant job for the position in the factory. But these risks were often more modest and provided on-the-job training, as Tracy's factory position had, whereas the men were more likely to move into positions that required prior knowledge they did not possess.

———

In this chapter, I have shown the people I met took three distinct paths to their most recent job loss: lockstep, transitory, and chronic unemployment. I also found that there were demonstrable gender differences within the lockstep (predominantly middle-class women) and chronic unemployment (men at twice the risk of women) paths. Even when paths looked similar, as they did on the transitory path, the meanings and the motivations behind them were often quite different. Across all three paths to job loss, we see that the men more often changed jobs (or stayed in them) for better opportunity while the women more often moved (or stayed) because of family responsibilities.

The lockstep group was remarkable in its stable work history—at a time when stable careers have become mostly a thing of the past. The people in the lockstep group had an average of two jobs and one job loss since they finished school, holding stable employment for lengthy periods of time, as Joan and Heather had done. Many were like Joan and Heather, having held one or two jobs right out of college or high school and then settling down with one main employer in an employment relationship that lasted for over a decade or sometimes even two. Most had experienced their first job loss when we met.

The transitory group had more job changes *and* more job loss, as we saw with Tracy and Heidi, averaging six jobs and one and a half job losses. Women bore more of the cost of family responsibilities, and men felt better able to pursue their career goals. Although Heidi had hoped being a CNA would make it easier for her to manage her family responsibilities, she thought it hadn't been true in the end, as the hospitals she worked for "kept getting rid of [people]." She sounded like she was describing a drive-through fast-food joint when asked about the relationship she'd had with most of her employers: "It was just like, 'Next.'" Her unstable relationship with her employers meant that her job was often at risk when cost-cutting measures were taken.

The gender divide in the final group, the chronic unemployed, is also striking, with men at much greater risk than women. But perhaps what is most striking is how accustomed to job loss those who have followed this path had become. Sounding eerily like Anthony in chapter 1, Dennis said about his most recent job loss, "I was not upset when they fired me. I'm not gonna cry over it. I mean I liked the job, it's just, I look at it this way—it is what it is." Even though Dennis's family, including his stay-at-home wife and two stepchildren, relied on his income and his income alone, he had lost so many earlier jobs that he had a hard time getting particularly upset about this most recent job loss.

Dennis's and Anthony's reactions to their job loss baffled me, particularly at first. While Heidi tried to distance herself from her employer by using language implying that she worked for a "fast food" establishment (and in doing so, suggested that neither she nor her employer expected much from the relationship), Dennis and Anthony seemed almost indifferent to their job loss. There are many emotions at play when people lose jobs. In chapter 3, I explore how Joan, Neil, Tracy, and Anthony and the others felt about losing their jobs and examine what seemed to explain the varied reactions that I found.

3

The Ax Falls

REGINA DESCRIBED a job loss ripped from a movie scene. The printing manufacturer held an all-employee meeting in the cafeteria, but the meeting's topic was a closely guarded secret known only to the top brass. Wondering what was going on, workers whispered together in groups, mostly with their work units, but some sat with family and friends, as the company was the largest employer in the area. Although her mother worked at the plant, Regina sat with her friends from her department, whom she described as "family" because they had worked together for so long. But when the CEO of the company and "his posse" walked into the room (having flown in that morning from out of state), Regina said everyone knew instantly what was about to happen.

The CEO gave a short speech explaining that in a cost-saving move, the company would be cutting production, moving it to another plant in a different state. As soon as his speech was over, the CEO left the building. "I would have left, too" commented Regina. The people who had come with him completed the rest of the events. Regina recalled, "Then everybody with him had boxes with manila envelopes and you lined up according to your last name. And you stood in line and you got your envelope, and inside that envelope was your release date basically. So, that's how you found out whether or not you were done that day. Yeah, and after everybody had their envelopes, we were all told to shut our computers off and go home. We weren't allowed to touch anything. Uh, even if you [had a later release date], you had to leave for the day— they just wanted everybody to be gone."

It took Regina and her coworkers weeks to process the shock. Regina opened the envelope to find out that her job would be the last cut. Moreover, not long after it was cut, she was called back because her employers learned that the employees in the other plant did not know how to do Regina's job. She returned to do her work in a smaller operation, working remotely with the other plant. Nine months later she got the call from HR to go to a meeting, and she joked to her boss, "I'm not losing my job again, am I?" Her boss reassured her, but when she walked into the room and saw the manila envelopes for the second time, Regina knew it had happened all over again. After she received her envelope, Regina was asked to get in touch with the woman who would be replacing her at the other plant. "They made me train her before I left, and I had to do it with a smile on my face." When the entire plant closed, Regina explained it was shocking, but since she had almost a year longer to remain at work than most of her coworkers, most of her emotions were centered on her feelings of luck rather than frustration at the plant closing. But the second time around, when she learned that she had lost her job to people who weren't qualified for it, "that's when I had the bitter feelings," Regina explained.

Writing in the 1980s, Katherine S. Newman argued that one of the challenges in understanding unemployment was that mass layoffs were a collective loss—they devastated entire communities. Mass layoffs were common at that time, and Newman wondered if losing a job among a collective would ease the pain of the loss somehow. Yet even among people whose communities were wracked by job losses, Newman found evidence that people felt very hurt and angry, as if the company had laid off just them and not the entire workforce.

In my study, Regina's was one of the few job losses that looked like the mass layoffs of Newman's time. Most of the other job losses came either in smaller downsizing efforts (either of entire units or some people within a department) or sometimes as the only discharge in the entire company. Tracy's factory did not close; instead, it scaled back and she and eight others lost their jobs. Similarly, Anthony's natural extraction plant did not close; the company simply laid off one of the shifts of workers—Anthony and twelve others were gone that day. These jobs

were lost in what is commonly understood to be the downsizing process, which is how most people lose their jobs during nonrecessionary
periods, as companies try to correct for changes in their profits and
losses.[1] Joan's university lost the grants that had funded her, and Neil's
hotel group decided to "go in a different direction." Both were "no fault"
job losses but not part of a mass layoff; both Joan and Neil were the only
ones at their companies to lose their jobs.

It can be tricky to keep track of the terminology of job loss. Many of
those I met spoke of "being fired." In fact, Anthony's son (still in elementary school at the time) had taken to saying repeatedly, "You're
fired," echoing the infamous refrain of Donald Trump's reality television
show. Yet the Bureau of Labor Statistics doesn't commonly use the word
fired to describe people who have lost jobs through no fault of their
own; instead, it tracks layoffs (temporary, mass, and permanent), involuntary separations, discharges, and permanent job losers.[2] Regardless of word choice, everyone described in these pages lost a job that
the Pennsylvania unemployment office determined was a "no fault"
job loss.

The sociologist Arne Kalleberg argues that the changes in how people
lose jobs are the result of decades of changes in what is called "employment relations," meaning how employers treat their workers in the
United States.[3] Kalleberg and others argue that while in years past employers and workers used to share both the risks and the rewards of
operating businesses, in today's open market, businesses keep more of
the rewards for themselves and offload more of the risks onto their employees.[4] When profits shrink, employers no longer weather storms
with their employees. Instead, it has become common practice to lay off
some employees in order to cut costs even when the economy is strong.[5]
This means that employees are at greater risk of losing their jobs from
downsizing, as Tracy and Anthony did, or with the occasional grand
plant closing still occurring, as happened more often during the Great
Recession.

Three decades later, in this very different-looking landscape, would
the people I met feel angry or hurt by their employers? Did they blame
themselves for not having seen the signs sooner or not adequately being

able to find a new job ahead of time?[6] Or would they shrug and accept their fate as cogs in a *Metropolis*-like dystopian society, in which job loss has become an inevitable part of working in America?

Most people were still upset weeks and even months after their job loss. When asked how they felt the company had treated them, the vast majority said they had been treated poorly. People described themselves as "pissed," "sad," "heated," "angry," "bitter," "upset," and even "traumatized." Three job loss experiences seemed most likely to lead to these negative emotions: a *loss of identity*, companies making them feel *replaceable*, and making them feel *not part of the group*. Additionally, the *emotional toll of discriminatory firings* weighed heavily on the Black and Latina unemployed whose companies engaged in illegal discrimination in the dismissal process, leaving them with multiple emotional layers, including frustration and hurt that often combined with anger or outrage.

How did these experiences differ across gender and class? Most women and working-class men shared similar feelings of deep upset and anger. Joan described herself as deeply hurt, saying, "I mean, it's unfortunate, I think, but I worked for them for so long and made so many friends and colleagues and made the impact that I did on a national level. And they couldn't do anything for me. I think that's the part that stings the most. I put my heart and soul into everything I do." Joan's language suggests she felt she had given not simply her expected work effort but all of herself—"her heart and soul"—to her employer, and the firing felt like a dismissal of this gift. Tracy was devastated by the news. The people in charge of the layoffs walked around the plant letting each of the ten employees know individually. When it came time to talk to Tracy, she "cried like a baby. I think I made them feel bad." A few working-class men—mostly those who experienced chronic unemployment—were like Anthony, who reported being more resigned than upset. Remember that Anthony had described himself as "mostly numb" when he heard the news. He described his employers as "real apologetic about it," but Anthony had lost so many jobs that he had a hard time taking the news in.

Yet fewer than half of the middle-class men reported having these hurt or angry feelings—far fewer than the women or working-class men—and I wanted to understand why. I found the middle-class men reported much better treatment overall, and they had a much greater likelihood of receiving a severance than the women or the working-class men. Since severances are a way for a company to show responsibility for the worker, even after formal ties have been cut, the offering of a severance appeared to allow the newly unemployed middle-class men to maintain dignity in a way that few other company actions did.[7] Like most middle-class men, Neil received a six-week severance package when he was let go. But he also had what he considered a bad experience—his boss had taken him out for lunch, which had led him to expect a celebration, not a layoff. He was one of the few middle-class men to describe himself as "frustrated" with his job loss, although he also described it as an opportunity to "get out of the industry" and to spend more time with his wife. Thus, even in his frustration, Neil's perspective of his job loss looked quite a bit different from Joan's, Tracy's, or Anthony's.

A Loss of Dignity, Team, and Identity

What is it like, then, at the moment the ax falls? Over and over again, people spoke of feeling replaceable, like not part of the team anymore, or like they had lost their sense of self. It was both a loss of their identity as workers, as other sociologists and scholars of unemployment have noted,[8] but also a hard hit to their dignity and self-worth. While cutting costs by discharging people is a well-accepted business practice, it comes both with economic and emotional tolls that people experience when they learn their employers had priorities other than them.

Being let go to be replaced with cheaper labor was almost uniformly devastating, often engendering the "bitter feelings" described by Regina at the beginning of the chapter. Alana had five children, including two she was working to put through college. Her live-in boyfriend worked full-time, but money was tight with the tuition payments. For the last four years, she had worked as a salesperson at a local business. A friendly woman, Alana had the best sales numbers of the entire staff. She charmed everyone who came into the store, so her boss increased her target sales goals to match what she thought her potential sales output could be. When Alana started, her sales goals were $30,000 a month; her last month, her goals were $50,000. But despite this substantial increase in sales—an increase of 66 percent in only four years—her wages never changed from her original starting salary of $10 an hour.

A week before she was let go, Alana approached her boss and asked if she could have a raise or, barring that, if she could earn commission on her sales. She put together a pitch and explained what she saw as her main contributions to sales and why she saw herself as a valued employee to the company. Her boss said she would consider this request over the weekend. When Alana went back to work on Monday, she felt confident her boss was going to give her a raise. Instead, her boss told her in front of all of her coworkers, "'Yeah, we don't have enough money to give you a raise or do the sales thing. And I just want you to know that you've been replaced. So, we're not gonna need you anymore.'" While Alana knew she might not get the raise, she had not expected her boss would fire her for asking for one. It sent a clear signal that everyone was expendable—even the person who had been the top salesperson for nearly sixty months in a row.

Economists have long noted that in the bid to increase profits, companies can either increase sales or control costs, and one of the easiest costs to control is labor.[9] Over the past few decades, companies have focused more of their attention on keeping labor costs low in order to increase profits.[10] One of the seemingly easiest ways to reduce labor costs is to shrink one's labor force—with fewer workers, there are fewer wages to pay and overall costs are reduced.

Firing someone is not cheap. But it is legal. Economist Heather Boushey and her colleague, Sarah Jane Glynn, found that for both lower-wage workers like Alana and high-wage workers like Joan and Neil, businesses spend about one-fifth of a worker's salary in order to replace them.[11] But if a firm's goal is to sell more with lower costs, wouldn't firing their best salesperson (and taking on the high costs of replacing her) potentially be a bad business decision? At the time Alana was fired there were many people seeking work in her area, so after she was fired, Alana realized she would be easily replaced. Given that she had performed better on sales than her coworkers, Alana speculated that she might be replaced by someone who wasn't as gifted at sales. But it also seemed likely her boss thought it would be bad for business if Alana (and other employees) thought it was possible to ask for raises and expect to get them.

Yet there is broad evidence that any kind of turnover actually hurts companies. One study found that at small companies, like the one Alana worked at, when employees leave (either because they quit or because they were fired), customer service—how well customers feel they are being treated—declines.[12] The study didn't look at why this happens, but we can speculate that it might be because the best people have left or it might be because it hurts employee morale when other workers leave. Either way, it suggests that job loss isn't as good for companies as they might think it is. A recent review of multiple studies of turnover found that it actually hurts a large company's bottom line to let people go. In fact, when news of downsizing goes public, the value of companies' stock shares drops, hurting their investor's pockets.[13]

Alana was caught off-guard by her job loss, as were most people I interviewed. Many people found themselves, like Alana, losing jobs in public ways—in front of their colleagues and friends at work, which often increased the feelings of shame or loss of dignity that accompanied the job loss. Alana was "upset" and worried that she might become "bitter," even though she was normally a "pretty forgiving person," because her public dismissal in front of the staff was a painful moment. She remembers mumbling "Alright" and then turning and walking out of the store.

In the United States, the labor laws are very much in favor of the employer rather than the employee. In fact, the Organization for Economic Cooperation and Development (OECD) ranks the United States as having the absolute weakest laws protecting workers from dismissal in over seventy countries worldwide.[14] Pennsylvania is, like all states but Montana, an "employment-at-will" state, meaning that an employer can fire someone with *or* without cause.[15] In direct contrast, in the European Union (EU), companies cannot fire people "at will"; the EU commission states quite clearly that employers cannot fire their employees simply for "the wish of the employer."[16] Yet in the United States, there are very limited protections to the "at will" rule. If you have a union contract, your union may negotiate rules of termination, or if you are in a protected class, such a woman or a person of color or someone with a disability, you can't be fired for being in this protected class. For the most part, in the United States, there are little to no rules regarding how employers treat employees when they are let go.[17]

"I felt like we were thrown out like we were the trash," Monica told me. A married mother of two, she had worked as a medical transcriptionist for a local hospital. Sixteen transcriptionists were brought into a room by their supervisor and told that they had two months before their jobs would be outsourced to a local transcription company. If they wanted to, they could apply to work for that company; in fact, the company had someone with applications waiting for them outside the room. But the pay would be minimum wage—half of what Monica was making at the hospital after almost fifteen years—and they would receive no benefits. Monica, and most of the others, refused to apply. After that, Monica felt the hospital human resources staff played tough. The staff refused to help with even the smallest request Monica and the others made, such as asking for paystub printouts they were told they would need for their unemployment application (payroll was all online and Monica did not have a home printer). They would not answer questions about buying COBRA (the health insurance extension program), even though Monica knew that a woman who had recently left the hospital voluntarily had received information about this. Feeling disposable—like the company could easily throw you out and replace you with someone newer and cheaper—was often very devastating to workers.

Many of the working-class women had the feeling that they were being replaced by younger versions of themselves. Jodi felt very hurt by her job loss. She had thought that the temps she helped to train were there because business was expanding. Instead, "I was there for so long . . . I felt like they could have used me. And I was doing other things and they gave my jobs to temps that were there." Being replaced by people the unemployed had helped train was a common theme underlying people's upset feelings.

Losing the sense of belonging to a team was also hard on many workers. Many companies had policies that required workers to gather their things and be escorted from the premises after they are dismissed. I met Jill in my office on Penn State's campus because both she and her boyfriend had recently lost jobs and she felt like their house was "too depressing." She confided that she wanted the excuse to get dressed up and get out of the house, even if it was to come to the university to meet with me, rather than go on a "real interview." Jill had been working as an office manager for a tech company, and while she would have preferred a position that was only marketing (her field), she did all the communications writing for them. Jill found the whole process deeply upsetting. "They shut down your access to your computer system. They shut people out. They don't want people to make a fuss about it, so you know, they just kind of boot people out." Being shut out of the system felt hurtful to Jill and made it clear to her immediately that she was no longer part of the team. While this is a common practice among large companies worried about employees who might be unhappy after their firing or who may also want to protect sensitive documents from people whose loyalty is no longer to the company, it also is a practice that protects employees because they can't be blamed if something goes wrong after they learn about their termination. But Jill wondered why companies did not provide at least a couple of weeks' notice to employees to allow them to "get themselves together." Having her computer access terminated, her things packed up while she was in talking to HR, and then being walked off premises gave Jill the feeling that she was "like a criminal."

Brent had a history of chronic unemployment, yet it did not prepare him for his job loss. In fact, even when he was called into the human resources office, he did not realize he would lose his job. "When I got called by HR into the office there was another position that had opened up that I applied for and so I thought they were calling me in to talk to me about that position. So, then they called me in, I saw the paper, it said for termination and then I knew." While Brent's office was hiring for supervisory positions, they were letting people go at his level, and he was not under consideration for a position the next level up because he hadn't been with the company long enough. Brent described how his things were "held hostage," as someone from HR had emptied his desk while he was in the termination meeting and he was walked to the parking garage; he had to hand over his parking pass before he could get back his possessions.

Natalie was mad, too. One of the things that frustrated her most was all of the extra things that the company had done—the exercise boot camps, the book club groups, the yearly picnics, and Christmas parties—that made it seem like the company was more than just a company. It was a family—a group of people who cared about each other. Once her job was gone, she said, "I almost feel like I was taken away from a family." But while the company had fostered this family feeling, it did not mean that the company had a lasting commitment to Natalie.

Sometimes the worker wasn't walked to the HR office and handed a box to retrieve personal items at the desk. Some workers received a phone call dismissal notification and had company equipment removed from their home. Seth delivered medical equipment for his work, so he did not go into the office on a regular basis. Instead, he would call in or receive a fax and then use the company truck to make his deliveries. When he lost his job, as he recalled, his "manager showed up at my front door at eight o'clock in the morning and I wasn't supposed to start till eleven. Took my keys, my truck, my cell phone. They had given me a printer and a fax machine; they took everything from me that day and let me know that was it." Having them show up on his doorstep and strip him of everything they had given him felt terrible, particularly since his boss wasn't forthcoming with details. Even worse, Seth had not thought to keep the contact information for his coworkers on his personal phone (only on the work phone), so when he lost his job and the work equipment he lost contact with his coworkers, too. Only later would he connect with one of his coworkers on social media and learn that the two of them had been laid off that day and six others a couple days later. The company had merged and downsized. Seth lost both access to the company property as well as to his coworkers and friends.

Sociologist Dawn Norris has examined how people cope with the loss of identity after a job loss and how the job loss impacted their mental health. Ultimately, Norris argues that most people who lose a job cope with what she calls an "identity void" after the job loss; people have had part of their identity tied to work, and when they lose their job, that part of their identity is gone. In the weeks (and sometimes months) after they lose a job and before they find a new one, people must construct a new sense of who they are.[18] I found that this loss of identity was strongly felt by those in both the transitional and the lock-step group. Only those who had experienced chronic unemployment, like Anthony or Dennis, were less likely to emphasize the loss of identity as workers. This may be because the chronically unemployed spent much *less* time, on average, with their most recent job and had much *more* experience, on average, living with chronic unemployment; being unemployed had become part of their identity.

The Emotional Toll of Discriminatory Firings

As I noted in chapter 2, Black Americans experience unemployment rates at nearly twice the rates of whites in the United States. Discrimination explains part of these differences.[19] Recent studies that have taken a closer look at workforce practices have found disturbing patterns of clear harassment of Black employees by white employers and of discriminatory firing practices.[20] Moreover, when someone engages in discriminatory practices, it is usually not the discriminator but the person who faces the discrimination whose job is lost.[21] Additionally, Louwanda Evans, a scholar specializing in race and emotion work, has found that the persistent experience of racist microaggressions at work and the dismissal of the importance of race as a social structure can lead to an increased emotional burden on workers of color.[22] Taken together, we can understand why the *emotional toll of discriminatory firings* weighed so heavily on Black and Latina workers.

Latoya had particularly good cause to be upset about her job loss. Multiracial (Black and white) and middle-class, she had never lost a job before. She'd worked for her prior employer, a large health care conglomerate, for a number of years, working her way up the ranks in the human resources department. Like so many others, her identity was tied to her work; she told me, "I've been working for a very long time. It makes me feel very good about myself to have a position, to have a job, and to know that I'm holding my own and contributing financially." She'd impressed her boss so much that her boss promoted Latoya several times and put her into a training program. The training program even included funding for her to earn her master's degree, which she had started part-time. "Things were going great and then they fired our human resources director and they brought a new one in. The third day she was there she just said she didn't like me. And about three months later my job was mysteriously eliminated." While she'd had no complaints on her file and no previous interactions with this new boss before being told she wasn't liked, Latoya lost her job once this woman became her new manager. Latoya asked her new boss for a reason for the firing and was told, "'If I could have picked someone to work here, it wouldn't be you.'" This language, combined with their lack of interaction, convinced Latoya that the only reason for this level of animus from a new boss could be race. After she lost her job, Latoya was not simply "livid," she took legal action and filed an Equal Employment Opportunity Commission complaint (which she would eventually win). Her sense of injustice at the way she'd been treated motivated this decision. She explained, "My goal is to have her removed from that position and have the company have to take other steps that will hit them in several areas to make sure that doesn't happen again." Latoya sought justice for herself and protection for other workers of color who might follow in her footsteps.

Latoya wasn't the only woman of color fired because of her race. Even in a study as small as mine, multiple people of color experienced job losses under discriminatory circumstances. Christina, a Latina woman, had worked as a social worker for a government agency and was exploring her options for suing the agency for wrongful dismissal when we first met. She felt her new boss hadn't liked her because she was an opinionated woman of color. She'd never had a problem in her several years working there until this new boss came on the scene. A unionized worker, Christina knew her union had negotiated a clear procedure that needed to be followed before an employee was fired. There were to be documented write-ups of problematic behavior from a supervisor or written complaints from a family. But Christina never received a write-up from him or a complaint from a family. Her firing came as a complete surprise and violated the terms of her union contract. She learned the news and thought, "How dare you?" Explaining this sense of outrage, she described how she had always gotten along with her coworkers and the clients they served: "The case workers and the frontline staff, they do a very good job and they're amazing people." Christina went on, "If I deserved it, I could understand that. But I've never had any warnings, nothing. . . . Or if it was downsizing, that would even be different, but that's not what this was." As a result, she was left with one feeling: "angry." After our first meeting, Christina sued and settled out of court. Recent research finds that both Black and Latino workers, particularly women, are less well represented in managerial positions in the public sector than they were in the past, and that their wages compared to whites have been on the decline.[23] Discriminatory firing practices as experienced by Latoya and Christina may contribute to the underrepresentation and lower wages that Black and Latino workers face and, like other experiences of racial discrimination at work, they may even harm health, increasing a worker's risk of stress or hypertension, as earlier studies have found.[24]

Severances, Dignity, and Middle-Class Men

There was one group that did not feel nearly as upset and angry as the rest; they also were protected from gender or racial bias in the workplace, as none reported having discriminatory experiences. These people told me the company just had to make the decision to let them go. As one said, "It's just business is business is business." This group was white middle-class men. A national study found that white middle-class men were much less likely to be the target of downsizing than women and men of color, which meant that white men in professional jobs were often the last to go or the sole survivors when layoffs arrived.[25]

In fact, a number of the white middle-class men had survived earlier layoffs at work or had been the ones instigating those layoffs. Some even said their companies had treated them well. The quotes from this group are in stark contrast to the primarily angry feelings described by the women and working-class men. "They did it as professionally as they could," said one. "I got the feeling they didn't really want to let me go," said another. "They treated us really well," replied a third, while a fourth reported, "It was a respectful thing." One man went so far as to say it was "no fault of the company, and I'm not blaming them in anyway." This final quote is particularly striking because the company had, of course, let him go, but he wanted to make sure I understood that he did not fault the company for that.

In the 1980s, Newman argued that the "culture of meritocracy" is so strong in the United States that it led some of the middle-class men she met to support their employers' decision to fire them. This "culture of meritocracy" hinges on what scholars have recognized as a particularly American belief that people achieve their successes and failures solely based on their own merit (and not, for example, because they may have benefited from having well-educated parents). Two decades later, writing about workers who lost jobs before the Great Recession, Allison Pugh found both working- and middle-class men and women generally accepted their job loss as a matter of course, not because of American meritocracy, but because of what Pugh called the "one-way honor system" in American workplaces, in which workers devote themselves to companies but do not expect such loyalty in return from their employers.[26] Looking at the unemployed who, again, lost jobs before the Great Recession, Ofer Sharone found that American white-collar workers (but less so blue-collar ones) engaged in a "self-blame" game.[27] Yet in her study on the reorganization of work in the 1990s, Vicki Smith found middle-class workers who said "it hurts to realize that the employers are not going to give to employees."[28] A post–Great Recession study likewise found that the unemployed—particularly the long-term unemployed with college but not advanced degrees—were likely to blame employers for their inability to find work.[29] Thus, there have been mixed results in the existing research on the middle class and their feelings about job loss.

I think there are a few reasons why the middle-class men were likely to agree with the business arguments for their firing and why they weren't as angry about their job loss. As a whole, the middle-class men were overrepresented in occupations where they had high degrees of autonomy and had reached high levels of success in their careers. They were most likely to be in management and to have done the firing in previous rounds. They often had survived other downsizings and appreciated that their companies made an effort to keep them on. They may have identified more strongly with the ones who were firing them than the women or the working-class men in this study would have, and they were also more likely to be employed in architecture and engineering or computer and mathematical occupations. Having achieved a sizable amount of success in our meritocratic system, the middle-class men perhaps felt more obligated to support the existing system, even when things didn't work out as well for them.

Overall, the middle-class men were treated with greater respect when they lost their jobs and appeared to feel like they retained more of their dignity. Most had experiences that were similar to that of Jerry, a white middle-class man, married with three children, who was told privately what was happening in the hospital where he worked in management and reassured by his supervisor who told him, "'I will give you an exemplary reference.'" His boss even offered to start making calls that day to help Jerry find a new position. This level of outreach by an employer was almost unheard of outside the circle of middle-class men. Jerry also had the experience of being walked out of the building on the day he was let go, but Jerry had done this to other employees himself when he was a manager and felt differently about the experience. He had gone through management training and saw being walked out as a protective step by the company—for his sake as much as his former employers—because it removed the possibility that momentary hurt feelings could cause bad decision making, and it protected him from any liability should anything happen in the hospital work environment after he received the news.

There is an additional answer for why the middle-class men felt so differently about their employers after their job loss than the other participants did. Almost two-thirds of the middle-class men were offered a severance package when they were let go. In striking contrast, not even a quarter of the middle- and working-class women received a severance, and none of the working-class men got one.[30] In 1988, Newman wrote that severances are "potent symbols of esteem." Severances let employees know that the company respected their work and their years of service, and they also suggest a level of continued corporate responsibility to the employee even after their formal relationship is severed. In addition to the social and psychological rewards, severances also provided real tangible financial benefits to the newly unemployed. Unlike unemployment benefits that pay, at most, half of someone's salary, severances extended the period for which people received their full salaries for weeks and often months. This allowed middle-class men to put into place more frugal spending practices in the time leading up to when they would start to receive unemployment.

In addition to being treated with a great deal of respect and being told he'd get a great reference, Jerry got a large severance package: nearly eight months' salary at full pay. Jerry felt his severance package was justified because, as a management-level employee, he couldn't be allowed to continue to work once he was given noticed. He explained, "Management, when you resign, typically depending on how long you're in that position, you give four weeks [notice] at management level. Unfortunately, with termination, for management it is immediate. You're literally given notice and you're walked to your office; you're watched as you're cleaning your office and then you're walked to the parking lot. Because of management—it's because of security, you know—I had access to computer systems that regular staff doesn't have access to." Because the security protocol required immediate termination, Jerry said, "most managements will get some sort of severance depending on how long they've been there and [in my case] it was for eight months' time. That was my severance."

But many workers—like Tracy, Joan, and Anthony, as well as others we met in this chapter—didn't receive a severance package, including many who were walked out in a similar manner. They were simply let go. (And many, like Tracy and Anthony, did not even receive any notice.)

Jerry's severance pay covered a long period of time, and it gave him the ability to search for new work while not working and before he started collecting unemployment (he was eligible for full unemployment benefits once his severance ended). While it can be easier to find a new job when employed, searching for work when not employed can be easier, as there is more free time in which to apply for jobs and go to interviews.

Severances were made more complicated when they came with strings attached or when they were offered by companies that had bought out previous employers. Frank had worked for nine years for the same company and enjoyed his work. He received nine total additional paychecks—one for each year he had spent with the company. While he appreciated the severance pay, he was disappointed that it came with a noncompete agreement, which stated he would not be allowed to work for a competitor, and that he had a very short time period in which to sign it. He told me, "We were given twelve hours to sign our severance paperwork. And in our paperwork, it says feel free to get a lawyer to look over it. I'm like, 'Yeah, I have a lawyer on retainer?'" Frank felt that twelve hours was not enough time to carefully consider signing a noncompete agreement, even though there were "not many competitors in that market." While federal law requires that workers age 40 and older be given a minimum of seven days to consider a severance package (and more time if more than one employee is being terminated), younger employees, like Frank, have no such rights.[31] Thus, even a generous severance (nine paychecks, or four and a half months before he would have to go on unemployment) can feel less generous depending on the restrictions placed on it.

Not everyone who was offered a severance package took it. Barry, a high-level executive, explained, "Well, I was offered a severance package, but I had to sign a severance agreement and there was a noncompete and some clauses in there that I didn't want to lock myself into. I did not sign the severance agreement, so I did not get a severance package." Despite not taking the offered severance package, Barry felt little ill will toward his company. There was a merger, and in the course of business his position and a few others were eliminated. Barry explained that with this sort of merger, it would have been unexpected for him to keep his job, so as soon as he heard the merger was happening, he began net-working and looking for a new position. When his bosses asked him to make the several-hours drive out to the new corporate headquarters, he knew what was in store for him that day. Despite spending almost all day in the car to get to a "ten-minute meeting" in which he was let go, Barry exhibited none of the resentment or anger expressed by the other participants. He said that he understood why it had to happen this way and that the severance he had been offered (and declined) had been more than generous.

Severances didn't guarantee that employees wouldn't be upset about their job loss. We remember from earlier in the chapter that Neil still felt upset despite a six-week severance. When people felt that they had lost their jobs unjustly, it was not always enough to be sent away with a fairly tidy sum of money. But, as we will see in the following chapters, it could ease the challenges of unemployment considerably. Sometimes receiving a severance that was less than what was understood to be stan-dard for the industry could lead to harsh feelings about the company. Nathan, an architect, was particularly put out with his employers because he felt that his severance was fairly shabby. He told me, "I only got two weeks of pay from here and I figured that stinks." He was com-paring his most recent severance to that of his former employer who had given him two months. Perhaps compared to his past severance package, two weeks' pay was low, and even compared to the other middle-class men, Nathan's severance was less than average. But, when compared to what the middle-class women and the working-class indi-viduals were offered, Nathan's full two weeks of pay set him clearly well above most people who lose their jobs.

Among the women, it was much more common not to receive sever-ances. Pamela, for example, had been with her former employer for al-most three years and had accrued vacation time but was not given a severance; in fact, she wasn't even allowed to take her remaining vaca-tion time or receive it as a cash payout. In contrast, many of the middle-class men took for granted that their owed vacation would also be in-cluded in a final lump-sum payout. Dean, for example, got all of his accrued eight weeks of vacation and sick days paid. Pamela "was so mad" when she realized she would receive nothing from the company. Rita wasn't even paid fully for her last day of work. While she was upset that she didn't receive severance after nearly seven years with the company, she was outraged that she wasn't paid for the final hours she worked; it was, she said, "just a horrible mess." While scholars (myself included) have often pointed out that women's motivation for participating in paid work is complicated and tied to more than what they can earn, it is important to note that what people earn is both financially important as well as a social signal of how that worker is valued by the company (and, perhaps, by society at large). In perhaps a sign of how much working-class jobs have changed in the last four decades, none of the working-class men reported having received a severance. In fact, Timothy remarked, "No place I've ever been [that] let me go, gave me severance pay." Both the women and the men understood that severances were a sign of a company's respect and responsibility, but only the middle-class men had regular access to this reward.

When I first puzzled over the differences in severances between the middle-class men and everyone else, I resented the Jerrys and Neils of the world—why did they get these benefits that the others did not? But the more I thought about it, the more I realized that I didn't really want Jerry, Neil, and others like them to have less; I wanted Regina and Joan and Tracy and Anthony to have more.

Most of the middle-class men still lived in a world in which their companies acted as if they owed them something for their efforts and their hard work over the years. In the first months of the 2020 global pandemic, differences in access to severance pay were widespread, with hourly and contingent workers reporting a much lower likelihood to receive a severance than those who worked in managerial positions. Several new tech companies, like Airbnb, made the news for their relatively generous severances, while large media conglomerates, manufacturing plants, and hotel chains were blasted by employees for their lack of such offerings.[32]

In the years after World War II, companies and workers both benefited from economic growth—a growth that was shared by employers
and workers.[33] But in recent years, companies have resisted sharing the
profits with their workers, and we have seen the relationship between
wages and profits come apart. Jacob Hacker argues that there has been
a decline in corporate responsibility toward the workforce: while
companies once felt responsible for providing for their workers' re-
tirements and health care, they no longer do so.[34] Christine Williams,
a sociologist of gender, race, and class inequality at work, argues that
these corporate changes systematically disadvantage women, making
them particularly vulnerable to layoffs.[35] Where was Regina's boss's
loyalty to her when she asked her point blank if she were about to be
fired and her boss blithely answered no, before walking Regina to the
room where she would, a second time, receive that manila envelope?
It was not, Regina felt, directed toward her.

As we will see in the next chapters, severances provided middle-class
men additional financial security that would have lasting implications
for what would happen next in their ability to make home payments and
maintain their health insurance, in their job searches, and in other areas.
The middle-class men already had the advantage of being, on average,
the best paid before they lost their jobs; most of them now had the
advantage of delaying receipt of their unemployment insurance. In
chapter 4, we will take a closer look at the financial devastation facing
some families in the wake of their job loss and the ways that other families managed to avoid many financial repercussions.

PART II

The Fallout

4

Insecurity after the Job Loss

CAROL'S WEEKS, even before her job loss, were centered around her daughter. Carol's fifteen-year-old was her only child and a promising traveling-club soccer player. The family often drove far distances on the weekends for soccer meets and had other expenses related to the daughter's soccer. After her job loss from a medical billing company, Carol was determined not to allow the family's financial challenges to intrude on her daughter's ability to play the game. She remembered, "[My daughter] asked me about soccer and I told her that I wasn't going to let anything ruin what we had going, and that I would make sure that we made all the tournaments." It was a tough goal: There were costly fees involved in certain leagues, plus the cost of outfits and equipment, not to mention the travel expenses. But Carol felt that participation in a team sport would be a crucial component of her daughter's college application. Carol's parents hadn't, she thought, really understood what it took to apply and get into college. In her mind, they had allowed Carol to drift into an associate's degree in foods and hospitality that would prove of little use for full-time employment. She never found work in the field in which she held her degree. Carol wanted things to be different for her daughter, explaining, "I want her to think about the future," and in order for her daughter to plan better, Carol focused on "showing her the opportunities" so that her daughter was better prepared for the world of work than she had been.

But after her job loss, finances became tight for Carol and her family. She and her husband struggled to pay their bills. With only half of her regular income coming in, the family cut back on all extra expenses (save for soccer) and a few necessary ones. Carol and her family stopped using one of the family cars, so they would only need to put gas in one. Carol started watching flyers for food deals and cutting coupons; they reduced some food purchases, although not the healthy foods her daughter needed. They stopped eating out, instead packing sandwiches and water bottles on days they would travel for soccer. Carol stopped her gym membership, cut back on cleaning supplies, stopped using fabric softener in her laundry, and started hanging the clothes out to dry to save on electricity. Vacations were a thing of the past, and even short drives to see friends were not taken to reduce the cost of gas. Her daughter continued her soccer playing, for now, but she was not allowed to participate in the team's social activities any longer, like going out for ice cream to celebrate after a win. That was hard on Carol's daughter—and on Carol, who hated to deny her this fun. She summed up, saying, "Right now we're just balancing out, just trying to live. We're getting exactly what we need, nothing extra, nothing extra at all."

In 2014, Carl Van Horn, a professor of public policy at Rutgers University, set out to understand how losing a job and experiencing unemployment was affecting people in the wake of the Great Recession. He and his research team surveyed both employed and unemployed Americans and asked them about changes in their lifestyles after the recession ended. They were particularly interested in those who were long-term unemployed (meaning they had been out of work for more than six months), but they also looked at people who hadn't been out of work that long—those like the people in this study. What they found raised alarm bells. Under the heading "diminished living standards," Van Horn and his colleagues reported that the majority of the recently unemployed reported their job loss had changed their lives.[1] Overall, Van Horn and his colleagues warned, the trend appeared bleak for Americans who lost jobs.

Despite the importance of this report, I found it did not provide a complete picture of the variation in how people's finances were affected by their job loss. About a tenth of the people I interviewed, like Carol, had barely enough to pay their bills and sometimes went without essentials and often without extras. Some were much harder hit; over a third did not have enough money to pay their daily bills. Those in this group regularly went without essentials, reducing their food purchases and electricity use, missing bill payments, and even eliminating some children's necessities. Yet a little over half of the sample had enough money—some even more than enough—to cover their daily bills; these people made much more modest changes to their spending.[2]

As we have seen thus far, gender and class shaped many aspects of job loss and unemployment, including the degree to which households felt the pinch of a job loss. Of course, changes to one's lifestyle when one makes $25,000 annually look different from changes to one's lifestyle when one makes $78,000 or $178,000, which the Pew Research Center estimates as the median incomes for households at the bottom, middle, and top in earnings in the United States.[3]

While Van Horn's study did not specifically look at gender or class differences, other research has. Asking whether women and men faced the same repercussions after the Great Recession, the Institute for Women's Policy Research found women reported greater material hardship than men did after losing their jobs; in fact, both married and single women reported being more likely than men to struggle to pay bills, to experience hunger, to have fewer savings, and to have a greater inability to fulfill their children's needs.[4] Some qualitative research offers insight on potential class differences in experiences of unemployment. Ofer Sharone, the author of *Flawed System/Flawed Self* about job searching and unemployment, suggests the working class may face greater financial precarity after a job loss. In his 2013 book, Sharone notes that "blue-collar job seekers are generally closer to the financial abyss" than middle-class job seekers in his study.[5] Looking exclusively at the working poor, Kathryn Edin and H. Luke Schaefer argue unemployment can be devasting, leading families to live on as little as $2 a day.[6] They write about low-income workers (some with high school degrees) in areas where jobs are scarce, temporary jobs are lost, and families rely on food stamps and face hunger and homelessness when new jobs can't be found.

Yet much of the research on middle-class workers has focused not on the material challenges but instead on the grave *feelings* of insecurity that they experience, particularly when they are among the long-term un-employed.[7] While Carrie Lane, the white-collar unemployment expert, argues that "jobless tech workers also face very real material challenges," she notes that "few of the jobs seekers I met were in danger of losing their homes or being unable to feed or clothe their families."[8] Yet Lane's participants often felt insecure. Still other researchers find many of the emotional strains experienced by upper-middle-class men stem from marital fissures caused by the anxieties about finances.[9] Feelings of fi-nancial insecurity may vary in married-coupled households, not based on income but on whether it is the husband (which seems to increase family insecurity) or the wife (which seems to decrease family insecu-rity) who has lost a job, according Aliya Rao, author of *Crunch Time: How Married Couples Confront Unemployment*.[10] Rao's research suggests that families worry more about finances after a husband's job loss and do more to help a husband return to work than when it is a wife who has lost a job.

In this chapter, I parse out exactly what kinds of material challenges people face and how they may differ by class and gender. There is evi-dence to suggest that unemployment may be particularly hazardous to people who have lower wages to start with and those who don't have a working spouse.[11] The hardship that can ensue after a job loss can be severe; by some calculations, about 40 percent of those who enter pov-erty do so after the person on whose income the family depends loses his or her job.[12] This suggests that, for some, the material challenges likely do include the possibilities of losing homes, facing hunger, or hav-ing the electricity turned off.

Among those I met, unemployment was a fast track to impoverish-ment and great hardship, but not for everyone. Unemployment benefits were an important component of this differentiation. In the state of Pennsylvania at the time of the interviews, unemployment benefits were calculated based on prior earnings (highest average quarterly earn-ings of any two quarters of the last four quarters). Thirty-six other states use a relatively generous formula to calculate unemployment insurance, calculating based either on the *highest* quarterly earnings (as in Penn-sylvania) or on the highest earnings over multiple quarters.[13] Thirteen states use either annual wages or average weekly wages, which can be much lower. This is worth pointing out because it means that Pennsylvania's benefit (while not the most generous) is certainly among the better plans in the nation (and we will see that this generosity still left so many in dire financial straits).

People received roughly half of this average (up to a maximum threshold), which meant that higher-earning folks received more from unemployment than did their counterparts. Middle-class men were often the most secure, as Neil was, removed from the worst unemployment can bring by multiple layers of resources, including higher unemployment benefits (as well as the severances I discovered in the last chapter) and, most often, a dual-earning wife who provided an additional layer of security. Middle-class women, too, had the greater protection of higher unemployment benefits (though their benefits were rarely as high as middle-class men received), greater savings, and a working spouse. Unlike the middle-class men, middle-class women like Joan rarely received a severance. Working-class men faced greater financial peril, having lower benefits, fewer savings, and being the most likely to have a stay-at-home spouse to support, as was the case with Anthony. Finally, working-class women were, by far, the most vulnerable as they reported the lowest unemployment benefits, the lowest savings in reserve, and a low likelihood of receiving severances. Working-class women were also the most likely to be single moms, like Tracy, which puts all of the financial burdens on one set of shoulders. We can see how, then, very early in the process, interactions with the institution of unemployment, including eligibility and benefits determinations by the state unemployment system (as well as differences in workplace severances) began to differently shape how the unemployment period would be experienced by Tracy compared to Neil.

Great Insecurity in the Working Class

Immediately after their job loss, the majority of working-class women said they either had not enough or barely enough money to pay their daily bills.[14] Among the working-class women, over half reported at least three of the following: bills going unpaid, food being reduced, children's necessities and extras being eliminated, savings (if they existed) being depleted, and household supplies being reduced. Some had been forced to turn off the electricity, and others reported that phone bills were the only bills regularly being paid (because they knew phones were necessary to find a job, although many had spoken with the phone company to change their plan). Unlike the vast majority of their middle-class counterparts, most of the working-class women had no savings to start with. They were also unlikely to receive severances.

Not only did the working-class women have few resources in reserve, they also received the lowest unemployment benefits, on average. In chapter 1, we learned that Tracy's unemployment compensation was $154 a week, or $616 monthly. How far would that have stretched during the years I interviewed the unemployed? For the year 2013, the U.S. Department of Agriculture (USDA) estimated it would cost about $479 a month using a "thrifty" budget to buy healthy meals to feed a mom and two children the ages of Tracy's kids.[15] Had Tracy followed this recommendation, it would have left her with $137 to pay her rent, her bills, and everything else. But Tracy had long been a saver of food. When we met, I noted how her pantry seemed stocked with dried goods, although in Tracy's eyes, her pantry was depleted, having been heavily raided and not replenished in the three months since she lost her job. This helped Tracy keep her children fed, as did the SNAP benefits (the Supplemental Nutrition Assistance Program that replaced food stamps) they received, but she was not eating as regularly as she used to. She wanted to make sure her kids had enough, and if that meant that she had to go without, she expected that was just part of what she would have to do.

Bills were being paid on time, though. Tracy made sure of that. She didn't want to lose their electricity or their phone, so she'd called both companies as soon as she lost her job to see if she could renegotiate her rates. Unfortunately, the person from the electric company didn't quite understand her predicament and had renegotiated a rate for her that spread out her payments evenly across the year, which he mistakenly thought would be helpful since she had electric heat. But since Tracy had lost her job over the summer, the renegotiation left her worse off in the immediate aftermath of her job loss, as she ended up owing extra money for future heating payments, which meant putting nearly a third of her unemployment compensation toward her electricity bill. When she called to complain, the company said she wasn't allowed to renegotiate the payment plan again until the new year.

Tracy explained, "So we have a home and we have TV and lights, but we can't go anywhere." The sparseness of their lives weighed on Tracy. Her children's father paid no child support, despite a court order; Tracy said, "I don't know how he gets away with it, but he does." Although he was rarely in the picture, when he asked if he could take the children to a local amusement park for an outing, she felt she couldn't refuse her kids the opportunity.[16] But she resented that he got to give them an exciting day away from the hardship while refusing to help with the daily work of financially providing, caring, and raising them. Sighing with frustration, she said, "He's pretty much a joke." Sociologists Kathryn Edin and Timothy Nelson have found that as men's paid work opportunities have decreased for those with a high school education or less, men have attempted to redefine what it means to be a good dad—a definition that no longer necessarily includes providing financially for their families.[17] They find that dads who have unsteady or infrequent employment, like Tracy's ex, contribute little financially to their children's household and, instead, make grand gestures by purchasing special gifts for children—gifts that mothers who are maintaining the household costs cannot afford. Tracy's ex certainly fell into this category as he took the kids out for a day and left her behind (literally and figuratively) juggling bills and the daily costs of supporting their children.

Tracy's life in the weeks and months after her job loss were marked by notable hardship and not enough government support to prevent her family from falling deeply into poverty. The fall into poverty was one experienced by many working-class women. Tamara and her kids started eating at soup kitchens, Tonya and her children were grateful to gain access to SNAP, and Vanessa explained that she'd sold just about everything she owned. "Next thing to go is that TV," she said, pointing to the only television in the house, but she thought her kids would take it badly. Most of these women were single mothers, which further exacerbated their economic insecurity because there wasn't anyone to help pick up the costs or help with the childcare. Almost all of the working-class women who had young children pulled them out of childcare after their job loss. It was impossible, they reasoned, to afford without their salary (although as we will see in chapter 7, searching for work without childcare was very difficult).

Not as many working-class men faced this level of hardship, but just under half (most of whom had been chronically unemployed) reported that they also didn't have enough or had barely enough money to cover their costs. Under a third of the working-class men reported three of the following: bills going unpaid, food being reduced, children's necessities and extras being eliminated, savings (if they existed) being depleted, and household supplies being reduced. Anthony and his family relied solely on his unemployment benefits. While he, like most working-class men, earned more than the working-class women, his unemployment benefits were not enough to pay his bills. Since working-class men like Anthony were the most likely to have had a history of chronic unemployment, they had often tapped out their financial reserves. Anthony explained that at some point, he had simply stopped trying to keep track of all of his bills. He could not keep up with them, and he could not pay off his credit cards. Even when he found employment again, the cumulative effect of having had so many job losses was financially devastating. He told me, "I struggled from that point on, even during good-paying times, to pay my bills on time." Being back on unemployment again made things for the working-class chronically unemployed much worse.

While working-class women, like Tracy, were the most likely to be single parents, working-class men were the most likely to have a stay-at-home wife. Being a breadwinner in what is typically called a "traditional family" with a stay-at-home mom was different from being a single mom, as the breadwinning working-class men could rely on their wives for childcare and household labor (work that the single moms had to do themselves, for the most part). But the men did feel the financial burden to provide for their families. Moreover, even if their wives did look for employment, they often could not find work that would help out the family because they had been outside of the paid labor market for so long. If their stay-at-home wives had found employment, it would have been for very low wages because of their lack of work experience (as I describe in my first book).[18] The families would then need to decide if women without much labor market experience should attempt to work for pay and whether the little money they could earn would be worth the need to juggle child-rearing responsibilities or even pay for outside childcare help.

Anthony's wife stayed at home, and they decided it didn't make sense for her to try to search for work. They also strongly considered her going back to school and thought her best bet was nursing; there had been a shortage of nurses in the area. But his wife didn't have the education credentials to get into an RN program, so she would need to take courses to help her get into that kind of program first. And, of course, they were struggling to pay their bills. His church was providing their groceries. Although sending her back to school might have solved their problems, it was not a solution they could afford.

It likely made sense for Anthony and his wife to have reached this decision. They had young children for whom she was caring and without any work experience, she was unlikely to find work that would have paid well enough to balance out the immediate cost of childcare. Nobel laureate and economist James Heckman called this the "shadow wage" placed on women's employment—the cost of covering childcare.[19] This is a complicated calculation, because children aren't only women's responsibility, and we could imagine the costs of childcare coming from both spouses' wages, yet this isn't how many families think about this cost.[20] Moreover, lost wages add up over the years, and just a short time out of work can mean a significant earnings penalty in older age for women.[21] But, as my collaborator Adrianne Frech and I found in a national study, while a majority of women work steadily through their childbearing years, many others either temporarily reduce their work hours or leave the labor force entirely for a time.[22] My first book suggests that white women like Anthony's wife, who had a working-class husband who was employed full-time and relatively poor work options herself, were particularly likely not to work.

Low unemployment benefits—stemming from institutional rules about minimum length of job tenure—could lead to great insecurity even with a working spouse. Roy had only recently started his new job as a welder on a probationary period at the plant. This meant that he wasn't eligible to join the union yet and wasn't eligible for the job benefits. Unfortunately, the plant had hired him and a couple hundred of others in anticipation of a new contract—a contract that was canceled within the first few months after Roy was hired. His previous work experience let Roy survive the first round of layoffs but not the second (only the unionized workers survived those). He hadn't even worked there long enough to earn unemployment from the company, according to state unemployment rules—he had to draw unemployment from the company he worked for before he took this job, where he'd earned a much lower wage.

Everything seemed to go wrong for Roy after the job loss. He and his common-law wife felt overwhelmed by their bills. "What I get in unemployment is basically barely enough to even feed us . . . or pay the mortgage, or pay the other bills, or keep gas in the car or day care." He explained, "Every month, if we pay something, we're falling behind in everything else."

Food scarcity hit Roy's family hard. While they were used to grabbing food out at fast-food restaurants, these types of quick and easy meals were no longer possible. In fact, with three young children to feed plus childcare support to pay for two of Roy's older kids, his unemployment did not fully cover their grocery bills. Roy's mom convinced them to lower their pride and accept food from the local food pantry. Roy's mom also gave them some expired food that they decided to eat because they couldn't afford to be picky. But they learned recently that the nearby food pantry was "closing down so we can't even use them" as an avenue of support. The authors of *Pressure Cooker*, a book about families and food in the United States, note that food pantries became prominent in the United States in the 1980s when the government safety net started shrinking rapidly.[23] But most of these programs are funded by private donations rather than being public programs, so they can shrink or even close when areas experience periods of economic contraction.

Yet families like Roy's needed more help just as these types of social supports were less able to provide it.

A history of chronic unemployment left a few working-class men at risk of losing their homes. Seth, who lost his job delivering medical equipment in a company merger and downsizing, and his family actually did lose their home. Without his income, he and his wife, a stay-at-home mom, could not afford to make their rent. They had been late on the last payment, too, because his paycheck had come late (because of the merger, as he learned much later). There was no wiggle room when the rent check came due; they were forced to leave their apartment and move back home to his mother's house with their kids. Seth had a history of chronic unemployment, and this latest job loss hit him at a time when the family had no savings and no second income. At its worst, then, unemployment brought hunger, loss of electricity, and loss of a home.

Steadier Working-Class Finances

Not all working-class families experienced such hardship. Writing in the 1970s about working-class families living on Clay Street in Washington, DC, Joseph Howell described two types of blue-collar families: the "steady" and the "hard living." The "hard living" families of Clay Street had less access to stable employment than did the steady families, so when things went wrong, they went really wrong. The steady families on Clay Street had better jobs, which gave them more resources with which to stabilize themselves; overall, they just seemed to have greater access to a stable life. Today, sociologists might characterize the steady families as having had "good jobs," the kinds of jobs that are less common but when found have better pay, health insurance, and fringe benefits like pensions or retirement accounts. Within the working-class today, there still exist some "good" or "steady" jobs that provide access to the kind of stability needed so that when a job loss comes, the family may have enough reserves to get by.

Having this kind of good job is so important because, as should be clear by now, if unemployment compensation is approximately half of what you were making (at its most generous), then you need to make a decent wage in order to be above the poverty line when your salary is cut in half. You also need to have earned enough to set some money aside in savings in order to weather the financial storm that would follow a job loss. But many Americans don't have the financial savings to withstand this kind of storm. In fact, over the past three decades, there has been a decline in the amount of wealth held by the bottom 90 percent of all families.[24]

Those working-class families that had enough to cover their bills generally had dual earners in the family who both worked at steady jobs, earning well above the minimum wage. They also had a spouse whose earnings could help keep the family afloat. Finally, they often had savings set aside that could be used for emergencies. After eight years as a foreman overseeing a team of mechanics for a national trucking company, Joel had been upset when he was let go, but in the six weeks since he'd lost his job, his family had not yet experienced any daily hardships. His son's birthday was coming up—and with a Halloween birthday, they had two big events to celebrate and they didn't plan to skimp on them. Joel said, "He's in Boy Scouts, and we haven't cut back or slashed or anything like that. Everything's still pretty much going."

Joel decided to empty $10,000 out of his 401(k) in order to tide them over until he found a new job. He hoped to be able to replace it before he'd have to pay the tax penalty for using it. He did still have his pension from the large trucking company, and while he wouldn't be able to touch it until his retirement, he was glad for the security that it provided. His wife, who worked about thirty hours a week as a waitress/cook, had increased her hours to nearly full-time, but that seemed fair to Joel, since he'd been the one working full-time for so long. Joel explained that they were "just trading places" for a little bit, but his wife had told him to expect that she'd be switching back to part-time work as soon as he found full-time work again. Overall, Joel was on steady financial ground for now, but he and others like him were less common in the working class.

Relying on retirement savings and on a spouse's income is what many families do when times are hard, as we learned from Joel. While some women (like Anthony's wife) who haven't been in the workforce have a hard time entering the job market, women who are already working could either increase their hours or maintain steady work and provide a cushion to family finances in that way. In my first book, I found that families were able to depend on women's income to help provide increased security during difficult times. While women's earnings typically cannot replace men's in the household, owing to the wage gap in income between men and women, the overall rise in women's employment has been critical for families' financial security in the United States. While women's labor force participation rates actually rose fastest among those married to the highest-earning men, women's labor force participation rates have risen among all married couples, helping to stem the tide of shrinking wages among the working class.[25]

Middle-Class Security

At about three months after their job loss, the vast majority of middle-class workers remained on solid financial ground. Over three-quarters of the middle-class men said that they had enough to cover their daily costs, as did two-thirds of the middle-class women.[26] In fact, among the middle class, it was more common to report that security was achieved without touching retirement savings than for people to empty their 401(k) plans. In fact, both Neil and Joan emphasized that they expected not to touch their retirement accounts during their period of unemployment.

This did not mean that nothing changed in these houses. Prior research has noted that most middle-class households are built on the assumption of two incomes, and the loss of one of those incomes can pose an immediate challenge.[27] But the changes were, for the most part, much smaller in magnitude in the first few months than they were for the working class. In chapter 8, we will take another look, one year later, to see if more financial sacrifices had to be made. But for now, most workers in the middle class reported fairly modest changes. Neil explained that he and his wife were eating out less frequently. He thought that previously they had been spending between $800 to $1,000 a month on groceries and meals out for two people and had tried to cut back. They had been eating their leftovers more often, rather than throwing them away.

Neil's income had been relatively high, so he was bringing home slightly less than half of what he'd made, as he had hit the maximum benefit allowed by the state. But his wife had a substantial salary, and Neil had received a severance pay of six weeks, some of which he had been able to set aside in preparation for when he would receive only the unemployment insurance. Neil and his wife also didn't have children, which meant they had no one else to support, unlike most other people I met. Even though he had had a history of chronic unemployment, Neil historically had bounced quickly from one job to the next with little time off in between, rebounding better than most of the working-class men.[28] Neil explained his wife had started "buying stuff online through Walmart and trying to buy bulk" household supplies. Their typical summer vacation was happening in the fall this year because the cost would be lower in the shoulder season rather than in the summer. And they decided not to run the household air-conditioning, using the ceiling fans instead and running the AC only on the one day that it had hit over ninety degrees. But none of these changes brought Neil and his family close to the insecurity that the working class experienced in the immediate aftermath of the job loss.

Joan's family had made even fewer changes to their spending than Neil had, even though Joan had been the family breadwinner before her job loss. She, too, brought home the weekly maximum in unemployment insurance. Joan also emphasized her husband's ability to be the breadwinner for the time being, similarly to how Aliya Rao's unemployed women emphasized their husbands' work—although Joan was unlike most of Rao's participants in that she emphasized the importance of her own work.[29] (Joan, like most of the women I met, identified strongly with work.) Her husband had, in Joan's words, "a good job and a great income." She explained that food "is the one area that we really have not cut back because we're trying to be healthy." They had put off going on vacation, but they had kept their son in his day care, had kept up with their bills, and had purchased a new bed. They had "been contemplating getting rid of the landline," Joan explained, but, she added, "I love my landline. I'm kind of old-fashioned."

Some middle-class families were even more secure than Neil and Joan. About a fifth of middle-class families reported making no changes in their spending habits (not even the relatively minimal ones Neil described) in the first three months after their job loss. In contrast, nearly all of the working-class families made some changes to their lifestyles. These families often had substantial savings in additional to higher unemployment benefits and high-earning spouses. Many reported having enough money in their daily-use checking or money market accounts from which they could draw; most maintained that they would not touch their retirement accounts. Some talked about "the rule of thumb" being that you wanted to have about three to six months of income set aside in case of emergency.[30] Rodney, an IT specialist, and his wife had substantial savings; in fact, his detailed recounting of them all took up a significant portion of our time together. This difference in savings can be seen across the United States. According to the Federal Reserve Board, the "bottom 50 percent [of Americans] has very little wealth," which may help explain another Federal Reserve Board finding that about 40 percent of all families would find it difficult to pay for an unexpected expense of $400 or more.[31]

Most middle-class families hadn't been living paycheck to paycheck before the job loss. In other words, unlike many working-class families, middle-class salaries were high enough that they were not immediately spending all (or nearly all) of what they earned in a month. Yes, there might come a time, Rodney reported, when "the checking account gets down to a level where it needs [to be] replenished." But they hadn't gotten there yet, and when they did, he knew they could turn to the online savings account, which, for now, hadn't been touched. Rodney and his wife were solidly upper-middle class (although like many Americans in the top quintile, they might have been surprised to be described as such), but they wouldn't be described as rich, not reaching the top 5 percent or even 10 percent of Americans in family income.[32] But even three months after Rodney's job loss, he and his wife hadn't seen any noticeable changes to their expenditures.

Greater Precarity in the Middle Class

Not all middle-class families were so comfortable. In households where there had been previous periods of unemployment—particularly when those periods had been lengthy—families found that finances got tight fast. Black middle-class families also were harder hit by job loss than were white families largely because of differences in savings and debt, which scholars have noted is largely the result of both historical and current discriminatory practices that have excluded Black Americans from access to wealth through homeownership and better employment opportunities.[33] Finally, middle-class families that relied on only one income were also more likely to see their finances tighten more substantially.

Jeff, a thirty-six-year-old, white middle-class man, had lost an earlier job and was out of work for nearly eighteen months. A probation officer, Jeff had earned his college degree and was excited to find his first job, working in the probation office and doing work with the local courthouse as well as with the local schools. He also wrote federal grants to support his work to help people fight addictions. Jeff remembered thinking at the time, "I really love my job," which was why he felt so devastated to lose it and then to be unable to find a new one. During Jeff's long job search, his wife had continued working full-time, but she worked in social services with a relatively low salary. Jeff's earnings were double hers when he'd been working. Looking back, he recalled that things didn't feel financially tight during his first job loss, but now he realized that it was mostly because they were putting things on the credit card when they couldn't afford to pay cash. Since one of the credit cards was in his wife's name only and tied directly to the bank account that was only in her name, he didn't have a good sense of how much credit card debt they were accruing on that card. Likewise, one of the other credit cards was in his name and tied to his account, and his wife didn't have a sense of how much debt they were accruing on that card. By the time Jeff found a job, he and his wife were surprised to find they had amassed close to $25,000 in credit card debt.

This time around, Jeff wanted to plan differently. After he had found his most recent job, he and his wife emptied their retirement accounts in order to pay down the debt. But once he lost that job, it was easy for credit card debt to creep back up; already he had $6,000 on his credit card, and he feared a similar amount was on his wife's card as well. Again, they weren't sharing their card information with each other. With so much debt and such little income coming in, he didn't know how they could make a better plan. Ultimately, he explained, "Credit card debt is one of those things, if there's ebb and flow, it's really not that big of a deal. But, if you don't have the money coming in to make above and beyond the payments, then you're screwed." While Jeff found it impossible not to fight over the little things—such as "Do you really need to spend fifty bucks on that?"—he was not going to start a larger fight over the credit card debt because he wasn't sure where it would lead.

It is important to note that Jeff and his family's economic decline (which was among the worst I saw in the middle class) still looked quite different from Tracy's or Anthony's experience. Jeff and his family were living a much less financially strained life than many of the working class—they weren't experiencing hunger and had even still taken a vacation the year before. Jeff noted that the time at the beach was shorter than usual and not as relaxing, but they had made it there nonetheless. Tracy, in contrast, wasn't sure if they would ever have a family vacation, period. She certainly did not plan to take one during her time on unemployment. Jeff's family hadn't changed phone or electricity services and made mostly modest changes to household supplies. The one large change Jeff noted (other than reducing the vacations) was that he liked to shoot for target practice, and he had mostly stopped that hobby because ammunition was too expensive. They also were eating out a bit less.

Much of the toll that Jeff and his family bore was the emotional and psychological costs of the uncertainty they faced. Stanford sociologist Marianne Cooper notes that even when everyone in the household is employed in high-status careers, people can feel insecure about their own and their children's financial futures.[34] In middle-class households that had experienced a measurable decline in their financial fortunes, there was new tension in the house about how long this insecurity would last. For Jeff and his family, there was anxiety about the likelihood that things could get worse if Jeff didn't find new work.

Black families often seemed harder hit by a job loss because they had fewer resources than their white counterparts. Many of these differences can be traced to differences in wealth in Black and white America— differences that scholars agree are tied to the legacy of slavery, Jim Crow laws, and racist homeownership policies that persisted in the North in the post–Civil War era.[35] Latoya and her husband both had solid middle-class jobs, but they had less savings than many white families. Their adult children also relied on them to help out from time to time, and they contributed to their college-age daughter's school costs. This increased their financial pressures. White Americans are most likely to continue to receive financial gifts from their parents long into their adulthood, which can help explain some of the differing financial resources between white, Black, and Latino families.[36] In contrast, Black Americans can find themselves more likely to provide financial support to their elderly parents.[37] Latesha, a Black woman, did not have a history of chronic unemployment or long periods of unsuccessful work searches. Instead, both she and her husband had had long periods of stable employment and were part of the stable working class. They had both been the first in their families to go beyond high school; each earned advanced technical and vocational certificates/degrees. But Latesha and her husband accrued significant student debt in order to do so; Black students typically accrue higher debt for schooling than their white peers due to the historical differences in wealth between white and Black families.[38] Her mother lived with them, as did their three children. When her mother became sick, they put some of her health care costs on their credit cards (health care costs are the largest cause of bankruptcy in the United States).[39] In total, she said, "Our accumulative debt, which is including my student loans and [his student loans, her mom's health costs, plus some credit card debt from when they were young], is a total of, like, $63,000." This debt load put Latesha and her family at greater risk after her job loss because they could not always pay the minimum amount on all of the bills. While her husband's job plus Latesha's unemployment was enough to cover their daily living expenses, their debt was an outsize burden that greatly increased their overall risk and their financial worries.[40]

Some of the middle-class families that struggled the most were those headed by single mothers. Being in a single-parent household meant all of the financial and emotional pressures were left in one person's hands. When Christina lost her job as a social worker, she and her twelve-year-old adopted son stopped eating out, and she even felt stressed about what they bought to eat at home. "When I go to the store, I'm only getting necessities. I'm not buying my favorite chips or his favorite cookies. I'm just buying whatever is on sale or least expensive. If it's not needed, I don't get that. And I pretty much freak out—I think that's the only term I can use—when he comes home and hasn't eaten his lunch and now it has to go in the garbage. Because he just wasted it and I'm just like, 'You're wasting food.' So that's on my mind—what are we wasting." Although Christina and her son were in much better shape financially than Tracy, she faced greater uncertainty than either Jeff or even Latesha. With only one income coming in, once the unemployment checks stopped, there would be no income coming in at all. Thus, even though Christina could afford to pay all of the household bills currently, the possibility that the unemployment checks would stop before she had found a job made her family's financial situation seem perilous.

Most middle-class families, then, had greater security than most working-class families, but risk remained, nonetheless. Among the middle class, certain families—those with chronic unemployment risk, lower overall savings, lower salaries (and thus lower benefits), single parents, and families of color—faced greater risks than others.

The Emotional Cost of Job Loss

Economic strains and stresses weren't the only tolls people described to me; they also grappled with what it meant to have lost a job. When people lose jobs during a period of recession, such as the Great Recession, social stigma surrounding job loss is lower; the strain of losing a job appears to be lower as well when everyone is losing jobs.[41] But when job loss happens during times of economic growth and when job loss and unemployment are less common (as it was during these interviews), the social stigma surrounding job loss returns. Researchers have argued this experience of social stigma may be strongest for the middle class because job loss is typically less common among their peers.[42] I found about a third of participants experienced strong emotional costs from their job loss, including a small number who felt a great deal of shame associated with being fired and a slightly larger group who reported feeling depressed about the job loss. These feelings led some to avoid friends and others to lie to family members about their job loss. Some people went so far as to say that their job loss had brought about suicidal thoughts.

Christina, the social worker who was thinking about moving if she had to, explained that she was avoiding everyone she knew except her parents. She also hadn't told her son about her job loss; she kept their daily routine exactly the same and got ready as if to go to work when she got him ready to go to school. She told me, "I don't want to be around anybody, I don't want to talk to anybody. I really, I just hate being at home. I'm tired. I get stir crazy, but I also don't want to go out. First of all, I don't want to spend the gas money. Second, I just don't want to risk people asking me, 'Oh, why are you off? Are you on vacation?' It's embarrassing."

It was not common for people to keep their job loss a secret, but I did meet several people who decided to do so. All of the people who kept their job loss a secret were from the middle class, and Christina was the only woman who did so. It seems possible that middle-class workers (and mostly men) might have felt that their friends and family would have had less sympathy for their job loss. They also were more likely to have enough resources to weather the job loss on their own, which may have made them feel like they didn't need to share this information. Like Christina, Barry and his wife had similarly decided against telling anyone—including their parents and their children. He explained that they could "go for eight months without really changing outwardly." Since the family's finances didn't need to change, Barry and his wife decided that they would keep the news to themselves and just "watch how we approach things and interact" with friends and family.

Keith went one step further and kept his job loss not only from friends and family but also from his wife. A middle-class man with two advanced degrees, Keith felt completely caught off-guard by his job loss. He also felt confident that with his experience and education, it would not take long for him to find new work. So, he decided not to tell his wife in the hopes that he could avoid causing her stress as she tried to get her own small business, an independent day care center, off the ground. To keep up appearances, they would both leave for "work" in the morning; Keith would go to a local coffee shop, and when he was certain his wife was out of the house, he would return home. But Keith's decision not to tell his wife had large financial repercussions, as the family did not make any financial changes to respond to his job loss. Reflecting back on this decision, Keith said, "It's still embarrassing to think how . . . how stupid it was to make things so much worse by not being honest about the fact that I was having trouble finding work. I'm sure I could've found a job faster, I'm sure I could've managed our income more wisely if I could've just said, 'You're the only one getting a check, so we have to use your money to get by as much as we can.'" Instead, Keith kept his job loss from his wife for months until it became very clear to him that he would not find work locally and that they likely needed to talk relocation in order for him to find a job with a salary similar to what he had made.

It was more common for participants to report they felt depressed about their job loss and that it made them feel bad about themselves than it was to hide unemployment from others. Dawn Norris, the sociologist who studies the mental health effects of job loss for the middle class, argues that for many in the middle class, jobs are very much tied to people's identities.[43] When they lose their jobs, they lose their sense of self, and they don't really know how to get it back so easily.

I saw this loss of self-worth happen to about a quarter of the people I met, among both the middle class and working class. This happened even in the most financially stable families. Frank's wife held a job that paid exceptionally well, and his job loss hadn't changed their finances appreciably. His was one of the families that hadn't even had to draw on their savings after he lost his job in marketing. An affable white guy in his midthirties who talked about "karma" when he described the need to temper his reaction to his job loss, Frank was delighted by the extra time he was now able to spend with his toddler daughter. But he also worried that he hadn't found a job yet and that his past job had been very specific, and the skills he gained there would not translate clearly on his résumé. Frank explained the frustration he felt building over the past months: "I've always had a job and I've always left on my terms and I had something to go to. And so being on the other side, where someone says we don't want you anymore, yeah, it's an ego hit too. It's like, 'Well, what did I do?'" Frank wasn't a slacker, and he wasn't slacking on his job search—but he still wasn't finding work.

Losing a job can strike at the heart of people's identity—both those who are strongly attached to a career, like Frank, and those who aren't. Dawn had a transitory work career, but her last job was the longest one she ever held, lasting over ten years. She'd been the manager of a restaurant, and she'd seen the restaurant go through ownership changes before, but none that had threatened her job. When she learned that the owners were preparing to sell the land and the property and that the restaurant would not reopen, Dawn felt "devastated." She said, "I was heartbroken. I lost my identity more than my job and that's the hardest part." Tracy also felt this loss of identity keenly. She explained, "I hate [not working]. It makes me feel less of a person." Sociologists have long acknowledged that many people tie their identity to their work, and this may be particularly acute after a job loss.[44]

While Dawn, Tracy, and Frank experienced different financial tolls from unemployment, their experience of devastation about the meaning of their job loss and their (at the time) inability to find new work was actually quite similar. The pain of job loss and unemployment is one of the few areas where we see differences diminish in the face of a singular experience: the emotional toll of job loss. In my first book, I argued that too often both the public and scholars dismiss the meaning of paid work in working-class women's lives, seeing the work they do as unimportant or unskilled—adjectives that devalue this labor.[45] Yet we see here that for Dawn and Tracy, as for most of the women I met, their work was meaningful to them and the loss of it wrenching.

Job loss and unemployment can be devastating to one's mental health.[46] Brent experienced chronic unemployment in the IT service industry. His wife stayed at home to raise their nine-year-old daughter, and they depended on their church and friends for support, which was hard on his self-esteem. He confided in me that he'd had suicidal thoughts, but that his religious faith made him realize that he couldn't think that way. He explained, "It is quite depressing. . . . I have [experienced] that sense of 'Would my family be better off if [I died]?' And it's something that I have. It's one of those thoughts that go through [my mind] and then you have to realize this isn't the right way to be thinking. But at times still, [I think] like what if I got hit by a bus—would my family be better off because I'm not bringing income in. So, it does take its toll in that sense of depression."

Some in the working class also pointed to their anxiety and depression as stemming from the real limitations they would face in finding new work. Joyce explained that her depression came from her concern that future employers would view her as "worthless." She told me, "Yeah, because I . . . pretty much feel like I'm not worth anything anymore, 'cause I'm forty-seven years old and I can't do the stuff I used to do." Although she wasn't yet fifty, Joyce felt her body looked worn well beyond its years from decades of service jobs and manual labor. She'd worked low-wage jobs at fast-food restaurants, and her doctor told her that her breathing problems were likely caused by years of breathing the cooking oils and other fumes in the kitchen. She'd also spent some time working as a self-described "carnie" for a traveling circus—a physically demanding job that was hard on the body. With close to two decades to go before she hit retirement age (and fears that even if she made it to retirement age, she could not afford to retire), Joyce worried that her ability to find work would be very constrained.

It's important to note that not everyone experienced these feelings of embarrassment, loss of self-worth depression, and anxiety. In fact, some participants (particularly among the middle class) reported feeling like their period of unemployment (if not their job loss itself) was a good thing. Multiple people described it as a "blessing in disguise"; others said they were "enjoying" their "time off," and some said that it was the chance to think about what they wanted to do with their lives. So, while it was certainly a toll on many people, it was a toll that was not evenly felt—not financially and not emotionally. But, when experienced, the emotional costs of a job loss seem to be spread more evenly across class and gender than were the financial ones. There were exceptions, as middle-class men were more likely to go to lengths to hide their job loss, but women, too, felt shame, and both men and women reported depression and anxiety about their job losses.

———

Nearly 100 years after the Great Depression, I found evidence of great financial and emotional tolls of unemployment. Why was there such financial precarity among people eligible to receive unemployment in a decade of nearly unprecedented growth in America? The Great Depression brought us people in breadlines, but it also gave us the New Deal from the team of Frances Perkins and Franklin Delano Roosevelt. Today, it seems like we should be farther away from the fates faced by families who experienced the Great Depression—families on the edge of starvation when fathers lost their jobs because we had no safety net in place when the economy collapsed. In 1929, there was no unemployment compensation to catch people in a safety net. When President-elect Roosevelt asked Perkins to become his labor secretary—the first woman to hold the position—she replied that she'd take the position only if he would agree to implement a laundry list of policy items, including unemployment compensation. Under her supervision, unemployment compensation was set up to work like an insurance program—workers' payments would be pooled, and they would have access to that pool should they lose their job and need a safety net to prevent them from experiencing the devastation that involuntary unemployment wrought during the Great Depression. But over the years, the federal government and the states have unevenly funded unemployment compensation, leaving it vastly underfunded today.[47] In fact, the Federal Unemployment Tax Act (FUTA), which pays for the administrative costs of unemployment insurance and half the cost of extended unemployment benefits, collects only $42 a year for each full-time year-round worker; since its inception, the value of this tax has declined 800 percent.[48]

But why have we let the unemployment system collapse (and with it the fortunes of so many unemployed)? In the United States, there has been a long history of casting a suspicious eye on the unemployed, as if their lack of employment was caused by personal fault rather than broader economic changes.[49] I saw evidence of this derogatory view of the unemployed in my own state of Pennsylvania while I interviewed the people in this book. In 2013, then-governor Tom Corbett stirred up controversy when he suggested the unemployed couldn't find work because they were drug users.[50] Corbett's remarks are part of a long tradition in the United States, in which politicians have portrayed people who are out of work or in need as suspect or immoral.[51] Today, almost everyone who works pays into the unemployment system through employer taxes.[52] Yet, as we saw so vividly in this chapter, for many, these benefits leave them and their families below the poverty line.

Severe financial losses characterized the experiences of most of the working class, particularly the working-class women and chronically unemployed working-class men, suggesting that very few in the working class received sufficient unemployment benefits. Among those who faced such financial strains, there were also the psychological strains of wondering how long they could continue to live with such uncertainty. Moreover, even among middle-class workers who had much greater financial reserves, I found evidence of stress and strain, brought on by people's reluctance to rely on their social networks, fears of future uncertainty, and the emotional tolls of being jobless. Both self-doubt and even thoughts of suicide were present among the people I met. Even in homes that seemed safe from the financial worries brought by job loss, unemployment took its quiet toll.

5

The Guilt Gap and Health

WHEN SHE LEFT her waitressing job for the factory, Tracy had finally found a position that provided health insurance. After nearly two decades of being uninsured or on minimal Medicaid plans, she got on the company plan and started treating several health problems. When she lost the factory job, she lost her insurance and was, yet again, among the country's 44 million uninsured.[1] Tracy's choices became ever tougher as the days passed after her job loss. While her factory job had brought her health insurance, her time on unemployment plunged her back into poverty and left her with not enough money to pay all of her bills. Thus Tracy, like many others, had to make tough choices about paying for health insurance and seeking necessary health care. Between tears, she told me, "I lost my health insurance, so I'm screwed on that. . . . I have a tooth—I had a temporary filling put in [before I lost my job] and then I haven't gone back, and it's been over eight weeks. I've got to go back, but I'm just like, 'Ahh.'" She made a pained sound, touching her jaw gingerly. Tracy went on to describe yet another problem that she had stopped treating. She explained, "I have high blood pressure. I'm not going to get checkups like I should." Tracy had stopped taking her blood pressure medicine, which made her similar to one-third of Americans who reported in 2017 not receiving necessary medical care because they couldn't afford it.[2] Throughout our discussion, Tracy choked up several times and had a hard time finding the words to describe how she felt about her inability to have the necessary follow-up care.

In the United States, 75 percent of full-time workers get their insurance through their employer.[3] What this means, practically speaking, is that when workers lose their jobs, they lose their health insurance, too. About 60 percent of those who lost jobs during the Great Recession, or 9 million people, lost their health insurance.[4] Recent estimates from the unemployment crisis during the global Covid-19 pandemic predict that the number of uninsured increased by more than 50 percent during this period.[5] And like Tracy, most of the unemployed didn't just have to worry about replacing their health insurance. Without a job, the cost of maintaining one's health is an expense that becomes harder to bear, regardless of insurance status.[6] Everyone, then, had to decide whether to continue to seek medical care. Those who lost insurance had a second decision to make: whether or not to purchase insurance.

A large majority of the people I met lost their health insurance when they lost their jobs, with the working class reporting this change at higher rates than the middle class.[7] The gender differences came later, in two separate decisions many of the unemployed made about their health care. First, people decided to seek or *not to seek* insurance for themselves after they had lost it.[8] Middle-class men who lost insurance were more likely to regain it than were the women. Significantly, some working-class men and middle-class men reported insuring themselves but not their wives or their children (no women reported this as an option they considered).

The second decision was whether to continue to seek medical care. The gender differences in not seeking necessary health care (either doctors' visits or medications) were also stark: Women (both working and middle class) were more likely than men to report that they went without necessary care, as Tracy had.[9] Women were also more likely than men to report that they had stopped taking necessary medications. Most men were like Neil, who explained, "I'm diabetic, so we don't skimp on that kind of stuff [meaning medication]." Finally, some men (but no women) said that their wives or their children (but not themselves) were forgoing necessary care. With his job loss, Anthony and his wife had remained uninsured, but the loss of insurance only affected his wife because he had, in his words, "good health for myself. Um, and kids have been covered [through CHIP]."

The Affordable Care Act (ACA) had passed only three years before I started my interviews and numerous provisions of the act—including mandated individual coverage—would not be implemented until January 1, 2014, halfway through the initial interviews. I found many people I spoke with weren't always clear about what the ACA was, perhaps because of the many ways it has been bandied about. In fact, one person told me he was very much against "Obamacare" but glad he was able to sign up for the ACA; he didn't seem to realize they were the same. An incredibly complex piece of federal legislation, the ACA set up a health insurance marketplace run by the states to allow people to purchase their own health insurance. It also provided a tax credit to people purchasing health insurance through the state marketplace if they earn between 100 percent to 400 percent of the federal poverty level (although this doesn't cover the total cost of the insurance), established that insurance companies cannot deny people coverage based on preexisting conditions, required that people be insured (either through their employer, through public insurance, or through the marketplace), and allowed parents to cover their children until the age of 26.[10]

Already the significance of the ACA implementation could be felt, because a few participants had used the marketplace to purchase insurance before they lost their jobs and about a dozen purchased it after they lost their jobs. But the inadequacies of the law were also manifest, because for those who had just lost their jobs, purchasing health insurance could be an enormous financial burden. Even the lowest-tier plan in Pennsylvania, as my respondents were quick to point out, was quite costly and came with expensive deductibles and co-pays. This meant that even when people purchased insurance, they were reluctant to use it. The cost of purchasing insurance made some willing to accept the federal penalty fee that was added to tax payments through 2018 rather than comply with the mandate to purchase insurance.

Children were much easier to insure than adults, thanks to a federal program known as CHIP—the Children's Health Insurance Program.

The program was signed into law in 1997 and covered many children whose families were not quite poor enough to qualify for Medicaid but who were nonetheless unable to insure their children because health insurance plans are costly and the families did not make a lot of money. In 2013, 1,576,935 children were enrolled in either CHIP or Medicaid in the state of Pennsylvania.[11] In other words, just over half of all the state's children received their health insurance from the state that year.[12]

Being able to insure her children through CHIP was a huge relief to Tracy. The insurance from her job at the factory had been too costly to cover her kids, so they had been covered by the state's CHIP program and were able to stay on the state's CHIP program after her job loss. Moreover, her kids were relatively healthy and didn't have to go to the doctor that often, for which she was very grateful. In the immediate aftermath of her job loss, Tracy was so focused on making sure her kids were insured and that the bills were paid that her own health had been relegated to the back of her to-do list. As we talked, she admitted she hadn't looked into whether she might qualify for Medicaid now that her unemployment compensation was the only household income. She said, "I need to call my caseworker because I just think he needs to re-evaluate me." But her health, despite her high blood pressure and aching tooth, was not high on her priority list.

Without insurance, the cost of maintaining one's health skyrockets. As we remember from chapter 4, many of the unemployed, particularly working-class women and men, struggled to pay daily bills after their job loss. In such a context, good health seems like a luxury one can't afford. Health costs have risen steeply in the United States since the mid-1990s, and most of that increase is borne by workers, not employers or health insurance carriers.[13] The political scientist Jacob Hacker has called this part of the "great risk shift," where the burdens of the economy have moved from the employers to the shoulders of the workers.[14] The economists Jonathan Morduch and Rachel Schneider go a step further and argue that since the workers actually bear the costs of many of these risks, that it has been a "great cost shift."[15] Today, many families have more bills that they can't regularly pay, even when they aren't facing a job loss.[16]

With or without insurance, people had many bills to pay and had to make difficult decisions about what they could afford. In the years I conducted the interviews, the Centers for Disease Control and Prevention estimated that approximately 20 percent of Americans could not pay their medical bills.[17] Nationally, about 70 percent of those who had lost their insurance because of a job loss during the Great Recession reported going without necessary medical treatments over a two-year period.[18]

In sum, then, people had to make two or three difficult decisions about their health: whether to purchase new health insurance if it was lost, to seek health care and continue medications, and to continue healthy behaviors, like eating well and getting enough sleep. Even if people had enough money to decide to purchase insurance or seek treatment or continue to maintain their health by sleeping and eating right, they did not always decide to do so. Moreover, I saw large differences in how people made this decision according to their gender. This suggested to me that there was more going on than could be explained by economics. In the next sections, I explore how these decisions played out very differently between the women and the men.

Women's Self-Sacrifice

In her 1980s study of job loss, Katherine Newman argued that one of the most difficult aspects of losing a job was the sense of guilt that accompanied the job loss for middle-class men.[19] These men, Newman argued, had come to accept that they must be the family breadwinner and when they failed to meet this responsibility, the guilt they experienced was often traumatic. She wrote, "Downward mobility strikes at the heart of the 'masculine ideal' for the American middle class." As a result of their guilt, some men lashed out at their families; others drank or sank into depression. Newman's research echoed some of the earliest findings on the effects of job loss on men and their families from the 1930s by Mirra Komarovsky.[20] Komarovsky found the unemployed men felt they had failed in their "role as family provider." The idea that men feel strongly obligated to serve as the family breadwinner has been

further confirmed by scholars such as Nicholas Townsend and Marianne Cooper, both of whom have argued that breadwinning is a core
component of being a man in America.[21]

Yet studying men who had lost jobs during the recession in the early
2000s, Carrie Lane found a striking reversal in this trend.[22] The men she
interviewed seemed surprisingly free of guilt about their job loss. Yes,
of course, they were worried about finding a new job. Yes, they did not
like being unemployed. But they displayed little of the guilt or shame of
being dependent on their wives that had so troubled Newman's respondents. It seems possible that the men in Lane's study had come to understand that unemployment was part and parcel of employment in the
new economy—which is very similar to what we learned from the men
I met and interviewed, as described in chapters 2 and 3.

In contrast, the women Lane met "felt guilty." They didn't like being
a burden on their families, and they hated the loss of independence
that they experienced when they lost their jobs. Like the middle-class
women on the lockstep paths and the working-class women on the
transitory paths, Lane's women had not yet become accustomed to
job loss—it was not yet part and parcel of women's experience of
employment.

Likewise, I met many women who felt guilty about losing their jobs
and with it their health insurance. This guilt led many women to make
decisions to prioritize family needs other than their own health insurance or health needs. It was decisions like these that amounted to what
I call a *guilt gap* that emerged between many of the unemployed men
and the women when it came time to make important health decisions.
Consistently, both in the decision to insure themselves and, as we will
see, in decisions regarding going to the doctors, taking necessary medications, getting enough nutritious food, and sleeping well, women were
less likely than men to prioritize themselves. While middle-class women
were most likely to find insurance through a spouse, they were also most
likely to remain uninsured. This surprised me because, as we saw in
chapter 4, they didn't have the same financial challenges many in the
working class faced. But women—both in the middle and the working
class—emphasized their responsibility to put their children's (and

sometimes their husband's) needs ahead of their own. Not all women explicitly made the connection between their decision to not care for themselves while privileging their family, but their decision *not* to prioritize their own health spoke volumes.

Writing in 1990 in the *Washington Post*, Ellen Goodman also used the term *guilt gap*, although quite a bit differently than how I use it here.[23] In her article, Goodman described a parenthood guilt gap, or "worry chasm," the amount of time mothers and fathers spend anxiously thinking about their children.[24] Unlike Goodman, my use of the term *guilt gap* does not focus on the worry that parenting produces. Instead, I focus on the guilt that women describe about their job loss and the way many of them tied this guilt to specific actions they took after their job loss (in terms of their health, seen here, and, as we will see in later chapters, of their housework and job searches). Women's guilt about their job loss and subsequent unemployment led them to prioritize their families' needs instead of their own. The "gap" comes in because men, for the most part, were less likely to describe feelings of guilt and much less likely to prioritize their families during their time spent unemployed (in health, housework, and job-seeking activities).

When describing their guilt, women often sounded a lot like Kimberly, who explained the guilt she carried with her after she lost her job and her family's health insurance along with it. Kimberly explained, "I feel bad that I'm not contributing anything. This whole time I felt like this whole situation is my fault because I'm the one that lost my job. It's like I have all this guilt. I still have this guilt, like this is my fault—this is my fault we're in this situation because I'm the one that wasn't doing my job, and I'm the one that got fired, and I'm the one that caused all this. So, it's hard to deal with that." Although Kimberly attributed her job loss to the fact that she "wasn't doing her job," she lost her job when the budget for her department was cut and the entire department was shuttered. Since her husband's job hadn't provided health insurance, they both started looking for new work. He found a job that provided health insurance first—in another city—so they had to move. Kimberly carried a lot of guilt about the cascading events that followed her job loss: their health insurance loss, her husband's search for a new job, and their eventual move. Finding fault with herself, she even exaggerated her role in her job loss, rather than recognizing the role of the budget cuts, which served to further fuel her guilt.

After a job loss, many women thought of their own health insurance as an added luxury to the family budget—most middle-class women who lost insurance remained uninsured.[25] Ruth was the primary breadwinner in her middle-class family because her husband had cancer and was out of work for years. His cancer was in remission when she lost her job, and they wanted to make sure that it stayed that way. They made getting insurance for him through the ACA exchange a top priority for the family, while deciding that Ruth should go uninsured. When asked if she worried about her husband's health, Ruth said, "He's covered so he'll be okay." Yet Ruth's decision not to purchase insurance meant that she was avoiding important preventative care and other doctor visits. She explained, "My mammogram is due, and I can't have that done because I don't have insurance now." As we will see later in this chapter, Ruth's decisions contrasted sharply with some of the decisions men made when faced with similarly difficult choices.

Most working-class women who lost insurance with their job also remained uninsured.[26] Emily learned she could get insurance for her son through the state CHIP program and did so. Her husband was insured through his job, but when he went to add her to his insurance, he learned they would have needed to purchase the family plan, which would have been quite costly. Not long after her job loss, he found new work that paid better and made the switch. This job also came with better insurance. "With his new job, he could add both me and my son for not much," Emily said. "For very normal reasonable amounts." Yet while they were considering the family plan, for the moment, the family had decided against it. Emily had debilitating migraines, as do about one in four women in the United States.[27] Being uninsured meant that she would no longer have access to the medicine that made her headaches— which were often accompanied by vomiting, auras, and extreme sensitivity to light—manageable. Describing her migraines without her medication, Emily said, "It's going to knock you on your butt and you can't, you can't get away from it and nothing helps. You just want to die."

This made Emily's job search more difficult, as she had to search for jobs while dealing with a chronic health condition.

Repeatedly, I saw the women make the choice to insure their families but not themselves. Perhaps, if they had only made decisions regarding the cost of insurance, it could be chalked up to their different responses to handling financial challenges. But women also sacrificed taking care of their own health for their families' other needs. Women were more likely to go without necessary doctor visits, medicines, or medical treatments. Just over half the women said they were not treating conditions such as heart problems, asthma, and diabetes in order to prioritize family needs.[28] Women were also more likely to report that they had been treated for mental health conditions before their job loss and had stopped treatment after their job loss. Often these mental health treatments were discussed as being a "fringe" benefit of working that could be set aside in the wake of a job loss.

When I first noticed this trend of women not taking care of their health in order to prioritize other family needs, it was among women who were saving money by borrowing inhalers from neighbors when they were needed. Hearing these stories made my body tense up; I knew a girl growing up who needed an inhaler, and watching her body sputter and gasp for breath as she searched in her backpack for it stands out as a terror-filled memory of my childhood. So, it was hard for me to wrap my head around the idea that women were saving money by not purchasing their inhalers. Instead, they were counting on neighbors to be nearby in case they needed them.

Brandi explained, "I do have asthma, so as far as my inhaler goes, actually, I'll be honest with you. A friend of mine let me use theirs. If it gets that bad, I call her." A registered nurse, Brandi understood that her asthma was a serious condition; she described to me having an attack and calling her neighbor and running up the road to borrow her inhaler. Before her job loss, she and her husband had earned over $100,000 annually combined. They also did not owe money on their mortgage because they had inherited their home from her grandparents, so things were not nearly as financially constrained for them as they were for many families. Why did her inhaler count as a luxury? Brandi didn't seem to have a ready answer for this. The family hadn't even touched their savings account yet or their retirement account. But Brandi was clear about one thing: her needs came last, after her husband's and her son's.

Women have long faced expectations that they sacrifice for their families. In the middle of the 1800s, Catherine Beecher and Harriet Beecher Stowe wrote a wildly popular book, *The American Woman's Home*, that would be read for generations. In it, they argued that it was a woman's duty to balance out the cold, calculating world of business through their own "self-denial," thus creating a cheerful and welcoming home to which their husbands could return after a hard day of work.[29]

The expectation women (particularly white women) sacrifice for their families has not gone away.[30] Economist Nancy Folbre argues that it is built into our economic system, as women continue to be primarily responsible for child-rearing while men remain more responsible for the world of paid work.[31] Why do women remain in charge of the home? Work-family scholar Jean-Anne Sutherland notes that when mothers do not put their children ahead of themselves, they can find themselves shamed by family members, friends, and even strangers.[32] I've found in my own research that women feel obligated to talk about putting their families first when making decisions about work, so as not to appear to prioritize their own goals at work over their families.[33] They do this to escape the judgment they expect will follow if they are seen to be doing something for themselves. A study looking at moms in the United States, Germany, Italy, and Sweden found not being able to prioritize kids over work can leave moms with strong feelings of guilt.[34] The cultural anthropologist Riché J. Daniel Barnes notes that expectations of self-sacrifice are often tied to the nuclear families of white women and that Black women have long relied on extended kin to help provide care.[35] Yet community responsibilities—the expectation that they "raise the race"—demand much from Black mothers as well, Barnes finds. Thus, despite all this progress, moms still have an impossibly fine needle to thread when it comes to work and family.

Many women evoked self-sacrifice when explaining that they would rather skimp on medications or doctors' visits than allow children or even spouses to bear financial repercussions from their job loss. Although most women could not prevent their families from feeling the financial squeeze of unemployment, they often framed their decision not to seek health care as a way to give their children (and spouses) more while giving themselves less. Even women who could afford medications and treatments avoided them so as to not shift any of the cost of their job loss onto their families. Middle-class mom Christina emphasized how she would go without before she would let her job loss impact her son, saying, "I try to take away from what I would normally get, making sure he has what he needs." She had stopped taking one of her medicines to manage her depression and was taking the other medicine every other day. The medicine was too costly, she explained, to take daily. Christina had more resources than some, including savings that she was not tapping into when she decided against taking medicine that she had previously deemed medically necessary. While financial cost was clearly part of the calculation here, we can see the specter of motherly self-sacrifice in her words that she "takes away" from herself so that her son "has what he needs."

Sacrificing health care to provide for children's "needs" was a recurring theme. Vanessa's explanation was striking: "I don't take any of my medications. None. . . . You know, my kids' school clothes and their food and stuff . . . it's worth more than your health." Vanessa explicitly stated that she valued her kids' need for food but also *school clothes* and *stuff* ahead of her own health; she wanted to make sure that her job loss disproportionately affected her instead of her children or her partner. After Victoria lost her job at a distributor plant, she told me "the first thing I did was take myself off medication." Doing this saved her quite a bit of money because she'd lost her insurance when she lost her job. It also allowed her to continue to prioritize her college-age son and his needs. She explained her thinking to me this way: "I'll go without before he will." What the kids were not giving up was either not described (what Victoria's son isn't going without is not stated) or broadly described (as in "what he needs" in Christina's example). Moreover, mothers' medical care often was weighed against the unspecified potential needs of their children, such as the "stuff" Vanessa broadly invokes.

Thus, even when children didn't have clearly defined needs that would benefit from the act, women sacrificed their own health.

Women also prioritized their husbands' health over their own. Kathy had had two heart attacks before her job loss and a family history of breast cancer, but her husband also had significant medical concerns. Although they did have health insurance, she felt they had to decide whose health to prioritize because co-pays and prescription costs were not cheap. "I made sure that [my husband] kept up all his visits. He has to with his situation. I, on the other hand, I've kind of passed on my own things to make sure that he gets what he needs." In this example, instead of prioritizing children's needs, we see Kathy prioritized her husband's medical needs ahead of her own. Kathy and her husband were not as financially distressed as some of the other families who made decisions to forgo care, but she still did not maintain the treatment she'd been receiving.

The high cost of care sometimes shut the door on possible treatment. Tamara's doctor had found a lump on her breast and masses on her thyroid. Her doctor recommended follow-up procedures to investigate whether the tumors were malignant. But then Tamara lost her administrative job and with it, her health insurance. She and her partner tried to scrape up the money to purchase insurance through the ACA, but they found they couldn't afford even the cheapest plan. "It's never been tested for cancer because I'm not on insurance. Um [soft crying], I haven't been able to get scripts. . . . [The welfare] office said, 'You can't get on medical, I'm sorry, because you have unemployment.' I said, 'Well, man, I can't afford [what] they are charging me.' She said, 'Oh, I don't know what to tell you.' [Inaudible] I was in tears." While not many participants had health crises as urgent as Tamara's, five participants reported having cancer and a sixth said that her spouse did. Tamara was the only one not receiving treatment.

Not all women made such choices. Some women, like Joan, decided to maintain their health after their job loss. Joan explained that "I kind of hit a wall recently, and I realized that it doesn't matter how much it costs, I really need to take care of myself because I was in a pretty bad place." She explained that her acid reflux had been bothering her and she decided to seek new medications, purchase special foods, and pursue alternative treatments, including visits to an acupuncturist and a nutritionist. The decision to maintain health was more common among middle-class women than among working-class women. And sometimes these decisions came after women realized, as Joan did, that they could not ignore their health when it started to deteriorate. At first, Joan explained, she had reduced the supplements and vitamins that she had been taking and not prioritized her own health (in fact, she still wasn't sleeping well). But then she realized that her health was declining, and she decided that needed to change. She did not describe herself as prioritizing her own health exclusively, though. Instead, she explained that as a family, "we're trying to be healthy." This focus on the whole family (she also described in detail her husband's health regime) cleaves from some of the stories that follow about how men made decisions about prioritizing their own health. In the end, Joan was glad she had refocused attention on the family's health, saying, "It's really helped a lot." It was possible, then, for women to prioritize their own health care; although, as we saw in Joan's case, it was usually done in the context of taking care of the health of everyone in the family.[36]

Men's Lack of Guilt

The men were much less likely to sacrifice their own health in favor of their families' health or other needs. Compared with the women, they were far less likely to report going without necessary medical treatment, far more likely to report their spouses and children went without care, and more likely to insure themselves alone (and not spouses or not the family).[37] Moreover, men discussed purchasing health insurance or continuing medical treatments in pragmatic terms noticeably absent of guilt and self-sacrifice, with a few notable exceptions.

Middle-class men rarely made a trade-off around health insurance. Most either remained on their wives' plans, switched over to their wives' plans, or purchased health insurance through COBRA.[38] Congress passed COBRA in the 1980s, requiring group health plans, like the ones provided by employers, to allow group members to purchase a temporary continuation of coverage after their participation in the group ended. This means once you lose your job, you have the right to continue to buy (at full price) your health insurance through your employer for a limited amount of time. Neil remained on his wife's plan, explaining that they'd made "no changes in that." Since he was relatively healthy aside from his diabetes, Neil hadn't been going to the doctor very often before his job loss, but he didn't change anything afterward.

Remaining on an existing plan was typical for middle-class men. Consider Derek. When asked about doctors' visits and medications, he brushed aside the questions, explaining, "My wife has a full-time job and all of our insurance is through her, so there're no issues there." An IT professional, Derek and his family didn't need to adjust their health insurance or their health care at all because they'd always been covered through his wife's plans. Other men purchased COBRA. A former executive, Barry had been one of the highest-paid individuals who participated in this study. Although his wife worked at a hospital, they decided her insurance was inferior to his and, despite the cost, purchased COBRA through his former employer. It was important to maintain their insurance because his "wife has three scripts that she takes for respiratory problems. . . . She really can't cut back." In Barry's narrative, health care wasn't optional—it was an expense the family had to have. Unlike other men, Barry emphasized the importance of paying extra to ensure his wife's health was covered; he also had great financial capacity to do so.

But for those middle-class men whose families did have to make changes, there was a noticeable lack of guilt about the changes to their families' health insurance in some men's discussions about the changes to their family's lives. Robert's wife had to increase her work hours from part-time to full-time in order to gain insurance at the bank where she was employed. He'd been the general manager of a large manufacturing plant, and when he lost his job, the family lost their health insurance. There was a lot of tension at home after his job loss. Robert explained, "So what irritates her is the fact that she has to work for the health care. . . . So, do I feel guilty about it now? No." Robert had missed a lot of time with his kids when they were younger, working long hours and having an especially long commute. It seemed fair to him that his wife take a turn supporting the family. Unlike Kimberly (from earlier in this chapter), whose job loss also led to a change for her spouse and guilt for her, Robert did not feel guilty about this shift in circumstance.

This lack of guilt about changing family responsibilities was fairly widespread among the men. When we talked about the change in health insurance, Dean focused on how he'd been able to "maximize" his health insurance and time off. Dean had a time-demanding professional job, which meant that he'd been putting off a back surgery his doctor wanted him to have. He also hadn't used many of his vacation days that year. His boss let him know that his job would be ending six weeks before his last day, which allowed him to schedule the surgery during those last weeks of work. He explained, "I took sick days to deal with the back surgery and the back injury and all that stuff and I kept all my vacation days I had amassed, and I got paid for those, too. So, I basically got paid for a month off." Afterward, Dean purchased COBRA insurance for himself but not for his children who had been on his plan until that point (and who qualified to stay covered on it). He switched his kids over to his ex-wife's insurance. He then took a monthlong trip to Europe.

Dean admitted to facing pushback from his ex-wife about switching their kids to her insurance plan. But he reasoned that although paying for his kids' health insurance was part of his custody agreement with his ex-wife, it seemed OK for his ex-wife to take a turn paying these expenses. "I had the kids' health care and the primary part of their educational expenses through my job. So that's changed, and so that indirect support is right now not there, but I've been doing that for four years." Again, note how Dean did not express obligation to ensure his kids' insurance was covered by him or guilty about his ex-wife needing to take a turn.

What was particularly striking was that eleven of the men decided to insure themselves and not their wives.[39] This was in stark contrast to the women, as none of the forty-nine women insured only themselves when faced with similarly difficult decisions. And this was not the only instance, as we will see, in which the men—but not the women—decided to privilege their own health above other family priorities.

A foreman who had run the mechanics for a national shipping company, Joel had been in a car accident a couple of years before his job loss. While he'd mostly recovered from his injuries, he did not want to go without health insurance, and the cost of purchasing COBRA through his former employer was very expensive. But his wife needed health insurance, too, because she suffered from asthma and needed two different types of inhalers. Joel made a difficult decision about insurance. As he explained, "I can afford insurance through COBRA for myself, and myself alone." His wife's asthma medication would cost upward of $600 a month now that she was uninsured, which was too costly for them to afford. He had hoped they could get an exemption for a state Medicaid card for her because of her illness, but at the time of the interview they had not been successful in their attempts to gain one. For now, Joel's wife was making do without her inhalers.

Although over half the women sacrificed their health after their job loss, just a handful of the men did so.[40] In fact, men were more likely to report that their wives alone were forgoing necessary health care treatments (reported by about a quarter of the men).[41] Jay's wife needed medication, but medications weren't cheap, he told me: "It's just ridiculous how much it costs." He explained, "You know, she can always kind of fudge asthma, which she shouldn't but she can." Jay had lost his job working at a company that manufactured dental supplies. While Jay didn't have any known health conditions, he wanted to maintain his health. "I had just gone to see my doctor to try and make sure everything was good," which it was. When asked if he was having difficulties maintaining his health, Jay said, "I don't think so." Compare Ruth's decisions (from earlier in this chapter) to Jay's. Ruth also had a spouse who needed medication and insurance, and COBRA payments for two people were expensive. But in her situation, they chose to insure her husband through the ACA and not Ruth through COBRA. Here, we see Jay and his family make the opposite decision. Both families faced somewhat similar challenges: mounting financial bills and an inability to pay them all. Only one member of the family had a pressing health need: the nonearning member. Through the state exchange of the ACA, Ruth's family insured the nonearner (her husband). Jay's family insured the earner (himself) and decided to "fudge" his wife's asthma medication needs.

Even in households with very low incomes, the expectation that women should manage without necessary care was tied both to financial needs and gendered expectations about women's bodies. Curtis described how his wife could share an inhaler: "She needs it, but we got people here and there that get extra—that is, the same doses of what she gets." Because of their exceptionally low income and her health condition, Curtis thought it was likely his wife could qualify for an "access card," meaning state-provided Medicaid. But they hadn't signed her up because the co-pays would be too high without one of them working, and Curtis figured that asthma could be managed by his wife without medication. "It's not an everyday thing she needs. [It's] just if she starts getting stressed out and running around too much, she needs it." The implication was that if his wife could control her body, she would be able to manage without her necessary medication, saving the family money they could use for other things.

Some men conceived of their wives' inability to receive care as either the fault of their former employer or the fault of the federal government. Vincent had been in the U.S. Navy reserves, then active-duty Army, before retiring to civilian life as a long-haul trucker. They had both lost their insurance when he'd lost his job. After his job loss, he'd been able to qualify for Veterans Administration (VA) benefits and health insurance, but his wife couldn't get insurance this way. He'd looked into getting her insurance through the ACA but decided it was too expensive. He explained, "My wife was on some meds and she don't have insurance now, because of the way the Obamacare is." Even though it was his job loss that triggered his wife's loss of insurance and, with it, her inability to afford now-uncovered medications, Vincent blamed ACA costs. Unlike the women discussed previously, Vincent did not plan to sacrifice his own health care in order to help his wife maintain her health. In fact, the family still planned to take a trip to Disney World later in the year.

Not all men were devoid of self-sacrifice and blame. Keith, the middle-class man we met in chapter 4, tried to hide his job loss from his wife and kids because he felt such a deep sense of shame. But he never tried to stop his family from going to the doctor's office. In fact, he learned that the doctor's office often didn't employ some of the more aggressive creditor tactics that he faced with some of his debtors. He explained, "As long as you send them something, they send you another bill and you don't get any phone calls or anything like that." Plus, while he was able to convince his wife that he didn't feel like going out to dinner, it was harder (until he came clean about his job loss) to explain why someone couldn't go get a medical checkup. In Keith's case, his shame actually facilitated the family going to the doctor's office rather than keeping them away.

Marcus also used language of self-sacrifice when talking about giving up going to the doctor, although he noted that he had not gone to the doctor's office long before he lost his job, despite living with a tremendous amount of pain. He explained, "I don't go to the hospital. No matter what . . . for myself, I won't go. I will just deal with whatever I have. . . . I mean, don't get me wrong, I have a lot of back pain. I have carpal tunnel in my left arm. That I know for a fact doing the research myself online. But I know I've got carpal tunnel in my left arm and my back. . . . When I was younger, I had real problems with scoliosis. Now my back has actually gotten straighter, but the pain is still there. So, I deal with back pain all the time but I'm at the point right now where I can somewhat block it out and just do what I got to do." In Marcus's case, we do see evidence of men stoically bearing pain and avoiding health care.

Eschewing Healthy Behaviors

Women didn't simply make sacrifices around health insurance, doctor visits, and medications. They also were more likely to report eating less food and being more food insecure than were men, more likely to start bad eating habits, and less likely to develop healthier eating habits after their job loss. Women also were more likely to report sleeping problems after their job loss. Again, these findings cut across classes, suggesting that financial challenges were not the only factors driving the continuation of healthy behaviors. The Institute for Women's Policy Research similarly found women faced greater food insecurity after a job loss than men; while women's risk drops as their education levels rise (as I find), they remain at disproportionately higher risk than do men.[42]

Nearly a third of the women said that they were eating less than they had before they lost their jobs, while only a handful of men said the same.[43] A number of women explained there was less food available and they wanted their children to eat before they did. Tracy described herself as an emotional eater, and we shared a laugh over our mutual love of Oreo cookies. Although she recognized eating was a coping mechanism she often relied on in times of stress, she was trying hard not to do so this time around because "when you don't have [enough food] here you try not to. I've been really trying not to [stress eat], because what I have, I want my kids to have it." Tracy emphasized the importance of her kids getting the food in the household before she got any. Vanessa, the working-class woman who had eliminated her medications so her kids would have new school clothes, had also cut down on what she was eating. She said that her friends at work had always teased her because she was tiny but could pack away food. She was no longer eating like that. "But it's not that I'm not hungry, it's just we don't have a bunch of food." Any spare food would go toward the kids, not to Vanessa's appetite.[44]

Sometimes women described the trade-offs between what they ate and the other extras their kids could get. Ruth, who we learned gave up her health insurance, had eliminated fresh fruits and vegetables from her diet so that her kids and her husband could eat better. Because her husband had been unable to work for the past few years, the family struggled more than many middle-class families after her job loss, and they had to tell the kids they had to do without some extras. After giving her twelve-year-old son $10 to spend at a music festival on a Friday night, he threw "a fit" because he thought it wasn't enough money. She explained, "So that's the hardest part because I feel guilty, but then again they're not starving." Ruth was sacrificing plenty, but it felt like not enough. Some men, like Anthony, also experienced food scarcity, although many of the men described, as Anthony did, a scarcity that hit the whole family rather than one borne only by the unemployed parent.

Anthony's wife was making "more home prepared meals," and they received some food from their church from time to time to help.

Women also ate more junk food after their job loss, but this was less common among men.[45] Women's ability to purchase healthy foods may be constrained by poverty.[46] Some women said they were eating junk food because it was cheaper than healthier foods, which supports the findings of sociologists Molly Martin and Adam Lippert, who argue that poor mothers may be at greater risk of obesity because they are saving the healthiest food for their children.[47] This decline in women's eating habits was often explicitly linked to maintaining their kids' food supply. Jodi explained that after the job loss, "I didn't eat as healthy, either. I mean, I had to worry more about baby stuff. Like the formulas and the baby food. . . . But I always made sure [the baby] had everything." While Jodi described herself as skipping meals and not always having all of the food she needed in the day, she emphasized how she made sure that there was always enough food in the house for her new baby.

In stark contrast, some men, but few women, developed healthier eating habits now that they were home more.[48] They explained they had more time to cook and less access to unhealthy foods available at work. Allen explained, "I think I probably eat better not being in an office environment." Without the temptation of bagels and other food that was left in the staff room near the watercooler, Allen found that he was able to eat more healthfully. The lack of tempting snacks at home was a common refrain among men. They also pointed to having more time to cook at home. Neil was cooking more and "eating up the leftovers" for lunch instead of grabbing lunch out. Cooking is one of the few household chores that men have picked up over the last few decades, increasing their labor so that it equals and, at times even surpasses, women's in national time survey data.[49]

Women also differed from men in their sleep habits, having more trouble falling asleep and more difficulties staying asleep over the course of the night.[50] Prior research has consistently found that women have more interrupted sleep than men, particularly when they have caregiving responsibilities.[51] It also seems likely that changes in other health arenas may have affected nighttime sleep either indirectly, as anxiety about the job changes may have disrupted their sleep, or directly, as discomfort over untreated conditions or poorer healthy behaviors might also have kept them awake. It also could be a combination of all of the above, as seemed to be the case for Vanessa. Vanessa's poor eating habits and lack of usual medications may have played a part in her inability to sleep at night. She explained, "I just want to sleep. I don't sleep at night at all, but I get tired during the day." Despite feeling almost exhausted during the day at times, by the time bedtime rolled around, Vanessa's stress about her job loss would ramp back up and she wouldn't be able to sleep. When asked what was keeping her up, she just repeated the same word: "Worried-worried-worried."

While women told me (and often themselves) that they would be OK without insurance and that the only thing that mattered was insuring their children, perhaps some of the strain that caused the lack of sleep came from knowing they were now uninsured. It is hard to know if these kinds of subconscious fears kept women awake. Many women, like Renee, who was herself uninsured but had insured her child through CHIP, simply weren't getting enough sleep. The consensus of prominent American sleep researchers is that adults need a minimum of seven hours of sleep nightly.[52] Yet Renee was avoiding sleep by watching TV until two or three in the morning when she had to be up by 6:30 or so to get her son ready for school—meaning she often slept less than half of the recommended number of hours. "I kind of feel guilty, almost, like right now, 'cause I feel like there's something I should be doing that I'm not doing. I think, it's almost like I should be held accountable," she said. These feelings of guilt seemed to consume many women but not nearly as many men, preventing the women from partaking in many necessary healthy behaviors, like getting insurance, going to the doctors, eating well, and even getting enough sleep.

———

In general, when not looking at the unemployed, research has found that women are more likely to go to the doctor and engage in a greater range of healthy behaviors than men.[53] But research has also found that women are also much more likely than men to prioritize caring for their children's health and caring for their spouses' health.[54] Unlike dads, moms feel obligated to monitor what their kids eat and how they exercise. Needing to take care of everyone else takes a toll on moms—they run out of the energy they need to take care of themselves.[55] This likely ties in to the ideas about guilt and shame that scholars like Komarovsky and Newman first found in unemployed men and then Lane found in unemployed women. If circumstances align to make it difficult for women to prioritize both their own health and their families' needs, who takes priority? Not women. In the wake of a job loss, women put their own health care on the back burner. Yet men did not.

Caring for oneself was often framed by women themselves as fundamentally conflicting with caring for family members, particularly when the family budget was squeezed, but not only then. It was not only that families could not afford for women to take care of their health—although, as we saw in Tamara's case, sometimes the costs of care were too great—it was that very often, families put women's health at the bottom of their priority list. We remember that Tracy said during our interview that she needed to reach out to see if she were eligible for state-run Medicaid, yet she hadn't done so because she was too busy prioritizing other family needs. Men's health needs rarely fell so far out of sight. Those who needed care got it. In the end, while our culture expects men to be the ones to provide for their families, it is women who are the ones who make the most sacrifices in an attempt to make up for their job loss to their families. Here, we see how they do this with their health. In chapter 6, we will see them do something similar with household labor as they attempt to make up for what seems like too much time.

6

The Guilt Gap and the Second Shift

DRIVING DOWN HIGHWAYS through green rolling hills, I marveled at the beauty of the mountains as I made my way to meet Victoria. I was also impressed by the remoteness of her location; I was often the only car on the road, surrounded by trucks making their way across the state. We met at Victoria's favorite diner (located in a large truck stop) because her son was home from college and she felt the diner would give us more privacy. Victoria was small and wiry, with messy brown hair that she kept pulled back in a ponytail from which strands kept escaping. In chapter 5, we learned Victoria had stopped taking her necessary medications after she lost her health insurance and her job working for a shipping plant for a large national corporation. She lived with her boyfriend; her son, a college student, came home almost every weekend. Upon his return, she did his laundry, cooked his meals, and enjoyed their visits. Until her son left for college, it had always been just the two of them; her boyfriend hadn't moved in until after her son's high school graduation.

Before her job loss, Victoria and her boyfriend had a fairly equitable division of labor. She cooked and he did the dishes; they decided it was fair if they each took care of their own laundry. While Victoria's boyfriend flatly refused to clean the toilet, he had done the vacuuming before her job loss. Since her son had moved out before her boyfriend moved in, Victoria had done all of the childcare when he was growing up. But her boyfriend did help her son, now a young adult, when he needed it, and they were quite close. Household labor expert Daniel L. Carlson and his colleagues have found that low- and moderate-income families like Victoria's are increasingly likely to share tasks like dishwashing and laundry.[1] That Victoria's boyfriend also did the vacuuming was an added bonus. This is, perhaps, because they weren't married; marriage can decrease men's household labor and make couples more traditional.[2] Overall, Victoria felt that before she lost her job they had a very fair division of labor (even though she did a bit more household work than her boyfriend).

But after she lost her job, Victoria greatly increased her work in the home: "I feel guilty if he comes home and I'm sitting down. That doesn't seem right to me." Victoria took on all of the vacuuming as well as the laundry. Her boyfriend stopped doing the dishes. She also took on many of the traditional "male" chores, including mowing the lawn and taking out the trash. On the nights they were supposed to bring the garbage to the curb, he now routinely went outside for his evening walk without taking out the trash unless specifically asked to do the chore. Victoria had started doing so many household chores that she thought her job loss had made her boyfriend a bit "lazy." Despite this complaint, Victoria had not spoken to him about pitching in more at home. Her guilt over her job loss led Victoria to feel like the division was fair. "I feel like I should be doing more because I'm not working," she told me. Just as we saw guilt in the last chapter over health care, here we see guilt emerge over household labor. In particular, for women, this guilt was often connected to their newly found "free" time (perhaps because women are used to having less leisure time than men have).[3]

When you lose your job, one thing you gain is time. Some people reveled in their newfound time, others felt anxious about it, unsure what to do without the structure of their job. But did this unstructured time fundamentally change how the newly unemployed's households divided the work of taking care of the kids and doing the chores? Prior research finds the unemployed do take on more household tasks and also suggests we should expect to find a gender divide here, too. In fact, national data finds that women take on twice as many household chores as men do after a job loss.[4] Although unemployed men with wives who work long hours take on more household chores than men with wives who stay at home, they still report doing fewer chores at home than do unemployed women with working husbands.[5] Aliya Rao's research on highly paid professional unemployed men and women suggests these divisions are reproduced by the elite as well.[6] Moreover, unemployed women continue to do more childcare work than do unemployed men.[7]

Since many of the people I met lived with a partner, I was able to take a look at what changed and why inside their home after a job loss.[8] (I looked at only people with a partner, because those who were single did most of the work even if they had older kids who could help some.) I examined both the work the couples did on household chores and the work they did caring for children. Family scholars have long considered these tasks separately, as household chores are thought to be less rewarding than those involving children.[9] Those who study household work typically go one step further and say that to understand how much labor goes into household work we also need to know how often chores occur and how much time they take to do. We call chores that are daily and time-consuming "routine," while those that happen less frequently and usually take less time are called "nonroutine." These phrases also help to signal which tasks are essential for the running of the household; most people can't go too long without completing routine tasks like cooking or doing dishes or the laundry (we run out of food or clean clothes), but most of us can avoid nonroutine tasks, ignoring the weeds in our flower beds or replacing the car's oil less frequently than recommended.[10]

When I looked at what kinds of housework people did, I found a striking pattern. Women did more of the routine household chores before they lost their jobs.[11] Afterward, almost all women and about half of the men increased the number of routine chores they did at home.[12] But men's routine chores increased just a bit; they were now "helping out" a little more than they had before, as we'll learn Neil did. In contrast, most women, including Victoria and, as we will see, Joan, took over so many tasks that they were doing all of the routine household chores. Notably, when women didn't increase their chores, it was because they couldn't; they were already responsible for *all* of the routine household labor. This was never the case among the men. When men didn't increase their chore load, it wasn't because they were already doing it all; rather, these men, like Anthony, had a stay-at-home wife who maintained the home and prioritized her husband's job search.

When I looked at childcare, I saw a similar pattern. On first glance, both men and women increased the time they spent with their children. But women did more of the childcare before they lost their jobs, and afterward the majority of them became primarily responsible for most childcare tasks. In contrast, only one man became solely responsible for all childcare tasks; the majority of men either shared childcare or had wives who continued to be primarily responsible.[13]

As we saw in earlier chapters, class continued to further shape these decisions. Middle-class women had carved out clearer bargains with their husbands about sharing household chores that fell apart after the job loss, leaving them primarily in charge of household and childcare labor (although most did continue to send young children to childcare or after-school programs). Working-class women often bore more household work both before and after their job loss, and the work of childcare (which middle-class women could partially outsource) fell disproportionately on working-class women's shoulders. Among the men, middle-class men took on a few new household chores (many fewer than the women) and then declared themselves "equal" sharers much more pronouncedly than did the working-class men, who also took on relatively few new tasks.

The Pew Research Center finds the majority of Americans—men and women—say they want a household in which both men and women share the responsibility for paid work and for the work done inside the home.[14] Many of the men and women I met said they wanted the same. Why, then, in the time these interviews were conducted from 2013 to 2015, was there such a large gender divide in the actual practice of how people divided household labor and childcare after a job loss?

Some of the answer lies in the ways that we continue to do gender at work and at home—even when we think we aren't. Men have increased their household labor by about 300 percent since the years when, in the popular Donna Reed television show, the titular character greeted her husband wearing pearls after having made a four-course dinner and cleaned the house for the umpteenth time.[15] Yet women still do more housework than men do, and married moms do about twice as much household labor as married dads.[16] Women also remain more responsible for taking care of kids than men are. Even as men's time doing childcare increased, women's did, too.[17] In her study of young adults living in New York City, sociologist Kathleen Gerson offers a clue as to why we see these persistent divides.[18] Like the Pew study mentioned above, Gerson found that most young people want an equal division of paid and unpaid labor. But when young adults thought about whether they could achieve this goal, they imagined that the demands of work would get in the way; if their ideals were thwarted, most of the men said they would fall back on more traditional family norms, in which men focused on paid work and left the unpaid labor to their wives. Thus, although our ideals for equal sharing are high, we have not yet escaped the institutional pressures of long workdays, the lack of available childcare, or the traditional gender beliefs of our past.[19]

Another clue can be found in *bargaining theory*, a popular economic and sociological explanation for gender differences in household labor. Bargaining theory expects that as women's earnings rise, they can "bargain" with their husbands in order to reduce their own time doing chores.[20] This bargain happens either as women's income increases relative to their husbands' earnings, which makes it easier for them to ask their husbands for more help in the home, or to a lesser degree, as women's income allows them to purchases services and goods (like someone to help with chores or takeout meals) that replace the labor women would have done.[21] Importantly, men's earnings don't appear to affect the bargain; regardless of their earnings, men can opt out of household work.[22]

Time availability matters, too, as people do fewer chores when they have less free time.[23] In fact, unemployment clearly gives both men and women more time to do chores.[24] Yet women do more household work on weekends than men do, and unemployed women pick up more household chores than unemployed men, suggesting that those pesky traditional gender beliefs work in conjunction with both time and earnings bargains.[25] Elaborating on this point, work and family scholars

Alexandra Killewald and Margaret Gough write, "There is something about the experience of being a wife, as opposed to a husband, that causes even high-earning wives to spend considerably more time in housework than their husbands, even when they out-earn them."[26]

That "something" seems to be about gender. Theories about why gender matters abound, but the evidence is clear: men appear better able to "resist" the demands of household and childcare labor than are women.[27] The "guilt gap" offers us yet another clue as to how gender operates in the household. Among the women and men, the guilt gap was present, yet again, in how the unemployed talked about their bargains, their time use, and their household labor. It was striking to me that unemployed women attempted to make up for losing their jobs by doing more household chores, but the unemployed men did not. The women and men did not simply talk about guilt differently. Rather, guilt was a regular part of women's language surrounding their unemployment as well as their household labor and childcare, but it was almost entirely absent from men's talk.

This was not simply a difference in how men and women spoke; their actions also spoke volumes. The unemployed women were not comfortable leaving chores undone for their working spouses; the unemployed men were.[28] Moreover, men did not connect feelings of guilt about their job loss to their additional free time at home or their need to do more household work, but women commonly did. These feelings of guilt are likely tied both to expectations about who should be doing what inside the home and how the men and women differentially managed their feelings of responsibility for their job loss and how that loss made them culpable for things around the house. In fact, some scholars have noted that modern motherhood involves a lot of mother-shaming and mother guilt at the inability to live up to sky-high expectations about what a good mom should be.[29] These ideals of good motherhood (which involve a lot of self-sacrifice) shaped the lives of the women I met.

Over the past several decades, researchers have noted a rise in the pressure mothers (particularly white moms) face to conform to what's called "intensive mothering" norms.[30] Sociologist Sharon Hays came up with this term for a phenomenon that she observed in a lot of moms (whether they worked for pay or not). They were expected to be perfect moms, who helped with their kids' homework, read stories, played games, and volunteered for the PTO.[31] White moms may be most likely to face the pressure of these norms.[32] Dawn Marie Dow, a noted University of Maryland professor, explains that racism historically excluded Black women from both the expectation of primarily maintaining the home and the protections afforded by it.[33] While Black women and men have often shared paid work outside the home, they have traditionally rejected the "private islands" of the nuclear households of moms, dads, and kids.[34] Instead, Black families tend to rely on broader support from kin when caring for children. Prior research continues to debate whether Black Americans may divide household chores more evenly because both Black men and women have worked for pay traditionally.[35] What scholars do agree on is that white men have been the main beneficiaries of the traditional division of labor in the household, as their wives' ability to do the daily tasks at home has allowed white men to focus on work and shrug off the demands of home.

We can see how white men benefit from the divisions of childcare and housework when we compare Victoria's experiences to Harold's. Harold had lost a job in the hotel industry. A sociable person, he wanted the chance to get out of the house for a little while, so we met in a coffee shop. He told me he would be easy to find, as I could look for the guy with the shiny head and, indeed, I found him easily; Harold was broad, with wide eyes and a large smile set in a round, bald head. When Harold met and married his wife, they decided they were going to have a pretty equal marriage. They would both work full-time and share the caregiving for the kids. This seemed fair to Harold. But even though Harold described himself and his wife as "sharing" everything, a close examination of their household chores revealed that both before and *after* his job loss, his wife took on the majority of daily tasks. After proudly telling me that nothing needed to change after his job loss because they were already great sharers, Harold seemed somewhat surprised to discover that his wife did many more daily tasks than he did. While he emphasized he did the dishes nightly, his wife's list of regular chores included meal prep and cooking, grocery shopping, laundry, vacuuming, dusting, bathroom cleaning, and many of the more routine childcare tasks, like helping the kids get ready for school and making sure they brushed their teeth at night. As he puzzled over my list of chores, Harold explained these differences emerged because his wife simply liked things cleaner than he did.

Harold's explanation that women just are "neater" than men is one that has been long deployed by men to justify their lack of participation in household tasks. This is what Arlie Hochschild calls a "resistance strategy" for avoiding housework in her classic book about gender and housework, *The Second Shift*.[36] Hochschild notes many of the men in her study, like Harold, complimented their wives for how super-organized and tidy they were, but she notes that this praise was very "convenient" for the men, as it let them off the hook for being responsible for these chores.

One of the problems of sharing tasks is that they can be split in ways that appear fair but actually aren't, such as dividing tasks into indoor and outdoor tasks (which is how the routine and nonroutine tasks are often divided). As Hochschild notes, again in *The Second Shift*, household tasks are often "gendered," meaning that the routine indoor tasks are primarily done by the wife, and the nonroutine outdoor tasks are done by the husbands. That's how Harold and his wife split the chores. The problem is, just as Hochschild described it so many years ago, this sort of division leaves the women doing the daily (and more time-consuming) tasks and the men doing the tasks that need to be done less frequently and on their own schedule (and are less time-consuming). The fact that Harold reported being fairly equal with his wife may have had to do with his perception of how things were divided—fairly evenly if you considered the outdoor versus the indoor tasks. But they were unevenly divided if you considered the time it took in a given week to complete most of the tasks. In fact, we can see the roots of the bargain in Harold's own telling of his story; he describes them discussing childcare and housework in their young adulthood and agreeing to share things equally, yet this bargain did not lead to an equal division even when paid work was equally shared. And now that Harold wasn't working outside the home, the bargain still wasn't altered.

Research on childcare suggests that, as with housework, there are divisions between routine tasks and play in how moms and dads approach childcare. These divisions can help us understand the differences between Harold's talk of "50/50" and his actual practice. While dads have increased time spent doing childcare, moms spend more time than dads taking care of routine tasks, like getting kids' teeth brushed, faces washed, and planning their next doctor's appointments.[37] Dads are also less likely than moms to spend time alone with kids—most of their parenting time comes when moms are also around—and when they do spend time with kids, more of it is spent recreationally, playing or reading, for instance, rather than doing routine tasks like bathing and feeding kids or taking them places.[38] Harold was pretty typical of most men—he was the "fun dad," and he left the more routine tasks for his wife. His wife's lesser bargaining power, combined with men's ability to ignore some tasks, left Harold with the upper hand: he could claim equality while not achieving it.

Did Harold increase his participation at home now that he was unemployed and his wife still worked full-time? If time alone drove these decisions, we would expect the answer to be yes. Yet it was not. Even though he acknowledged that his wife was "getting the short end of the stick," Harold declared he was satisfied with this arrangement. He did not plan to increase what he was doing at home, and he did not express any guilt over the fact that he was benefiting from what seemed like an overload of household tasks on his wife. The guilt gap here is clear: Victoria thought she owed her family a significant amount of extra household work to make up for her job loss, but Harold did not.

Collapsed Bargains, More Time, and
the Guilt Gap in the Middle Class

Did the unemployed middle-class women have such unequal bargains? Middle-class women (who, on average, have better-paying and more prestigious jobs than working-class women do) have steadier work histories, spending more time engaged in paid labor when they are in their twenties, thirties, and forties than working-class women do.[39] Their steadier and higher-paying jobs may give them the ability to ask for more work around the house from their husbands.[40] Cohabiting middle-class women have partners who are more likely to engage and increase participation when asked.[41] Middle-class incomes likely also allow both men and women to outsource some of the household and childcare labor.[42] And the middle class is more likely to hold more gender egalitarian ideals—that is, they say they want to be equal at home, just like Harold and his wife did (although Harold's wife wasn't able to negotiate more).[43] Yet, perhaps other middle-class women would end up able to bargain for a better balance than Harold's wife did.

Joan was proud to tell me that she had a "rock star husband" when it came to doing household chores. Like Harold, Joan said she shared most of her chores with her spouse, and she was pleased with how they divided things in their house. She was quick to point out that she "wasn't a stay-at-home mom," and she was looking for work to make sure that she didn't become one. As I started to read my list of chores, Joan interrupted to say most of the chores were shared. But she then acknowledged she did most of the grocery shopping, cooking, and bill paying and that her husband did more repair work. When I asked a follow-up about whether anything had changed after her job loss, Joan paused and noted she had taken on many more cleaning tasks and also most of the laundry. She was now responsible for getting her son to and from day care and for his nighttime bath and bedtime routine. Her husband still read his book at night and did more of the playing tasks. So, Joan had picked up more of the childcare routine tasks while her husband retained the fun. Plus, she was now doing the vast majority of the tasks inside the home. Yet Joan felt so conflicted about the changes that she contradicted herself as she explained them, telling me, "[My husband] was doing bath for a while but now I'm doing bath, but he'll do bath once in a while. [My husband] loves to do bath. It's . . . it's . . . it's very equal." Despite stating that she was now primarily in charge of bath (which she subsequently confirmed) and that her husband only did bath once in a while, Joan concluded our conversation about the division of labor around her son's bath by saying, "It's very equal."

What was going on here? The story Joan told me about how awesome her husband was at sharing the workload at home didn't seem to line up with what was going on at home. Why did she end up ignoring so many of the details of how much work in the home her husband really did?

In my first book, I argue that people tell "accounts" about their lives—it's a way we talk about our lives to make them line up with the way we think things should be.[44] Joan did not think of herself as a "stay-at-home mom." She must have told me at least a half a dozen times that she wasn't cut out for staying at home.[45] But she'd been at home for a while by the time we met. During that time, there'd been a creep in the chores. As time wore on, she'd taken over more and more of the tasks she and her husband used to share. She explained it just seemed fair to do more since she wasn't working. If they didn't have to scramble to get her son to preschool in the morning, that made life easier. Same with pickup. She was home, so she could make the house cleaner. While Joan saw herself and her husband as equals—they'd both gone to college and earned master's degrees—over and over they had prioritized his career over hers (even though she was earning about a third more than him when she lost her job). The bargain she'd worked so hard to craft and maintain (despite its flaws) fell apart without Joan's paid labor to help shore up her demands of equal partnership.

But Joan wanted to be an equal sharer, just like Harold did. So, she talked about herself that way. She kept her high aspirations for her family's division of labor inside and outside the home, even though they didn't live up to that ideal. Despite describing herself as a career-committed woman—and she was in fact one of the most passionate about her career commitment in the whole study and one of the few to significantly outearn her husband before her job loss—Joan ended up doing exactly what almost all of the women in the study ended up doing: almost all of the indoor housework after they lost their job and some of the outside chores as well. She also did most of the routine childcare chores, as most of the women in the study did (the most notable distinction between the middle- and working-class women was that middle-class women like Joan kept their kids in childcare, as I will discuss in detail later in the chapter).

None of the men did this. Not one man—even the most egalitarian among them—ended up picking up all of the indoor chores and most of the outside chores. Many (particularly the middle-class men) did more childcare than they had before, but it was often more recreational care than routine childcare. In fact, although about half of the men increased their household labor and their time with their kids, none of them took on as much work around the house as Joan did—Joan who said that she was married to a rock star of a sharing husband.

Men's bargains with their wives changed much less dramatically. This is likely related to the differing expectations we have of fathers in our society. Scott Coltrane writes that "compared to the complete self-sacrifice expected of mothers, being a father in our culture carries far fewer burdens."[46] Middle-class fathers may face high demands to be successful breadwinners, but as we saw in chapter 5, there is some evidence that in recent years, even these demands have lessened. Research on middle-class men who have lost jobs and started providing care for their families suggests that even when they are out of work for a long time, they do not take on identities as the primary caregiver in the family.[47] This suggests that middle-class men are unlikely to take on the full workload at home.

Neil was pretty typical of the middle-class men who increased their household chores a little bit. About half of the middle-class men shared a few more routine tasks with their wives/partners, although rarely did they take them on entirely, as so many of the women did. Yet, unlike Joan, Neil wasn't the family breadwinner when he lost his job. He was proud of how great his wife was doing at work—it was one of the reasons his period of unemployment wasn't more difficult. While she'd followed him for several different job transitions during their almost twenty years together, this time around she found a terrific job of her own. She made over 30 percent more than Neil in her graphic design job, and her career was beginning to catch on fire. He expected that if they moved again, it would be for her career, rather than his.

Given the newfound importance of his wife's job to the family, did Neil feel obligated to take on the lion's share of work at home? His wife had started calling him "Vacation Neil," because it felt like a vacation when she sometimes came home to find he had cooked dinner. But he had not taken sole responsibility for this task. Instead, it had gone from being his wife's responsibility to being one that they shared. According to Neil, cooking was "a big change . . . I'm doing more of it." It was the biggest change he'd made. They also both continued to share the grocery shopping, and he still washed dishes while his wife put the food away after dinner. Many more tasks remained uniquely his wife's responsibility, including cleaning, laundry, and bill paying. When it came down to the nitty-gritty of the household who-did-what list, while Neil certainly did more than Harold, he didn't do nearly as much as Joan (or even his own full-time working wife). Thus, while he had more free time and he had slightly changed the bargain he had with his wife, it was still weighted favorably toward him.

Neil did contribute more to the outdoor tasks, and this was where I saw the most significant changes among the middle-class men. Like other middle-class men, Neil had previously outsourced outdoor work, like the lawn care or home repairs. After their job loss, middle-class men were the most likely to take on new outdoor work and home repairs. Neil had done so, incorporating any necessary repairs and outside tasks into his new routine. When all was said and done, Neil was most responsible for the less onerous and time-consuming tasks, and he shared the more repetitive daily tasks. When asked how he felt about things at home, he replied, "I've been enjoying not doing anything but taking care of the homestead and just taking a break." Neil's choice of words— "taking care of the homestead"—indicate he was sharing the load, but his wife's high earnings had not earned her a bargain that was an *equal share* of that load. Moreover, some of Neil's new time availability was "break" time that he was enjoying and felt comfortable taking. No guilt attached.

One notable similarity between the middle-class men and women was their likelihood to continue to keep their children in either childcare or after-school programs. Most of the middle-class parents spoke of the importance of socialization for their kids or talked about how their children would not want to be home with them all of the time. They also sometimes explicitly linked the need for childcare to their job search activities (something I will talk about in greater detail in chapter 7). Talking about the decision to keep her son in childcare, Joan explained, "We were able to keep my son in day care 'cause he's thriving there . . . he's with the same group of boys that he started with when he was three months of age. [It's] his special place." While Joan remained primarily responsible for her son's care during the times he was home, she also continued to outsource much of his care during the day, which allowed her to maintain her job search. This "extensive" mothering, in which moms primarily maintain responsibility through a combination of outsourced care plus the care provided in the home has been identified mostly among middle-class mothers.[48]

Many middle-class men also framed childcare around their kids' needs. Frank placed a priority on what his daughter learned by being in childcare. He said, "Like day care, I could totally stay at home with her and be fine with that, but I think she would miss out on the interaction with the other kids she's known now for a little over a year." Thus, in the middle class, keeping children's routines and childcare was prioritized even when it was expensive.

Unequal Bargains, Guilt over Leisure, and No Childcare in the Working Class

Perhaps I would find a different response among the working-class men and women. There has been considerable debate among sociologists about whether class and available resources may lead someone to become more egalitarian. Some scholars have argued that because working-class families may depend on the income of working wives, husbands and partners may respect the work of those women more.[49] Sometimes when a community is hit hard by the loss of factories or other economic changes, the only work that is available may be work that is traditionally done by women in the service economy.[50] When this happens, working-class families may have to figure out new ways of being moms and dads and of earning and caring, leaving men to provide care at home.[51] This line of reasoning would suggest that, unlike middle-class women, working-class women might be able to negotiate stronger bargains.

Yet the types of jobs working-class women can find are often not particularly prestigious or well paying.[52] They can get stuck in the types of jobs that are often dismissed by the general public as being not particularly important and that I've found even women's families dismiss as not being very worthwhile (although both my research and that of others has shown that it takes skill and determination to remain employed in such jobs).[53] Stuck in poorly valued jobs, women may find they lack the ability to demand more equal marriages. In fact, sociologists Amanda Miller and Dan Carlson found that working-class women's low wages left them unable to negotiate out of undesirable chores.[54] Sharon Sassler and Amanda Miller find working-class women are less satisfied with the division of labor in their households and that they achieve less equal divisions.[55] I've found that working-class women's bad jobs can leave them subject to critiques from their husbands that they should quit work to do more at home.[56]

The existing research leaves us with a confusing picture, then. Do unemployed working-class women have more bargaining power in the house than unemployed middle-class women, or do their jobs leave them vulnerable to exploitation within their own homes? The answer lies somewhere in between. The majority of both middle-class and working-class women reported doing the household chores with little help from their husbands. Some of the differences lay in the emphasis: Almost all of the working-class women reported that they alone did the household chores, while about half of middle-class women said they shared some chores with their husbands (as Joan did).[57] An additional difference came because the working-class women had to do this work within the restraints of having far fewer resources. This means that in addition to shouldering solo more of the household burden, their budgets were too tight for the occasional meal out (and night off). Sometimes it meant that they grew their own food, started canning, or took on other household cost-saving measures that were less common in the middle-class households. Perhaps the biggest difference, which had an effect on their job searches (as we will see in chapter 7), was that working-class women were unlikely to keep their children in childcare or after-school care. As we saw, middle-class families most often continued to pay for care.

Short in height, with short blonde curls and an easy smile, it was clear to see why Leslie had been such a popular bank teller. Having worked at one bank for twenty years, by the end, she earned close to a middle-class wage with only a high school education. She was devastated when she lost her job. It was also hard on her family, as Leslie had been the family's main earner, earning sometimes close to double her husband's low-wage annual salary. She'd been taken by surprise when the bank had closed the branch; none of the employees had been given any notice.

Her first response when asked how she felt about her job loss: "guilty." Even though she'd done nothing to warrant the job loss and couldn't have prevented it, Leslie, like so many of the women I met, felt guilty— guilty to have lost her job, guilty to take unemployment, guilty not to be working, guilty to have more time with her kids, guilty to ask her husband to do anything at home since he was still working.

Her husband worked at a big box store in the warehouse on the night shift. He worked four nights a week for a ten-hour day. Although he hadn't been the main breadwinner in their family, he wasn't one to do much around the house even before her job loss. His mom lived with them, and she also didn't do any of the household chores. Leslie did almost everything, although before Leslie's job loss, she did have her kids help out with the dishes, the laundry, and some of the household cleaning. Leslie also did the majority of the repair work and the outside tasks, too. She explained that she was handier than her husband. "I can look at instructions and do it and it'll be done in ten minutes," she said. "He can look at them and look at them." Leslie's husband had helped with some of the routine childcare tasks before her job loss, because he wouldn't go into work until after she got home. This allowed him to meet the kids at the bus stop and, if necessary, address any problems that arose before Leslie got home. Leslie still did most of the carpooling to activities; she had worked out an arrangement with another mom who picked up the kids at school and brought them to their activity, and then Leslie drove everyone home once she was out of work.

Despite doing most of the chores and childcare before she lost her job, Leslie managed to increase her household labor after her job loss. She took over all of the chores the kids had helped with, simply stating, "I'm there to do it." Her older two girls were in a competition dance program, so she spent much of her weekend time driving them to towns in different counties in the state to perform, which kept her busy. The family had also started a construction project before her job loss: building a deck on the back porch. Without the means to pay the construction company to finish the job, Leslie was now trying to complete the project on her own. Plus, her mom had gotten sick and needed to go to the doctor for treatments, so Leslie added caregiving for her mother to the list and was now driving her mother to the doctor in a small city a half hour away a couple times a week.

When asked whether it seemed like her husband had more leisure time than she did, Leslie took a long pause and said, "I'm responsible for doing more than he does." She then paused again and corrected herself, saying, "He does a lot, so that sounds. . . ." Leslie's voice trailed off and she ended with a laugh. She finished by saying that her husband worked very hard because he worked nights and long hours. She then discussed his commute—which, at an hour, was longer than her half-hour commute had been—and concluded that he worked hard. Leslie did not expect her husband to do much work around the house before she'd lost her job, and she felt she owed her family more of her labor inside the home after she'd lost it.

Here we see the calculation of time availability shape Leslie's household labor but not her husband's. His long days meant that he worked four ten-hour shifts, so he had three days when he did not have to go to work, but these hours were not discussed when she calculated available time for chores. While it was important for Leslie to find a new job—she was the family's main breadwinner, after all—this did not prevent her from doing so much work for her family that it became almost a full-time job itself.

We also see the guilt gap rear its head. Leslie's guilt over her job loss, coupled with her newfound time, drove Leslie to do almost all of the household and childcare work as well the ambitious deck-building project, which she worked on over the weekends. Driving her daughter to dance added to the time she spent on childcare. She even clocked in a "third shift"—taking care of her mom. Naomi Gerstel has argued that women in midlife (with older children like Leslie's) can end up taking on both paid work and work around the home and what she calls a "third shift" of work taking care of their now-elderly parents; Gerstel argues this labor is rarely done by men.[58] Overall, then, Leslie's pattern fit the mold of women who seemed to do more than their fair share to start with and who increased their household labor even more after their job loss.

The only working-class women who did not increase their chores were the ones who could not because they already were doing *all* the work *before* they lost their jobs (none of the middle-class women had already been doing everything). There was not much more to do for Donna, a short, stocky woman with dyed blonde hair, because she was already doing almost all of the tasks inside the home. The one household chore her husband did that she did not take over was the cooking. A great cook, her husband did not want to give that task up after her job loss. She did try to take it over, because it seemed fair to do so, but he enjoyed cooking, so she was only able to make a small inroad there.

Donna had worked at the local courthouse and had been promoted rapidly there. She hadn't enjoyed the job after her promotion and had already started looking for new work before she learned that there were budget cuts that eliminated her position. She felt bad about her job loss and the hardship it caused her family and wished there were more she could do. Her husband was a maintenance man, and her job loss put the family on shaky financial ground. Their twelve-year-old daughter was an only child, and Donna and the girl were very close—sharing lunches and play dates now that Donna was home more often. Since she lost her job, Donna had decided against keeping her daughter in summer camps. This left most of the responsibility for entertaining her daughter during the day up to Donna, who said, "She definitely wants me to play with her, but luckily we do have neighbors that she plays with, too. . . . Usually, [I] play with her." Unlike the middle-class moms, most working-class mothers like Donna shouldered the bulk of the daytime childcare.

Since her job loss, Donna had more leisure time than her husband did. She lamented this difference in their time off, and she tried her best to minimize her downtime, stating, "I try not to have too much leisure time." So, she increased how much time she spent searching for work and cleaning the house. To be clear, Donna felt so bad that she created work for herself. This was also why she had tried to take over the cooking from her husband, so she could increase his leisure time. As she explained, "If he doesn't have to cook, well, then he has the rest of the evening to relax" after he got home from work. The guilt gap appears starkly here; unlike Harold or Neil, Donna was not "satisfied" nor did she view this extra time as a "vacation" or time to "enjoy." It was time she actively resisted having because of her guilt about having an excess of free time.

What of the working-class men? Did they, like the middle-class men, resist shouldering more of the burden of home when they found themselves with more time on their hands? Prior research on working-class men who have lost jobs suggests I would find that they would do a tiny bit more household work, but not much more than that.[59] Sociologists Elizabeth Legerski and Marie Cornwall argue that losing a job is a blow to working-class men's masculinity and that helping out at home can further chip away at their sense of identity. Sharon Sassler and Amanda Miller find that working-class men are more resistant to requests from their partners to help.[60] Others have argued the opposite. Working-class men may be more likely to help out with childcare while out of work and to search for work that allows split-shift childcare duties, thus prolonging their job search.[61] Men may step up and do more household chores in regions plagued by economic troubles, as the financial reckoning forces men to change their ideas about what it means to be a good dad.[62]

Yet again, we are left with a fairly conflicting picture. On the one hand, recent research paints a picture of working-class men who aren't as helpful at home once they lose their jobs. On the other hand, other research suggests that some of these men really do step up. What were the working-class men likely to do?

The working-class men most often got the better end of their bargains, even when their wives worked full-time, increased to full-time work, or stepped up as breadwinners.[63] But many working-class men had stay-at-home wives who facilitated their returns to work by prioritizing their time spent searching for work. Anthony's wife accompanied him to the lunch spot where he and I chatted for almost three hours. She mostly entertained their two children as Anthony and I spoke, but she occasionally chimed in and, when we talked about their division of household labor, she had a lot to say. Although Anthony (like Harold and Neil and so many others) described himself as doing many tasks, his wife often corrected him to say that the tasks were shared or that she primarily did them. Take grocery shopping, for example. When I started to read my chore list, they responded simultaneously but with different answers. Anthony said, "We do it together." His wife replied, "You don't do it at all right now." How to make sense of this conflicting picture? Further questioning revealed that Anthony picked up the groceries that the family received from their church (they were receiving some help to cover their food needs) while his wife continued to do the typical grocery shopping. Similarly, his wife reported she was primarily responsible for the laundry, but Anthony said it was "50/50." Again, further questioning revealed that "she puts it in [the laundry machine] and starts it and then I'll go and put it in the dryer and bring it back up." And then his wife folded and put the laundry away. As with the outdoor/ indoor tasks, laundry was divided in a way that felt "50/50" to Anthony, but the tasks his wife completed took more time than did his tasks. As for childcare, his wife retained all of those responsibilities, allowing Anthony to prioritize his job search. He was, however, "going on an all-day field trip with [his daughter]," which he wouldn't have been able to do before he lost his job. Anthony certainly did much more work at home than many of the men I met, but he also defined as "equal" any tasks that let him "help" but did not make him primarily responsible or even equally responsible for the chores.

Joel's workload was typical of what working-class men did. Tall and skinny with graying brown hair and brown eyes, Joel wore glasses perched on the end of his nose. A toolmaker of medical instruments, Joel was the family breadwinner, so his job loss was hard on his family. His wife had been working less than ten hours a week at her children's school when Joel lost his job. But after his job loss, she switched jobs and found a thirty-hour-a-week job that paid better as well. She also started going to school part-time at night to earn a degree in phlebotomy. She hoped to be able to find part-time work at a hospital when she finished her degree and to keep her current job. Between her paid job and school, she was outside the home more than forty hours a week.

Yet Joel was not picking up the slack at home like Leslie and Donna had. In fact, not much had changed since he lost his job. Joel's wife continued to do most of the grocery shopping, cooking, cleaning, laundry, bill paying, and the childcare. He and his wife both agreed he was the better cook. "She does the more daily cooking. I do it if we want something really yummy." If Joel was the better cook, why hadn't he taken over this one chore at least? He explained, "I do it because I enjoy cooking; she does it because it has to get done."

We see here how Joel was able to exercise a clear form of male privilege—the ability to ignore the immediate need of a daily task. Even though Joel recognized cooking as something that "has to get done," he could choose to do it on his own terms. He did this, despite his wife's apparent increased bargaining power, his increased time availability, and the entire family's agreement that he had more talent for the task than his wife did. Despite everything, Joel still did not feel obligated to participate in most household tasks and did not say he was sharing, like Harold or Neil had.

Joel expressed no obligation to do more at home. He never discussed guilt about his job loss or guilt about his household or childcare chores. When asked about his free time, Joel laughed and repeatedly said, "Too much, too much." When asked the same question about his wife, he said she probably didn't have enough free time, but that he couldn't do anything about that because his wife had everything done a certain way. "It's her routine, you know, and it's bam, bam, bam . . . and she's done." Like Harold, Joel used a "resistance strategy," saying that his wife was too quick in her routine for him to help with any of the chores. Since her work and school hours added up to more than a full-time job, it seemed unlikely that Joel couldn't find the time to get some of these tasks done before his wife completed them. Joel was satisfied with the current division of labor in his house—when asked if he wanted to change things, he said he would not. Of course, Joel had little incentive to change things as they currently stood—he certainly benefited from being the one who did little of the household labor and from bearing no obligation to do more.

Tall with short cropped hair, Troy had worked his way up at a local bank. His wife was hoping to start a new career as a realtor; so far, she was working a lot of hours but not earning much money yet. His job loss put a huge strain on the family's finances. They had four children, including one from his wife's previous relationship, and his father-in-law also lived with them.

Troy's wife had done most of the household chores before his job loss. His wife was in the house as he and I met, and she chimed in at this point in our conversation. They laughed as they teased each other about the bill paying, each agreeing that it was best that she continue with this chore (his checkbook had been a mess when they had met and married). But it wasn't the only chore she kept; like many of the other men I interviewed, Troy shared some more of the housework, but his wife still did more than he did.

Where Troy did make big changes—unlike most men—was in childcare. He took on many of the recreational childcare tasks, and I could see how excited he was about this. He particularly enjoyed the extra time he had to spend with the kids' sports teams. When he worked long hours in his old job, he explained, "I wasn't able to be part of the softball team as much. Now that I'm off, I can enjoy more of that. And going to my kid's football games. I'm able to be there for his football games now." He also took on some routine tasks, like getting the kids ready for school or taking them to their sports camps, sharing these activities equally with his wife. Troy was excited to have "more opportunities during the week to spend more time with the kids." These opportunities translated to much more childcare time with his kids than many men spent (particularly in routine care), although Troy shared this time with his wife and did not take these tasks over.

Finally, it is important to note that a key difference between the working class and the middle class was the working-class families' inability to continue to outsource childcare.[64] Many families had relied heavily on family members or, to a lesser degree, on paid caregivers to watch their children when they worked. The reliance on multiple forms of care—which I also saw—is particularly common for workers in the low-wage service industry.[65] As we saw previously, Donna and her husband relied primarily on the school system during the academic year and summer camps, which they had canceled for now. Roy explained that he and his wife had decided they could not afford childcare after his job loss. He asked, "Do we pay day care, or do we eat?" They decided against paying for day care and rearranged his wife's schedule so that she could provide more care during the day when Roy searched for work. Others had worked split shifts and shared care for children with their spouses, as Leslie had done. Splitting shifts, when one parent works days and the other works nights, so a parent is always home to provide care is more common in working-class households.[66]

While working-class families were more likely to rely on kin when they were employed, once they were unemployed, their family members expected them to take over care responsibilities. Carol, whom we met earlier, explained that her mom helped take care of her daughter after school when she was working. After she lost her job, all of those responsibilities transferred back to Carol. Leah and her husband were in a unique position in that they were both out of work when I interviewed her. As a result, they had decided to move in with his parents to save money. They had also pulled their son out of his paid childcare. But when asked who helped care for their toddler son, she replied, "Childcare—that's me." I asked Leah if her husband was able to help out at all, since he was also unemployed. She responded, "A lot of times he'll be going to the gym, or he's looking for jobs, or he's not really home too much." While she and her husband had similar work experiences and were both searching for work when we met, her husband's free time was given preference (to the point where she described him as often at the gym), but she was the one who did all of the childcare work. Regardless of how families had formerly managed childcare, during unemployment, working-class women shouldered the greatest childcare burden.

———

Gender reigned supreme in household matters once people were unemployed. Even in households that had once had fairly equal divisions of labor, women took on almost all the chores inside the home and many of the outside chores as well. Men took on relatively fewer tasks and ended up with far more free time than most of the women. Bargains, additional time, and the guilt gap appeared to play significant roles in these differences. In many households, expectations about what women were meant to do in the home guided expectations about household labor and childcare even before jobs were lost. Men's household tasks were often much more narrowly defined, and even when they expanded to include either cooking or dishwashing, men's chores remain limited in scope. Women also took on a much greater guilt burden after their job loss than did men. Often explicitly mentioning guilt or shame or fairness, women spoke of not wanting their partners/spouses to do too much around the house. In contrast, this kind of language was almost entirely absent from how men spoke about their job loss.

Some class differences did emerge in how men and women took on household tasks. Overall, women from both classes took on the lion's share of routine household and childcare labor. But working-class women bore an extra burden in that they alone shouldered almost all the childcare in their households. Middle-class women and men remained better positioned to outsource this labor, while working-class men either shared responsibility with their wives or avoided it entirely. Men from both classes were able to maintain their right to claim that someone else should continue to do more household labor than they did, even when they weren't contributing as much income.

As we continued our conversation about housework, Victoria recalled that when she had been employed, she would sometimes come home from work to find her boyfriend asleep on the couch. Since then, Victoria had been reluctant to sit on the chair positioned next to that couch, because she felt "guilty." She paused as she noted the difference in how she and her boyfriend had filled the free time until the other returned from work. Then, she resumed her story. For now, Victoria would make sure there was a homemade meal on the table when her boyfriend came home from work.

In chapter 7, I examine something else that the unemployed did with their newly acquired free time: search for a job. Many of the same questions of class and gender reemerge in that chapter, and we will see how the higher burden of caregiving, in particular, shapes working-class women's searches. We will also see how the discussion of enjoying one's free time continues to shape middle-class men's actions, even as they think about searching for work.

PART III

The Search

7

Attempting to Return to Work

I MET PAULA in her beautiful old farmhouse out in the country where she lived with her elementary-school-age son, Andrew, their dog, and some chickens they kept for eggs. While the farmhouse had "good bones," as Paula put it, it had not been maintained by the previous owners, which is why she'd been able to afford to purchase it two years earlier. Paula was slowly refurbishing, it and I was impressed with the work she'd done with the gorgeous woodwork in the kitchen. She wanted the security of owning her home, because after she and her husband separated, her finances had been rocky. Paula had grown up quite poor and had been the first in her family to get a college degree, in early-childhood education. She'd spent many years working as a childcare provider. Despite her passion for her career, she felt frustrated by the relatively low wages. With the help of a program from her previous employer, she'd gone back to school to earn her master of arts degree. While having an MA gave her access to better pay (about $45,000 annually), she still earned less than most women with her level of education (and her college debt load).

After her husband left, Paula and Andrew struggled. Unlike most middle-class women, in order to provide, she tended a large vegetable garden to help maintain their access to fresh vegetables, and she also hunted from time to time when things were very lean. After her job loss, Paula had even sold some furniture and some of Andrew's old toys, as well as some of the things her ex had never collected from the garage.

Just before her job loss, two good things happened for Paula and Andrew. First, she was hired to teach a night course at the college where she received her master's degree; it was a late-night class, so she was able to put Andrew to bed, call her mother to come watch him, and head into town to teach. This gave her the first real financial "cushion" that she had in a long time. Second, she received a large tax refund the following spring. While Paula worried about their finances after her job loss, these two changes left her less worried than she might have been. Without a job, she could forgo some weekly expenses, including most of the gas for commuting, Andrew's after-school costs, and other weekly incidentals.

This meant that when Paula thought about returning to work, she felt like she had some room to consider what jobs to take. She explained, "I'm sort of being strategic about what I'm applying for, so I don't put myself in a position of having to take a job that's not gonna pay the bills." Paula was using her networks, looking online, going to career fairs, even cold-calling local childcare centers to ask when they might next hire in order to search for a job that was the right fit. She explained, "I'm looking [for the right job] because I do recognize that if I want to continue to live in this fabulous place and provide for my family, [I] need a full-time job with benefits." Paula's cushion would not last forever, though, so she pounded the pavement in search of a good job that would provide for herself and Andrew.

Like Paula, the newly unemployed didn't only have time to do the household labor I discussed in chapter 6. They also had an important task: to find a new job. In fact, the state had a system in place to ensure the unemployed did just that. Individuals who received unemployment were required to check in online weekly and report about their job search. Pennsylvania had fairly strict rules about how to maintain eligibility for unemployment. First, everyone had to participate in a job search activity. Job search activities were broadly defined and included searching for jobs online, attending a job fair, going to an interview, or attending a meeting at the CareerLink Center, where my team and I recruited. This was, according to most of the people I talked to, the easy part of maintaining eligibility. The harder part was step two. Beginning three weeks after they started receiving unemployment, they had to apply for at least two jobs every week that they received unemployment. They were expected to apply for jobs as far as forty-five minutes away from where they lived, meaning they could be expected to commute for up to an hour and a half every day. But what if there were no jobs for which they were trained to do? If nothing was available in their line of work, they were expected to apply for jobs outside their trained area. Of course, workers could expand their search outside the state's mandated forty-five-minute commute or think about relocation to another area rather than search for a job other than for which they've trained.

Paula explained her take on the rules: "I have to apply for two jobs every week, so a lot of them I'm applying for I probably wouldn't take." Yet the state of Pennsylvania does not simply expect people to apply for two jobs a week. It also expects people to accept a job if offered to them. Paula went on, "Most jobs wouldn't pay enough, or be flexible enough to be a single mom . . . and there's some that I would be able to get but I'm not applying for them because it's not going to be enough money." Despite the state's expectations, then, Paula refused to apply for jobs paying below a certain level; she figured she could live with a 20 percent pay cut, but anything less than that would lead her and Andrew to lose their home.

Given Paula's stark finances (as well as the very real financial restrictions facing many others), are the unemployment rules actually good for the unemployed and, by extension, good for the people of Pennsylvania? A study done in West Germany, a country with more generous unemployment benefits than here in the United States, found an increase in benefits made it more likely that the unemployed would spend more time searching for work and thus increase the likelihood that they would find jobs that actually matched their skill set; a similar study done in the United States likewise found that more generous benefits decreased the likelihood of a mismatch between workers' educations and their new jobs' education requirements.[1] A study in the United States found that when comparing otherwise similarly situated job seekers, the unemployed who are almost out of benefits take poorer-quality jobs than those whose benefits have been extended, suggesting that desperation may lead to poorer reemployment out-comes.[2] Indeed, the higher unemployment benefits provided by the CARES Act during the 2020 recession did not appear to deter the un-employed from regaining work and may have provided a financial boost to the overall economy.[3] This suggests that the current rules may not align with either the worker's best interests or the state's long-term goals (which are generally not to see that unemployed worker back on the unemployment line).[4]

Yet in Pennsylvania, as in most of the United States, the unemploy-ment system is set up to get people back to work as quickly as possible. The type of work the unemployed find is less important than the goal of getting people off the unemployment system.[5]

Despite these rules, I found that not everyone started searching right away and that even among those who did search immediately, how people searched—what kind of job they looked for, how urgently they searched, and whether they felt able to decline a job—was often wildly different.[6] Among the people I met, four clear search strategies emerged in how participants considered reengaging with the labor market. I called these search patterns *Deliberate, Take Time, Urgent,* and *Diverted.* The searches were divided by gender and class, and some hewed closer to the letter of the unemployment laws than others.

The most common search strategy, *Deliberate,* followed many of the mandated Pennsylvania unemployment rules; these workers started their job search quickly and methodically after their job loss (some-times before a job was lost).[7] They treated their job search as if it were a job itself—clocking in and out and networking with colleagues to help them find work.[8] They wanted to maintain their positions and (ignoring the rules) felt able to decline a job if it was not good enough for them. Despite existing research about middle-class women and intensive mothering norms and their own increased labor in the home that I dis-cussed in chapter 6, more than three-quarters of the middle-class women reported an immediate methodical search.[9] Joan's search was typical of *Deliberate* searchers; Joan, our middle-class scientist, told me, "I've been looking for jobs for over a year now because I knew [my job loss] was imminent; I knew it was coming and so I started looking a long time ago." Joan's deliberate search involved networking, attending job fairs, and taking her job search very seriously.

Although past research has emphasized middle-class men's strong labor force attachment and the burden unemployment can be on them, I found middle-class men were overrepresented in what I called the *Take Time* search.[10] The name of this group stems from someone who stated he was "taking my time" to begin his job search, as those in this group did not immediately start their search after losing their job. In fact, almost half of the middle-class men reported "taking time" in the wake of their job loss, whereas none of the middle-class women did.[11] Despite rules that charged the unemployed to search for and accept work, these workers explained that they were deciding their next steps, considering a change of career, or enjoying time off before the search began. Like the others in this group, Neil, our middle-class hotelier, had not begun a search yet when he and I met. Unlike Joan, he seemed pleased with the idea of paid time off, adding that he hoped he would have the twenty-six weeks of unemployment and then he would "pray for an extension," meaning that he would want to extend the time he received unemployment benefits.

Urgent searchers found themselves in an almost frantic scramble to find work, with searches that began immediately. This group was dominated by working-class men. Not quite two-thirds of working-class men reported their need to find work demanded they search for any job (regardless of whether it fit their skills or prior experience) that would hire them as soon as possible.[12] About a quarter of the working-class women also reported the need to return to work quickly and to any job.[13,14] In stark contrast, none of the middle-class women and only two of the middle-class men undertook urgent searches. Anthony, our technical repairman, had searched urgently for a job, applying for every job that was advertised, even those that were unlike anything he had done before. When we met, he had taken a job that paid less than what he made on unemployment, meaning that it paid less than half of what he'd earned at his prior job.

Yet some had been diverted from looking for work and even seemed not to understand the rules of unemployment particularly well. Unlike the *Take Time* search strategy, this was not a carefully laid plan designed to provide some needed free time. In fact, calling being *Diverted* a search strategy seems a bit of a misnomer, as most of these individuals desperately needed to work, but they had not been able to begin and sustain a job search. A little over a third of working-class women reported being *Diverted* due to constraints in their attempts to return to work.[15] Although working-class women were more evenly dispersed across all four groups than their peers, they made up the vast majority of this group.[16] No middle-class men followed this pathway, and only one working-class man did. Tracy, our waitress turned factory worker, explained to me, "I hope to get back to work as soon as possible." But when I then asked her how her job search was going, she said, "I'm not going to lie, I haven't [looked]." Unlike their peers, the *Diverted* group wanted to search for work but could not.

Deliberate Searches

The vast majority of middle-class women like Paula followed this deliberate search pattern, with their gazes firmly set on regaining the employment they had lost; it was not as dominant, although not uncommon, among the middle-class men and was less common among the working class.[17] Most of the middle-class women were like Joan, who treated her job search as if it were a job; even her husband networked for her. In this way, Joan and the other middle-class women sharply diverged from the patterns described in Aliya Rao's research on more elite unemployed women, who were less likely to become what Rao called, "ideal job seekers."[18] Joan had started searching long before she was given six months' notice that the grant she was on was ending; her team had gotten smaller in recent years, as government funding had retracted.

The professor she worked for had tried to connect Joan with other faculty on campus, but her skills and degree were pretty specific to her old job. Moreover, she had worked there for nearly fifteen years, earning her seniority that gave her steady full-time hours and flexibility on her terms—what sociologists Phyllis Moen and Erin Kelly have called "schedule control."[19] She could go into work late if she needed to accommodate her childcare needs or leave early if her husband was traveling for work and she had to do the childcare pickup. She also had accumulated sick days, and because she had a good relationship with her boss, he trusted her when she said she needed to use them if her kid got sick. In the time leading up to her job loss, Joan did not find anything on campus that would provide these kinds of benefits. Describing one job, she explained, "They wanted to pay between like twelve and fifteen bucks an hour and wanted you to be extremely flexible. That's not enough money to put your kid in day care full-time, you know, and then be flexible." In Joan's calculation, the pay was a measly one-fifth of what she had earned, and they wanted her to work longer hours with less schedule control.

Joan did not want to settle for these jobs; they didn't pay well enough or allow her the time she wanted with her toddler son. As I've recounted in earlier chapters, I heard Joan say over and over again, she worried that if she stopped looking, she'd be taken for a stay-at-home mother. "I'm not a stay-at-home mom. It's not in me to do that. I need to be out contributing to society." Stay-at-home moms often get a bad rap in our country, facing criticism for doing what there is a lot of pressure to do—intensively care for their children.[20] Joan likely wanted to avoid this kind of criticism, although most women face criticism in one way or another, as my research has shown that it's difficult to avoid being criticized either for working or for not working.[21] She also wanted to avoid having a gap on her résumé. Her instincts on the gap were spot on; research has shown women's time off is viewed poorly by employers and that mothers face greater lost wages after being laid off.[22] So Joan started searching right away for work, and when her first plans didn't work out, she continued searching and started thinking and planning for a new line of work. I was surprised most middle-class women followed a deliberate search like Joan did, because I expected the demands of intensive mothering to get in the way of doing this kind of search, particularly since the middle-class women had taken on so much work inside the home.

A two-stage plan was common among many deliberate job seekers. They discussed time lines for expanding their searches outside the region and time lines for when they would have to consider jobs that they did not feel were comparable to what they had once had. Heather, who we met at the beginning of chapter 2, hoped to use the job search to transition back to something she had done before her most recent job. She explained, "I'm looking to move more into accounting. So, I was an accounting clerk when I worked at [an investment firm], and when I took the job at [an energy company], it was more marketing, land resources, and I worked some for the finance department, but not a lot. And I want to get a job doing accounting." Heather started applying for work before she officially lost her job (she was phased out in a large takeover), and she had a contingency plan: she would return to something similar to her more recent role if she couldn't find an accounting position.

In the not quite two months since she'd lost her job, Heather had applied for fifteen jobs. She'd also received a job offer she'd decided against taking. It was for nearly $15,000 less than what she'd made in her prior job, which was a lower salary than she'd expected and did not move her toward her goal of being an accountant again. She told me, "I'm more afraid of [being underemployed] than unemployment." Yet to remain eligible for unemployment benefits, was Heather technically allowed to turn this job down? No, the state expected Heather to take this job (although this expectation was laid out in the unemployment handbook that many admitted to not reading). But Heather felt she couldn't accept a job that paid so much below what she'd been making. She had three children; two of them were in full-time childcare and one was in an after-school program. Taking such a drastic pay cut was not feasible, particularly if it didn't align with her career goals. Since Pennsylvania, like most states, relies on the unemployed to self-police many components of compliance with the laws, Heather could decline a "bad" job. In fact, Heather, like most of the deliberate searchers, did not think she was skirting the rules. Instead, she saw herself as doing what was necessary for her and her family.

Recently, Heather felt like her plan was working out. When we met, she'd had several in-person interviews and she had a second-round interview at a company where she really wanted to work. She was hopeful that she'd land that position soon. While the position was going to be a step down from the management position she held at her old job in the energy firm, her husband encouraged her to take it and the possible pay cut. He reasoned that moving back into accounting in a different industry would give her more long-term stability. Heather agreed the trade-off was worth it.

Slightly under half the middle-class men also took deliberate searches. Harold, from chapter 6, told me that he wanted to complete the last class needed to earn his bachelor's degree. But for now, he said, "I just want to get into something similar to what I was doing. Maybe a hotel accounting position, something like that. That's not what I want to stay in. I'd like to finish that last class [laughter] and maybe . . . I've always thought that teaching would be good, like elementary or junior high teacher." While Harold dreamed of becoming a teacher someday, he put his dream on hold so that he could search for work in his current field. Ofer Sharone, the long-term unemployment expert, has found that the middle class, particularly at first, apply only for jobs that are similar to those they have recently lost.[23] American Studies professor Carrie Lane found the unemployed in the IT industry took a similar approach.[24] Sharone and Lane have both also found evidence that the middle class treated searches as if they were "jobs," which matches my finding of what the *Deliberate* middle-class job-seekers did.

Almost a quarter of the working-class women took deliberate searches; most had lost either office or health care jobs. These jobs—"pink-collar jobs," as National Book Award nominee Louise Kapp Howe termed them—were some of the best jobs working-class women could aspire to hold.[25] These pink-collar jobs placed them closer to the middle class and sometimes required additional training, certificates, or years of experience.[26] After high school, Latesha earned a certificate from a technical school in office administration. She hoped this degree would continue to give her an advantage over the deep pool of high school candidates in the area competing for a fairly limited number of jobs. She thought her education and experience might be paying off. In the seven weeks since she'd lost her job, she said, "I have fifteen job inquiries in and I've gotten two interviews so far." She was waiting to hear back from one of them. Latesha started her search the day after she lost her job and began applying for administrative jobs similar to the one she lost.

Four working-class men also took the deliberate search approach. These men had work histories from a time seemingly gone by—steady working-class blue-collar jobs. Paul was a carpenter, and his recent job loss came at a nonunion job. After his job loss, he explained, "I just decided, that's it, I'm gonna call the union." While Paul expected his search would take longer through the union, he believed this slower approach would lead to better pay and better long-term stability. Finding a job through the union meant "you get paid what you are worth, what you need to get paid." The working-class men and women who took deliberate searches had experience in working-class jobs that were more stable than many working-class jobs are these days, and they hoped a deliberate search would lead to better long-term prospects.

"Taking My Time"

Given the financial strains of unemployment and the rules of the Pennsylvania system, we might expect that people rolled up their sleeves and diligently searched for work. I certainly expected to find that to be the case, in line with what most of the qualitative literature on job searching depicts.[27] But about half of the middle-class men did not follow this path, including Neil.[28] Not searching for work was rare among all of the other groups: none of the middle-class women fell in this group, while only three of twenty-five working-class men did, and five of thirty-one working-class women did. When he and I met, Neil had not started looking for work. As I mentioned in chapter 1, Neil had lost his job during prime fishing season. He told me, "I'm an avid fly-fisherman and I was like, 'Wow, I could use this time to go fly-fishing.'" Instead of immediately searching for work, Neil explained, "Now I need to try to find out what it is I want to do." He wasn't even sure what kind of job he wanted yet, so how could he start looking for work, he wondered.

But how was this even possible? Didn't Pennsylvania require Neil to apply for two jobs every week? Neil explained this was an easy mandate to get around. He could set the search parameters for jobs for which he was unqualified and apply only for those jobs. In this manner, he could search and apply for nonrealistic jobs in one fell swoop, knowing he would not have to take a job before he was ready to go back to work.

Neil was unapologetic about using this strategy to enjoy the time he had on unemployment. He had paid into the unemployment system for decades; he felt he had earned the right to use the time as he saw fit. "I've been enjoying the past few weeks of not having much responsibility because it's been twenty-five years of more than most normal people would work, and the stresses. So, I'm like gosh, darn, it's my time." Just as we saw men's lack of guilt emerge in previous chapters, we see it again here. Neil was quick to point out that unemployment benefits weren't charity; he saw this benefit as something he had earned because he had paid into the system as someone who had worked (often longer than full-time hours) since he was a young man. He felt he deserved some time to enjoy his fly-fishing hobby and to figure out what he would do next. Unlike most of the women and the working-class men in this study, the middle-class men had a greater sense of entitlement to these benefits and to the time the benefits granted them in the wake of a job loss.

The past fifty years of research has emphasized middle-class men like Neil build their identities based on what they do for paid work.[29] So, I was surprised to find not just Neil but other middle-class men wanted to take time off. I was less surprised that middle-class men might feel justified in bending (or breaking) the unemployment eligibility rules. Research by sociologist Annette Lareau suggests the middle class learn at a young age that they are entitled to bend, or even break, the rules; this is something she finds working-class kids do not learn.[30] Many middle-class men felt it was OK to take time off and that it also would be easy for them to find another position. Having this kind of certainty (whether it was justified or not, as I'll explore in chapter 8) encouraged them to take some time. As Dean and I sat in a coffee shop, we discussed his plans to go back to work. He was not sure when he might start searching for work. He'd looked at jobs at his former employer, as part of his mandatory search obligation. Like Neil, he'd applied for jobs he didn't think he would get. Dean explained, "So this is almost a chosen unemployment at some level. . . . Even before I was unemployed, I could've gotten another job. There were other jobs that I can do that I could've applied for and I had zero motivation to do it." Instead of looking for work, Dean, and those like him, decided they wanted some time off first.

His daughter was in college, and while his job loss meant more of her college costs would be either on his ex-wife or through additional loans his daughter would take out, he still couldn't see himself searching for work anytime soon. He felt like he'd done his part working to fulfill his family obligations, and now he wanted some time to figure out how to find work that would fulfill him. In chapter 5, when Dean discussed the loss of his kids' health insurance, he did not express any guilt about how his job loss had changed his daughter's fortunes or his financial responsibilities toward her.

As he told me about his daughter's concerns about how she would pay for college, he wondered aloud if I would see him as selfish for taking time for himself. But he did not wonder (at least to me) about his obligations toward the state for receiving unemployment or about the state's expectation that he be available for work and actively applying for jobs. Instead, he elaborated on his earlier statement about his ability to find work easily, saying, "I would like not to work now, but I do know that I'm in a position where I could have autonomy [at work] and I have a skill set where I can do freelance tomorrow and basically call my shots and say [that] I'll work this much and I would like to make this much and I'll do it for this long. I could probably do that right now and work for people that I like." Dean felt very secure about both his ability to find employment and also about his ability to maneuver around the unemployment mandates.

As I've given talks about this research at various universities over the past few years, inevitably, someone will ask me some form of the following question: "Isn't it possible that the men are saying that they are enjoying their time off in order to avoid the stigma or the shame of being unemployed?" And, of course, this does seem plausible. Yet the middle-class men did not have detailed search strategies to describe to me, unlike the middle-class women (described above) or the working-class men (described next). Instead, they had stories about taking extra time for fishing, as Neil did, or taking a trip to Europe just after being laid off, as Dean did. (Dean received severance pay and was able to take the trip to Europe before he started his unemployment claim.) While it is possible these stories of taking time provided some social cover for men, I accepted that they had yet to meaningfully start their job searches, as these middle-class men reported little effort had been made to find work when we met.

The few working-class women and men in this group taking time to find work (there were no middle-class women) spoke less frequently about the need for time off to enjoy themselves and more about making the right choices now to find better work for the future. Roger explained his job loss was "a good opportunity to make a change. And do something more fulfilling with my life. So, with that in mind, I've kind of been taking my time. I don't want to panic and think, 'Oh, shit, I need to find another job right away.' So, I haven't really been looking for something, because I wasn't sure if I want something in that same field." The start of Roger's job search was paused while he reflected on what type of work he might seek.

Urgently Searching

About two-thirds of working-class men described urgent searches, searching for work immediately after losing their job (several even said they left their old job and drove straight to an unemployment center). About a quarter of working-class women also searched urgently, while the search pattern was uncommon in middle-class men and absent among middle-class women.[31] Unlike the deliberate searches, urgent searches were not thoughtfully planned out; the job seekers in this group didn't have that luxury. They also felt they could not decline a bad job—both because they needed the money and because of their interpretation of the unemployment laws. Most knew that if offered a job, they would have to take it. They even took jobs for which they were entirely unsuited and some, like Anthony, had found and lost jobs in between when my team invited them to meet with me for the study and when we scheduled our meeting a couple of weeks later. In fact, just before I met him, Anthony had lost a job. He'd been told it was a temporary position, but he thought that meant months, not two weeks.

Trained as a technical repairman, Anthony had used these skills in many different types of jobs. If something had electric components, he liked to think he could fix it. Prior research suggests the working class may search for positions that they think match their skills rather than look for jobs that are similar to those they have held before.[32] This is very different from what the middle class does. A lawyer, for example, typically would not apply for consulting positions even though many of the same skills are used in both jobs. But a working-class person like Anthony who has worked in repairing computer electronics might transition to repairing industrial air conditioners. While a working knowledge of repairs and electronics are necessary for both positions, there could be a steep learning curve to make this kind of transition, and it might mean a lateral or even a downward move.

Anthony's work history fit the description that prior research would suggest: He found jobs that matched his skill set rather than his prior experience. He'd worked in more traditional electronic repairs as well as in manufacturing, and his most recent layoff had been in the natural resources industry. He started applying for jobs immediately. He applied with an urgency that veered toward desperation and looked nothing like Joan's job search. While Joan was able to consider whether she would take some of the jobs on campus that paid quite poorly or had little flexibility, Anthony did not feel he had this ability. His wife was a stay-at-home mom, and they had two children in elementary school as well as his wife's elderly aunt depending on his income.

Not only was Anthony applying to every job that advertised for a technical repairman, he was applying for every job he saw within a forty-five-minute radius, exactly as mandated by the law. He had rewritten his résumé for a custodial position, and he found it difficult to "tweak his résumé" for "mopping floors" because he hadn't had much experience doing that particular job. For the most part, in his prior searches, Anthony had found work as a technical repairman before he'd found work doing something else. But once he'd been hired to stock shelves at a supermarket, he'd spent almost a year earning $8 an hour, working his way up to $9 an hour supervising other shelf stockers, before he was able to find work as a technical repairman. Taking the first job he had found left Anthony underemployed in a job where he didn't use his skills, because it was hard to work overtime (he'd worked ten- to twelve-hour shifts to make up for some of his lost wages) and search for work.

Now, yet again, Anthony was searching frenziedly, spurred both by his family's financial straits and by the clear provisions in the state laws. As he saw it, "When you're on unemployment, you have to be available, you have to be looking at jobs." Anthony interpreted the law more rigidly than Neil and Joan did. Joan was searching diligently and hoped to find a job, but she had clear boundaries about what she was and wasn't willing to include in her search. And Neil was only applying for jobs he felt certain would not hire him so that he could enjoy the time he felt he had earned. Here we see how unemployment, as an institution with formal rules, can be experienced very differently by people who know how to bend (like Joan) or break (like Neil) those rules versus those (like Anthony) who expect that the rules must be strictly followed.

Like Anthony, Seth didn't feel like he could wait for a job like the one he held previously, working for a company that sold home health care products. His wife had recently left work to take care of their toddler daughter and to prepare for the birth of their second child. They each had partial custody of one child from previous relationships, and his wife cared for them, too, when they were in the home. There were a lot of mouths to feed, and his unemployment benefits didn't stretch nearly far enough.

Already searching urgently, Seth turned frantic when, within a month of his job loss, he couldn't make the family's rent payment. Seth and his family lost their home and moved back in with his mother, three hours away from where they'd been. By the time we met, two months into his job search, Seth had applied for over seventy jobs and said the reality of his financial situation meant he was searching for "anything." Because he'd had to move, Seth couldn't rely on his local contacts to help him find a job. Seth preferred to find "anything that's paying decent. Factory work, getting in a hospital. [At a] hospital, you can probably start at twelve bucks an hour and they got the best health insurance coverage." But he worried the urgency of his search meant "the only job I can find still is McDonald's, because that's happening to a lot of people. So, I fear that the most." Men like Seth with urgent job searches understood it would be better in the long term to wait for a higher-paying job, but financial pressures rarely allowed such time.

While middle-class men were unlikely to take such an urgent approach, two middle-class men did. Both had gone through previous job losses and prolonged bouts of unemployment, and they were in more precarious financial shape than most of the middle class. While some middle-class men had faced chronic unemployment (three or more job losses), most bounced back quickly (unlike the working-class men).[33] It was when these unemployment bouts became extended that the family faced greater financial peril,[34] and that situation spurred urgent searches among middle-class men. Jeff, the former parole officer with enormous debt, had sent out over fifty job applications. Sitting in his house amidst several home renovation projects that were now languishing, Jeff discovered that his mood about his job search alternated from bleak to optimistic. He said, "I've applied for factory work, I have not gotten any calls. I've applied for other administrative work; I've applied with [a large nonprofit]. I did have an interview three weeks ago up in [a different county] for a chief probation officer up there. Unfortunately, I already heard back [and] I didn't get that position. So, that sucks." Jeff was particularly disheartened not to get the job for which he'd been trained, but he was also frustrated that he couldn't get jobs for which he seemed (in his eyes) overly qualified, such as work in a factory. Multiple job losses followed by prolonged periods of unemployment had left Jeff in greater precarity than other middle-class men and more willing to take almost any job he could find.

Diverted from Searching

Although she was a single mom to two children, Tracy hadn't applied for a single job. She explained, "I haven't looked. I haven't tried . . . I don't even know where to apply." Given Tracy's descent into poverty, at first glance, her diverted search was surprising. We remember Tracy and her kids were experiencing food insecurity. She wasn't getting the medical care she needed. But when I asked about her job search, Tracy seemed at a loss for words. Tracy thought the biggest barrier to her job search was "just stress." Despite wishing that she could work again, Tracy was too stressed to start her search. While working-class women took a wider range of search strategies than their peers, they made up the vast majority of those whose search was diverted.[35]

As we talked, it became clear that Tracy wasn't taking time for herself like Neil was. She told me not working made her "feel like less of a person." She'd always expected to work ever since she was a young girl. She liked going to work and getting out of the house and earning a paycheck. She didn't like being unemployed and she felt trapped at home by the lack of money. It is possible to see some similarities between the *Diverted* job searchers and those in the *Take Time* group, as neither started searching right away, but we can also see how different Neil and Tracy's experiences were. Neil wanted some time to himself; Tracy felt trapped in her home. Neil could afford some time off; Tracy desperately needed to get back to work.

But Tracy also felt overwhelmed. She was overwhelmed by the decisions she had to make on a daily basis about what bills to pay and how to make her unemployment check stretch far enough. If we think back to earlier chapters, we remember how Tracy struggled to pay her electric bill, to pay the mortgage, and to have enough money left over to eat regularly. If she managed to pay all the bills, there sometimes wasn't enough money left to put gas in her car. Psychologists Sendhil Mullainathan and Eldar Shafir have done research on the toll poverty takes on decision making.[36] In their book *Scarcity*, they write about the way poverty affects people's abilities to make everyday decisions about their lives. Every moment you spend deciding something like how to pay a bill lessens your ability to make a good decision later on that day about something else—something like how to search for work. In other words, your brain has a limited ability to make decisions over the course of the day, and the more decisions you have to make, the more drained you become.

Tracy wasn't just overwhelmed by the daily decisions; she was also underwhelmed by a dearth of opportunity. She lived in a tiny town in a rural area. This was nice if you wanted to know every neighbor's name but tough when you wanted to find a job. Jobs were few and far between. Her daughter was still in elementary school and needed adult supervision after school, and Tracy didn't want her fourteen-year-old son to take on that responsibility. He needed to focus on his education if he was going to have a better life than Tracy had had. So did her daughter. Tracy couldn't travel too far for work, then, because she couldn't afford the gas or childcare. Her options seemed exceptionally limited. Faced with an inability to make a decision about her job search, Tracy simply didn't begin it.

And what did Tracy do about the state mandate that she begin searching and that she document her search? Having not lost a job recently, she seemed confused by the state rules. She had intended to drive to the CareerLink Center again to have someone help her with the online system, but since she was in a remote area, it was over a half-hour drive to get to the nearest center. She didn't want to waste the gas. When pressed, it became clear that Tracy didn't realize she could lose her benefit eligibility if she weren't actively searching for work.

Being thrown into poverty wasn't the only reason women were diverted from their job search. Family responsibilities also kept women from searching for work. Many said a lack of childcare prevented them from searching for work. Kimberly had a "great support system" in the town she lived when she lost her middle-class job as an education director for a nonprofit. "I could take the kids to work and my friend [who lived nearby] watched [them]. . . . It worked out great; I had a great support system where I didn't have to pay a babysitter." But after her job loss, the family moved to a new city so that her husband could take a new job with better pay and health insurance to offset her job loss. In the new town, Kimberly was unable to find affordable quality childcare, and without her old support network, Kimberly did not attempt to return to work.

Family responsibilities also kept Samantha from searching for work as clerical support staff. Samantha lost her state childcare credit for low-income workers when she lost her job. She said, "I'm a stay-at-home mom now, again, because my day care was pulled. . . . I couldn't afford day care with the check I was making from [unemployment]. So, now I'm just home with the kids again." Although Samantha called herself a stay-at-home mom, she was not partnered, so she knew she would need a job once her unemployment ran out. In the meantime, with two young children and no childcare, she could not search for work.

The large gender and class differences in search strategies that we see here contradict some of the most recent research on unemployment and gender. Though some have argued the gender differences are revealed largely in how the emotions about the job loss are managed, other have found no meaningful gender differences in the early stages of the job search.[37]

Economic Incentives to Return to Work

Why did I find such striking patterns across gender and class? As I have argued throughout the book, unemployment widens already existing inequalities between people and creates new inequalities. We saw earlier (chapter 4) how financial differences before a job loss affected the likelihood of experiencing financial precarity. We saw how gender differences in family obligations shaped decisions about health and home (chapters 5 and 6). Here, we see how these differences then shaped people's abilities to search for work (and, in chapter 8, we will see how it matters for the success of these searches).

Since unemployment benefits in Pennsylvania are based on wages, earnings before the job was lost likely played an important role. Earnings also shape how much people could set aside in savings (if they had savings at all).[38] But there is some conflicting evidence about how wages may matter when people search for work. Economists have two guiding presumptions about wages and unemployment compensation that may shed light on how we think about this issue. On the one hand, knowing that you can earn higher wages may make you more eager to go back to work, while having a low wage may give you less of an incentive to go back. On the other hand, higher unemployment compensation may slow the start of a job search because you feel financially secure enough to wait to start looking, while lower unemployment compensation might force you to start your search sooner.

How wages shape benefits, savings, and potential earnings (and thus searches) is likely also complicated by people's gender and class. I expected there would be sizable class differences in people's wages and also for there to be gender differences as well, because of the known gender wage gap in the United States. The gender wage gap remains significant in the United States, with women earning about 77 cents for every dollar earned by a man.[39] Although working-class men have faced long-term declines in their earnings since the 1970s, and the wage gap has shrunk among low-wage workers, a sizable gender wage gap remains at all levels of the income ladder.[40]

The question of the importance of wages is harder to tease out because in many households, families rely on two incomes. This is particularly true in households of married couples with children, in which 63 percent rely on income from both the mom and the dad; even in households without kids, nearly half rely on income from both the husband and wife (less than 20 percent rely on only the husband).[41] Yet, historically, when men lose jobs, it's harder for these households to make up the income lost than it is when women lose jobs.[42] This makes sense when we think about the gender wage gap: Men make more than women, on average, so when they lose jobs, it is likely harder for women's earnings to cover all of the household expenses. But at the same time, unemployment is calculated based on a percentage of the lost wages, so men likely bring home higher unemployment benefits than women do. While there is a cap on wages for unemployment insurance that does shrink the gender gap (in unemployment benefits, at least), in most states, including Pennsylvania, men's average wages were at or near the cap while women's average wages remained quite a bit below it.[43] Thus, there remained more of a cushion, on average, from men's unemployment benefits than from women's.

As I discussed in chapter 4, I developed measures to gauge how financially at-risk people felt, based on whether they reported they had "enough" to cover daily costs from either unemployment alone, unemployment plus their savings, or unemployment, savings, plus their partner. This was contrasted with having "barely enough" (some essentials were occasionally given up, as well as many luxuries) or "not enough" (daily they went without essentials). Those in the final category reported food scarcity, missed bills, loss of basic services, and/or an inability to pay for daily needs of their children.

Over three-quarters of middle-class men and two-thirds of middle-class women had enough money to cover their daily costs, which made it possible to take time or follow deliberate searches.[44] Many were like Joan (in the *Deliberate* group) who had used her bank savings a little, but when asked about retirement she replied, "I have not dipped into my retirement, no. We've had other pots that we've been able to take from. No, I will not do that. I refuse to do that." Her certainty that she would not touch her retirement showed a broad sense of financial security. Even though Joan had been her family's primary earner (Joan earned more than 60 percent of her family's income), her husband earned enough to keep the family comfortable, particularly with Joan's unemployment benefits. Once Joan's benefits ran out, the family might have to make some tough decisions, particularly about continuing her son's full-time childcare. But she still felt quite confident about her financial security, as did most of the middle class. Rodney (*Take Time* group) explained his search decisions came down to how long his unemployment kept his family from tapping into their savings account: "We have enough in the joint checking account to live month to month." The middle class often had the financial resources to pursue either deliberate job searches or to take time off.

Taking money from a retirement account or increasing a spouse's hours gave some working-class families the financial security to take time or to be deliberate in their return to work. Joel (*Take Time*) said, "I had $10,000 in a 401, so what I did, I rolled part of that into my checking account . . . so we had that financial cushion." Some working-class families had a family member increase work hours to provide additional financial security. Heidi (*Deliberate*) explained that her husband had greatly increased his hours to keep the family financially stable while she took a deliberate job search approach. "Like, he would work two doubles in one week. Or he'd pick up an extra day." Her husband's extra hours made it possible for her to reject a bad job: "I don't want to do [a CNA job again]. That is like my last resort. You work so hard. It's so underpaid. . . . So, I'm trying to steer away from that." Her husband's additional hours allowed Heidi to keep her search expanded away from particularly poor options.

In contrast, almost two-thirds of working-class women and nearly half of working-class men said there was not enough or barely enough to cover their needs.[45] While this financial pressure led some workers to return to work faster, others were so constrained by financial insecurity they did not search. Marcus (*Urgent*), whose church was helping him with food donations, explained, "I'm looking for anything I can get my hands on. I need something." Wendy (*Urgent*) had sent out numerous applications. Wendy had fairly low expectations, explaining, "Hopefully it's comparable to at least what I'm making on unemployment," which was about "$150" less "per paycheck" than her last job. Urgent searches like Wendy's were often motivated by the fact that working-class women didn't see the advantage in waiting for a good job opportunity to arise; they expected their options would be poor but knew that the labor market was tight and that they would face stiff competition for even the poor options they did have.

As we saw with Tracy, financial strains sometimes diverted people from starting a search. Roy (*Diverted*) hadn't started a job search. He felt overwhelmed by choosing which bills to pay. "What I get in unemployment is basically barely enough to even feed us . . . or pay the mortgage or pay the other bills," he explained. "Every month, if we pay something, we're falling behind in everything else." Roy said all of his energy was spent managing bills, leaving no time to search for work.

Thus, differences in unemployment benefits and in pre-job-loss savings exacerbate existing inequalities and generates new inequalities by shaping how people search for work. Workers with higher education and earnings had a greater security net after their job loss, and these resources gave them the ability to undertake either deliberate searches or to take time off. Workers with lower education levels and earnings often approached or entered poverty after a job loss, leading them to either search for work with a desperate urgency or not to start a search because they were overwhelmed by their inability to pay their daily bills.

Gender and Labor Force Attachment and Family Responsibilities

In the last two chapters, we saw how broad social and cultural norms about what is acceptable for men and women to do can shape how men and women behave after they lose their jobs. Societal expectations about who should care and who should work influences what we do and what we expect others to think of us. What others will think shaped people's decision making about health care, the household division of labor, and childcare.[46] It then shaped their decisions about searching for work. Although sociologist Jennifer Sherman finds gender flexibility—the ability to share work and home tasks and to break away from traditional gender norms—can help families when they face economic challenges and during times of familial change, I find that not everyone has the same access to flexibility.[47] As we have already seen, women, particularly working-class women, faced greater demands to do more at home after their job loss. Working-class women's increased childcare responsibilities (which middle-class women shared to a lesser extent, as they had a greater ability to outsource childcare, particularly at first) played a critical role. Men, on the other hand, had a greater ability to avoid household labor and, as we will see, middle-class men were best positioned to demand some time for themselves, while working-class men faced strong breadwinning demands because of the likelihood that they had a stay-at-home partner.

While most of the middle-class men had anticipated a lifetime of full-time labor, unemployment presented an opportunity to rethink their relationship with work. Many of the men in the *Take Time* group pointed to their long years in the labor force and said they deserved this time off. A lack of guilt surrounding their job loss emerged, as the middle-class men expressed their entitlement to take time off. Neil said he was "enjoying my time," and Dean explained, "It's like I want a break. I just want a break. So, I'm going to let go of the appointment. I will figure out my next steps after I get to take a bit of a break. So that's where this ended up." Jason went so far as to say that his job loss was a "blessing in disguise" because it had given him the ability "to focus on [figuring out what I want to do] full-time."

Some middle-class men felt torn about their decision because they were not fulfilling what they (and their wives) saw as their responsibilities to their families. In the previous chapters, we saw guilt connected to actions in which women sacrificed health care or healthy behaviors or increased their household labor; here, a few men talked about feeling guilty, but not enough to change their search strategies. Jacob (*Take Time*) explained, "I feel terrible about it and I'm not doing what I'm supposed to do. If she wants to work, that should be her prerogative to do that as sort of an extra thing. I don't feel she should have to carry the burden of having to supply for her family like that." Although Jacob "felt awful," he was not willing to take "any job." In the prior two chapters, women's guilt was explicitly linked to their behavior—reduction in health care maintenance or an increase in second shift tasks. In contrast, here we can see how even when men expressed guilt, it did not lead to a new search plan; Jacob acknowledged that he was not living up to what both he and his wife agreed was his responsibility, but he did not feel bad enough to start searching for work. He wanted to take some time off before he did so.

Some working-class men also expressed a lack of guilt over the change in circumstances and their ability to take some time off. Joel (*Take Time*) explained that his wife's full-time work "doesn't really bother me. I know she said, once I do get back to work, she's gonna cut her hours down, but it's sort of a balance, 'cause I'm home all the time. I can do a lot more stuff that she used to have to do, whether it's laundry, cooking, cleaning, whatever, but since I'm there, it's just trading places." Some of the men, like Joel, had been doing the breadwinning for most of their lives and felt it was OK if their wives took a turn. Although, if we remember from the earlier chapter, Joel wasn't exactly trading places with his wife, because she was still doing most of the household labor when she got home from work.

If labor force attachment did not necessarily push men back to work, then how might work devotions influence women's return to work? In contrast to many middle-class men, both middle-class and working-class women repeatedly explained their attempts to return to work in terms of their work devotion and strong labor force attachment. Like Joan, the women also emphasized that they were not stay-at-home moms. Christina (*Deliberate*), explained, "I could never be a stay-at-home parent. . . . I do not have the strength to stay at home the whole time. And now, unfortunately, I've been doing that for two months and it's driving me insane." Unlike the men who were enjoying their time off, Christina wanted to return to work.

Both middle-class and working-class women emphasized the importance of work to their identity. Latoya (*Deliberate*), explained, "It's very important for my self-esteem and I like to work. I like to have a job. . . . So, yeah, for me it's been an obsession to find a position." Dana (*Take Time*), explained, "When I'm out working, I'm not 'the wife' anymore. I'm not the housewife. You're a person again and people notice you." Similarly, Peggy (*Urgent*), said, "I want to be working. I don't want to be . . . I am not a person to be not working. I hate not working." But unlike the middle-class women, many of the working-class women who reported this attachment to work experienced financial precarity, which hindered their ability to engage in a deliberate search. We remember Tracy had not happily returned home; she wanted to work, but burdened by decision making, lacking easy-to-find jobs, and without gas money to search for a job, she saw no easy way back.

Unlike most of the middle class, many working-class men and women reported that gendered family obligations shaped their searches—often brought on by the financial crises they faced after their job loss. While many middle-class men felt freed from work devotions, most working-class men felt burdened by their inability to provide for their families. Family differences may help explain this response. Although the vast majority of all participants were either married or cohabiting and had a child age 23 or younger who lived in their household and depended on their income, middle-class men and women were most likely to have a working partner.[48]

Nearly half of the working-class men who had an urgent search had a wife who worked either part-time or not at all.[49] In contrast, only two of the men in the *Take Time* group reported having a spouse who was either working part-time or not working. Having someone still earning a full-time middle-class salary made a huge difference in the lives of the middle class. The working class, on the other hand, did not have that kind of stability to fall back on. Marcus (*Urgent*) had started working part-time and was not reporting his income while he searched for new work, "And I'm not going to lie," he said, "I'm [working under the table]. I have no choice; I have to provide for my children." Seth (*Urgent*) said, "It just hurts my family because I don't have a job right now. And it hurts me, too." He was desperate to find work for his family, including his wife, who was not working.

Those on the diverted path were the most likely to be single and to have children. This often meant that they either had family obligations (like childcare) that prevented them from searching or they were dealing with multiple strains from poverty that stopped them from searching. Jodi (*Diverted*) faced both the challenge of raising her fifteen-year-old daughter by herself and also managing their below-poverty budget. She said, "I'm, like, living check to check right now. . . . I try not to get as much [food] so I can stretch it for the bills that come in." Managing the bills, plus watching her daughter and trying to get her ex to pay child support (which he was reluctant to do), left Jodi with little time to search for work.

As we saw in the last chapter, most working-class women increased their time on childcare and household tasks after their job loss. Some also said their job loss gave their husbands leverage to expect them to stay at home and continue to do this work. This was particularly true for working-class women, although two middle-class women also reported this situation. Pamela (*Diverted*), explained, "[My husband] was glad [I lost my job]. Now I could stay at home and he made a huge garden for me to have to work on, so that's what I'm supposed to do. . . .

But he feels at least I'm home where I'm supposed to be with the kids." Similarly, Nicole (*Diverted*) said her husband "was thrilled. [He] had wanted to me quit that job for years." Rhonda (*Diverted*) explained, "[My husband is] respecting me a little more, and I think he's realizing the treasure of having a woman home in the house. Because way back when, when his mom was a mom, that's what they did—they stayed home, they were the stability of the home." Although all of these women had previously worked full-time, their job loss opened them up to expectations from their husbands that they should remain at home to care for their children (and their spouse).

———

Ultimately, those in the middle class appeared doubly advantaged—both in their financial capabilities and in their ability to respond to the crisis without being as closely tied to traditional gender norms. Those in the working class appeared doubly disadvantaged—both in their financial precarity and in how their insecurity constrained their searches, leading women to stay at home and men to remain breadwinners in homes that could use a second earner. The middle class actively rejected traditional gender norms while the working class became more tightly bound to them in the wake of a crisis. Economic incentives were deeply interwoven with these gendered work devotions and family responsibilities in shaping how people responded to their job loss. Only those with enough resources could afford a deliberate search or to pause and take time before beginning their search. Yet not having enough resources could stifle the possibility of carefully searching for a new job, as those in the *Diverted* group found themselves too busy putting out fires to pull together a coherent search strategy.

Many middle-class men were pleased to take a short pause in their relationship with the paid labor force. These men seemed clear that they were going against traditional gender norms; many men noted their long devotion to work while explaining this step back. In this way, the middle-class men appear to have the privilege to redefine their gender obligations without much apparent social cost. In contrast, middle-class women made strong claims about their rightful place in the work-force. Many middle-class women invoked the image of stay-at-home moms when describing their own choices, suggesting that, unlike the middle-class men, their searches were constrained by what they feared would become their fate. In chapter 8, I will examine whether these differing approaches to searches led to differing outcomes in finding a job (and whether the middle-class women were right to fear what would come next).

Bearing the sole financial responsibility for the family was not something easily changed in the wake of a job loss, and it was a burden working-class men carried with them as they searched for new work. Breadwinning responsibilities forced many working-class men to search urgently and take jobs quickly. It also put them at risk for another job loss. This type of churning stemmed both from their poor labor prospects and from the greater likelihood that these men had stay-at-home or part-time working wives.

Many working-class women felt obliged to take on caregiving tasks that prevented them from searching for new work or they faced new pressure from husbands to stay at home. While prior scholars have noted employment allows working-class women to barter for more power in the home,[50] losing a job meant a loss of bargaining power for many working-class women and a undesired return to household tasks.

Although in the critically acclaimed novel *My Year of Rest and Relaxation*, the wealthy elite protagonist falsely reports searching for work in order to remain on unemployment while not seeking work, most public discourse surrounding rule breaking and misuse of government funds has focused on the poor.[51] Yet we see in this chapter that the people with greater economic security appeared to understand the unemployment rules better, which gave them a better sense of how to navigate the rules and even how to break them. While it may seem as if Neil and Dean, in particular, and even Paula, Heather, and Joan (when they didn't apply or turned down jobs they deemed to be "bad") were taking advantage of the system, we only need to remember Anthony's year in the grocery store to realize that the rules may not be set up in a way that leads to optimal outcomes. Paula was certain that following the rules to the

letter would lead to the loss of her home, and Heather and Joan felt the
rules did not recognize the need to find a job that covered the cost of
childcare. But is there a difference between how Neil and Dean responded and the decisions Heather, Paula, and Joan made? The white
middle-class men who took their time seemed to embrace a sense of
entitlement to more time, certainly, and perhaps to better outcomes as
well.[52] Perhaps, what we need is for the rules to be expanded so that
they do not push people into jobs like those Paula and Heather feared.
In order to understand whether different search strategies lead to different outcomes, I examine next what kinds of work the unemployed have
found one year later.

8

One Year Later

HAROLD FOUND WORK. Even better, the salary was about the same as his old job; it was, in his words, "a great job." Unlike others I interviewed, Harold, whom we first met in chapter 6 when he talked about sharing the household labor with his wife, did not enter the land of long-term unemployment. He found a job before his benefits had run out. Over the course of his period of unemployment, Harold (*Deliberate*) tapped into many of the resources I've explored in this book: his severance, his savings, his maximum-level unemployment benefit, and his wife's steady middle-class income. He also benefited from a lack of guilt; he maintained his health (even starting a new exercise regime) and did not increase his household labor. While he did feel they got a little stressed when it came close to "crunch time" (meaning when his benefits were set to expire), he stuck with his deliberate search plan until the end. With one offer already in hand and with the days ticking toward the expiration of his unemployment insurance benefit, he interviewed at one last company, hoping to land a better-paying and higher-status position. He got the job.

Harold's ability to marshal the resources he'd accumulated allowed him to find this "great job." His family used some savings (and used up his severance), but they never dipped into their emergency savings account, nor did they touch their retirement account. During his six months off work, Harold and his wife made relatively few financial changes; they stopped eating out regularly, and they put a couple of small home improvement projects on hold. They also did not go on their annual vacation, which typically involved plane flights and hotels. But they did take the kids on short trips to visit friends and family. They also all stayed on his wife's health insurance plan and remained relatively healthy that year. He was keeping up the daily walks he'd started when he lost his job, only now he did them on his lunch break, paired with longer walks with his wife on weekends. Harold and his wife also continued to "share" the household and childcare, allowing him ample time to search for work.

Once Harold went back to work, his family's finances straightened out quickly. He restarted a small construction project in the house, renovating the master bedroom closet. He thought his wife would love the extra space for her shoes. Harold found a job with a comparable salary and, even better, he'd found work as an accountant, but not in the hotel industry. This meant he had more regular hours than in previous jobs. He had "a huge sense of relief." Accounting wasn't something that Harold felt anyone could find "exceptionally fulfilling, spiritually fulfilling," except, he joked, someone who was "really into numbers." But he'd returned to the same pay, with better hours, and felt glad to have found work that returned his family to financial stability. While prior research has found that workers in the United States pay a high penalty for experiencing job loss and unemployment—about a 15 percent drop, on average, in their annual pay—there is evidence suggesting that some workers return to work either relatively unscathed or even better off.[1] Harold's new job both provided similar pay and better hours; he came out the other side ahead of the game.

The job loss period was a time of stress for almost everyone I met. But some, like Harold, navigated the process with more ease than others; many of the factors we saw in earlier chapters, including severances, financial constraints, guilt (or lack thereof), health insurance and health care access, household responsibilities, and search strategies, shaped decision making and job search outcomes. Unlike Harold, Tracy, Neil, Joan, and Anthony all paid a higher price than they thought they would, but the "toll" they paid for their job loss varied greatly. This chapter delves into how the unemployment period and the inequalities that grew during it shaped the details of their job searches and their new jobs.

One year out, some people had certainly moved ahead, a few were not quite maintaining where they had been, but the vast majority had fallen far behind. There are many ways to think about how the unemployed were doing one year later. But I was most interested in learning whether they had been able to find comparable work to what they had lost and how they fared financially overall.

About a quarter, the majority of whom were middle-class men, found good job opportunities and were moving ahead, as Harold had done.[2] Those who moved ahead found work that was either similar in pay or prestige (or both) to what they had done before, or they found something better.[3] Importantly, the resources they brought with them and that they gained during their unemployment period gave many white middle-class men a leg up in their searches. Most who moved ahead took a deliberate job search plan, although a handful of middle-class men who took their time to start their job searches managed to move ahead, leveraging resources that others simply did not have to advance when they reentered the labor market.

A smaller group of individuals also found work one year out, but the work was a step down either in pay or prestige, so they were not quite maintaining what they'd once had. Some experienced a step down in their lifestyles as well, although many had dual-earning spouses whose income kept the worst of the storm at bay. Yet again, I saw the middle class finding ways to come close to maintaining what they once had, while the working class were less likely to find themselves here.[4] After a slow start to his job search, Neil had found full-time work that was not quite as prestigious as what he had once done, and he did not return to his former salary, but his decline was slight and his wife's new promotion at her job kept them in a similar financial position. Deliberate searches propelled some middle- and working-class women into this category, keeping their target occupational goal within sight even if they couldn't quite attain what they once had. Despite starting their searches later, a handful of middle-class men who took their time also managed to keep their original goals within sight.

But, one year later, the majority reported a large decline, either in their wages, in their job quality, or most often, in both. And some people still had not found work. Almost two-thirds were falling far behind. Women often ended up in part-time work, like Tracy did, or in new fields, like Joan, and some reported they stopped looking for work altogether. About two-thirds of working-class women said they were worse off one year later.[5] Tracy found work as a waitress, but she had to settle for part-time work, which kept her finances on shaky ground. Working-class men were in similar straits, with almost two-thirds, including Anthony, unable to return to similar work.[6] Well over half the middle-class women took a big step backward in their careers, despite beginning with deliberate searches and high hopes.[7] Joan eventually found full-time work (at substantially lower pay) in a new field about sixteen months after her job loss. Most of the people who followed *Urgent* or *Diverted* searches for new jobs ended up in this group, as did a few deliberate job seekers and some who took their time.

Finally, my team and I could not find a sizable number of people we had met the year before. We had the most luck reaching the middle-class interviewees; most still had either the same cell phone number, e-mail, or mailing address. Sometimes, when all else failed, I found a few people through LinkedIn, which was used by many in the middle class but wasn't very common in the working class. Working-class women and men, particularly the men, were much harder to locate. We could not reach nearly half of the working-class men; phone numbers came back as no longer in service; e-mails bounced back as in-box full; letters were returned as no longer deliverable.[8] I never caught up with Dennis again, who if you recall had a long history of unemployment. When I could not find a way to contact people, I used public search engines to learn what I could. Sometimes all I discovered was through their original home address. If they lived in single-family homes, I could learn if their homes had been put for sale; sometimes I learned the homes had repeatedly dropped in price before they sold. This was usually the last bit of information I found. Now, this does not mean that everyone we could not contact struggled, but most people whom I interviewed did indicate that moving would be their last resort.[9] The changed numbers, addresses, and e-mails certainly suggested that those we could not contact moved, if nothing else.

Moving Ahead

Middle-class men seemed so often to land on their feet—either in better jobs than they'd started out in or in jobs similar to those that they'd been laid off from. While much of the sociological and economic literature on job loss has focused on what Markus Gangl calls the "scar effects" of job loss—the ways that job loss cuts deeply into people's future earnings and even their future health[10]—other research suggests there is a lot of variability in how much someone's next wages is affected by a recent job loss. In fact, some studies suggest as many as 40 percent of those who lose a job will go on to find a job that pays as well or even better than the one they lost.[11] In fact, in preliminary analyses that my colleagues Adrianne Frech, Jane Lankes, and I have conducted, we found that some of the most advantaged and successful men have had more experiences of unemployment than is typical for other men, suggesting that there is much more variability in unemployment outcomes than previously thought.[12]

In contrast to the often gloomy academic forecasts about the futures of the unemployed (and we've seen quite a bit of devastation already in this book), a number of the people I caught back up with had some good fortune in the year in between our talks.[13] The middle-class men seemed best positioned to take advantage of new labor market opportunities. The gains were not without costs: Some faced stress on their way to find jobs, others moved in order to move up, while still others took on longer commutes. Few escaped their job loss entirely unscathed, but most in this group hit fewer bumps than those in the other groups and, like Harold, they relied on the advantages we've seen them accumulate throughout the book to help them move forward. Surprisingly, the middle-class men in this group were evenly divided between the *Deliberate* job search strategy and the *Take Time* approach, suggesting that at least some of those who had taken some time off before searching had judged their job prospects well.

Receiving a severance, having substantial existing savings, not worrying about health insurance, and getting family support from wives and extended kin benefited middle-class men in their search. Corey (*Deliberate*) received a severance equal to one month's pay, and he and his wife also had substantial savings, including an "emergency backup fund" that they never tapped. He also received quite a bit of help from both his wife and his mother; his wife increased her work hours after he'd lost his job to give them more financial flexibility, and his mom came three times a week to help provide childcare to their toddler. About three months after his job loss, Corey and his wife decided it was time to expand his search geographically. He'd been part of a large layoff, and not only were local jobs scarce, but everyone from his old team was competing for the few local jobs. Additionally, his wife's skills (as a hospital nurse) made her employable in almost any state in the country. They also had significant equity in their home, which would allow them to sell and purchase a new home.

All of these resources gave Corey the time to search for the kind of job that he truly wanted. It also gave him the opportunity to search outside his local region when what he wanted wasn't available there. He reached out and used his networks extensively, asking for tips and leads from everyone he had worked with, as well as his college and grad school friends and colleagues. His wife's willingness to follow him to a new job (despite her own good employment in the area) further enhanced his ability to find the right match. Corey expanded his search out of state. Within a month, he'd found a new job. As he described it, "I am making more money now, and the subject matter is more interesting."

I do not mean to diminish Corey's experience of the strains of unemployment. Just as Harold did, Corey emphasized the toll of unemployment: "It was a lot of stress," he said. And Corey did have to move in order to find work that he wanted, so he faced real trade-offs. Marianne Cooper has written at length about how increasing precarity in the labor market can make even financially stable families feel insecure.[14] The unemployed whom I met, regardless of financial background, had a firsthand look at this instability and the feelings of insecurity that it generated. Moreover, the longer it takes to find a job, the risks that accompany unemployment grow, increasing financial instability and decreasing future employability.[15]

Yet, in addition to recognizing the seemingly universal tolls, it is also important to recognize that some individuals, like Corey and Harold, had a much better support system throughout their period of unemployment, that they sometimes gained resources during this time, and that they had better outcomes in the end. Recognizing these differences helps us understand how the institution of unemployment—through the company severances that are unevenly offered; the unemployment benefits that are based on a percentage of one's wages; the gendered expectations about self-sacrifice and health care; the guilt gap and the second shift; and the state-mandated rules about job seeking that some navigate better than others—operates to exacerbate and generate inequality. In other words, there is no singular toll of uncertainty; some people paid a much lower price than others and arrived on the other side with seemingly few scars.

Few other than the middle-class men managed to find jobs very similar to or better than the ones they held before, and the three middle-class women who did took deliberate searches. In chapter 3, we learned that Jill had been devastated by how impersonal her firing by her former IT employer had been. She launched a targeted search, hoping to find work in marketing and communications (her areas of expertise). Like the middle-class men in this group, Jill had many resources to support her job search. She was one of the few women in the study to receive severance pay (and it was substantial, six months), and she also had some money set aside as a "safety net." Additionally, money she'd inherited from her grandmother further enhanced her financial stability after her job loss. Her live-in boyfriend who had also lost his job at the IT company found work the week after she and I met for our first interview; his new job was a step up for him, too. They also did not have any kids, so they didn't need to manage childcare during her weeks being out of work. Researchers previously have argued that the introduction of children into a household strains a couple's sense of time and availability, often leading to more traditional divisions of labor.[16] Looking back on both her time off and her search success, Jill explained, "I was in a lucky situation where I could take a couple of months and really hone [in on] what I wanted to do." She searched only for jobs with large employers and in her target areas. Within four months, she had found work in her target area.

Paul (*Deliberate*), who we learned in chapter 7 decided to hold out for a union job, also found better work. Although he did not have nearly as many resources as his middle-class counterparts, Paul did have a skill that was in demand in unionized jobs. When he decided to return to the union, he felt confident that waiting to find work would pay off. He was right; he had a much higher base wage with the union, and the union also guaranteed he would be called ahead of other (younger) members because of his past union experience. Paul and his family maintained good health during this period, which was critical to his forward progress, as they had lost their health insurance when he lost his job. Even with the few months he had spent unemployed, Paul reported he was on track to surpass his wages from the year before. He said, "I've been in there, since January . . . [and] I've been pretty much full-time." The full-time union work came with benefits, including a retirement fund into which both he and his employer contributed. He explained, "Since January I have over $3,000 in my retirement." Having highly specialized skills, even when paired with more urgent searches, led some working-class men to find work in their fields before they had to turn to jobs that weren't as good a fit. All of the working-class men who moved ahead had specialized vocational skills that either led them back to unionized work or that allowed them to move into niche labor markets before their unemployment benefits ran out. Yet, although we remember that some of the working-class women had health care backgrounds, none of the working-class women had managed to move ahead one year later.

Overall, the middle-class men's overrepresentation in this category is hard to understate; both in sheer numbers and in proportion, they outnumbered everyone else. Their resources gave them an important advantage in allowing them to move forward one year later.

Almost Maintaining

Those who were almost maintaining their situation before job loss had found new work that was, either in type of work or salary (and sometimes both), a step down from what they had done before. Many faced a decline in their salary in the range of 10 to 15 percent, which was a hit. The biggest salary reductions came to the women, who sometimes reported salaries that were close to one-third lower, even though they'd found similar status jobs. If they did not experience a decline in pay, they had taken a step down in terms of status, but they were not so far from where they had been that their jobs looked unrecognizable. Deliberate searches led some middle- and working-class women to make their way back toward where they'd been, while a handful of middle-class men who had taken their time did so as well. The *Take Time* search approach only worked for middle-class men, in the same way that those who moved ahead were predominantly middle-class men.

Neil (*Take Time*) started his search in earnest about twelve weeks after he lost his job. During those three months off, he'd enjoyed some fly-fishing, thought about his long-term goals, and decided to move out of the hospitality industry. Once he started to search, he focused primarily on jobs outside his area of expertise. He studied and passed exams to sell life insurance. He networked with friends and neighbors. He redid his profile on LinkedIn and searched on multiple websites.[17] Unfortunately, this strategy of seeking a career in a new field backfired. Despite sending out upward of fifty applications, Neil did not receive a single interview in this new field.

Neil had several things going for him during this job search process. He had received six weeks' severance (full pay), which paid for some of his time off when he was not searching. He also had excellent health insurance through his wife. As a diabetic, he made sure to continue to take his medications, telling me, "We don't skimp on that kind of stuff." He also had his wife to rely on; she continued to share the chores equally, allowing him to keep his focus on his job search. While he was unemployed, she'd been promoted to a more demanding position at her organization, which also took away some of the financial pressure, and she still kept sharing those chores at home.

But unlike some of those who ended up moving ahead, Neil did not have significant savings to rely on. He'd been on a chronic unemployment path to this most recent job loss, and he'd relied on his savings during earlier periods of unemployment. As a result, despite the generous severance, he did not have as large a financial cushion in the bank as other men in the middle class (and some women) who moved ahead.

Right before his unemployment ran out, Neil and his wife sat down for a long conversation. Rather than scale back their lifestyle, they had taken on some credit card debt during his time off. When added to their college loans, it seemed like a significant amount to owe. His wife felt Neil couldn't continue to hold out for his dream job any longer, and she pushed him to start searching for jobs in the field in which he had experience. Neil was still working on switching fields at that point. He explained, "I actually studied and passed my exam and was in training with a company here locally to sell insurance." Despite his reluctance, Neil understood her point. He started applying for jobs he'd sworn to avoid, and a few weeks later, he was offered a position working for a large restaurant group. He took it. Once Neil started looking within his field, he was able to find work right away. Had he not taken time off before his search or had he not searched for jobs outside his field, he might have ended up in the moving-ahead group, despite his lack of savings.

Four months after he started his new job and just over a year after his other job loss, Neil was unhappy in his new position, stating flatly, "It's not the job that I want to be in. Trust me." Although it had better hours, it was a step down in status, and he did not love the job or his new boss. He also made less money—about 10 percent less than he'd made in his previous job. Neil's new job was fairly typical of what many who lose jobs experience; on average, workers in the United States can expect earnings that are lower than what they'd made before and often in jobs that are slightly less prestigious than what they'd previously held.[18]

But a closer look at his family life and future job prospects suggested a better overall picture. Neil's wife had gotten a promotion and a salary raise—a significant one. She was now earning substantially more than he had when he lost his job, so their two salaries combined left them a bit better off than they'd been before he'd lost his job. After her promotion and his new job, they'd gone to their bank and "rolled the high-interest rate credit cards to a low-interest rate bank loan." While it didn't erase their financial stress, it did immediately decrease their financial payments and substantially lowered what they would owe over the lifetime of the debt.

Neil was also hopeful about his own job prospects. He'd finally heard back from some of the jobs he applied for outside the hospitality industry; he'd been talking to friends and neighbors and using his networks to reach out for opportunities. He had a third-round interview for a new position, found through a network connection, and expected to hear back about that job soon. He hoped being reemployed gave him a better shot at switching industries.

In the end, Neil had had a tough year. He landed in a job he didn't like and that paid a bit less than the one he lost. He was almost maintaining his prior status. Yet between Neil and his wife, their income placed them well into six figures, or at the top of what the Pew Research Center estimates was the middle third of American households at that time.[19] And Neil's new job prospects appeared fairly good. They also had enough equity in their home to allow them to get a low-interest loan to relieve the pressure of the credit card debt.

Importantly, all of the middle-class men who were not quite back to where they'd been were from the *Take Time* group, having started searches later than most. While I can't say for certain if they would have moved ahead had they searched right away, some of them did wonder about this very question. Dean had hoped the time away would help him figure out what he wanted to do, but after six months out of the labor market, he had become somewhat less competitive in his field. He had not expected employers to take such a dim view of his time spent out of work. When he was first offered a position that paid significantly less than what he made before, he dismissed it. He was "holding out for something that was closer to [what he'd done] or that would be meaningful to me as opposed to just a job." But when we caught up later, he shared that he was surprised he hadn't found a comparable job.

At the time of his follow-up interview, Dean no longer believed it would be easy for him to find "the same quality job" as he'd had. When he first lost his job and decided to travel abroad rather than search for work, he'd assumed a new job would be easy to find. A year into the process, he realized that "it was actually going to be a lot harder and more difficult than I thought . . . and I started to really fear that I had let this go too far." As someone who joined the ranks of the long-term unemployed, Dean certainly was right to be worried; this type of unemployment can be the hardest from which to recover.[20] Yet, like many other middle-class men, Dean had the advantages of savings, a severance, health insurance, and someone else to assume the household duties. He had a high-earning partner with whom he lived, who had offered to marry him should his finances get to the point that he needed additional help. As it was, she was no longer asking him to contribute to the daily household expenses (and the mortgage was in her name), so Dean had relatively few bills to pay. Not long after the follow-up interview, Dean did find work with his former employer, relying on the networks he had built there. It was a step down from where he'd been, and his salary was not what he'd hoped, but it would allow him to be creative and set him back on the path he saw himself.

Dean felt frustrated with the challenges he faced when he decided to start searching for work, but like Neil, Corey, and other white middle-class men, Dean, too, had the ability to activate and use a network of social connections to move ahead and find somewhat comparable work. Writing about Black professional men's access to social networks, Adia Harvey Wingfield notes that their ties both to whites and to other Black men are key to their success, yet Black professional men are also keenly aware that white men have more expansive social networks that give them access to a wider range of opportunities than the Black professional men have.[21] In my own research, I've found that access to social networks may be something that key institutional gatekeepers may be willing to share more readily with white job seekers than with people of color.[22] Ofer Sharone has written extensively about the importance of networking for the unemployed, particularly those who have been out of work for longer periods of time.[23] Broad social networks were clearly accessed by white middle-class men when they needed to find work and were an important part of their ability either to move ahead (as Corey did and Neil hoped to) or to come close to regaining what they had before (as Dean did).

Like the middle-class women who managed to move ahead, the middle-class women who were almost maintaining at work had more advantages than most during their time unemployed. But they faced several more constraints. Heather (*Deliberate*) had a relatively straightforward path back to work. Unlike most women, she'd received a severance package from her old job, and she and her husband had continued to save during the time she was unemployed. Yet Heather had taken on most of the household and childcare during the time she was off work. Her search was also confined by her husband's job parameters and her greater family responsibilities; she wanted a job that would allow her greater flexibility, as his job did not have much. Heather hoped to find work again as an accountant, and she already had turned down a job that paid too low and was not in accounting. When she finally took an accounting job, it was relatively similar in status and tasks as the last job she held. The biggest downside was the pay decrease; Heather took an almost 35 percent reduction in pay. Having declined a slightly worse position for a slightly greater sum of money, Heather felt unable to decline again, as her search had led her to believe she might find the job she wanted, but it was unlikely she could find it at comparable pay.

Most of the working-class women who were just maintaining did so at a level several notches below where they had started. None found work that paid as well as they had made previously, but some found jobs that were comparable, and others hoped that the work they moved into held the promise of better tomorrows. Carol (*Deliberate*) managed to find work that was almost identical to what she had done before. She had previously worked in billing for a medical company and found work at a hospital doing similar tasks. She found work after only a few months of unemployment, making her one of the few to experience a relatively short unemployment duration.

Yet despite using a deliberate search method (searching daily and sending out nearly sixty applications) that yielded a job in her intended occupation, Carol had to accept many trade-offs in her new job. She made $3 less an hour, reducing her salary to $13 an hour. Her commute nearly doubled from twenty to almost forty minutes each way. Additionally, she now worked in an environment in which she had to take mandatory overtime every week, working forty-five hours a week instead of thirty-five.

Unlike the middle class, Carol had few resources to rely on during this process. This meant that once she found a job in her targeted area, she did not feel able to turn it down, despite its numerous drawbacks. Carol did not receive a severance when she lost her job doing medical billing, and she and her husband had relatively little savings in the bank. During the period in which she was unemployed, the factory where her husband worked full-time started to cut back on employees' hours; despite his full-time status, he was no longer regularly scheduled for forty-hour weeks. Prior research finds working-class workers may often find their hours cut despite an employment status of full-time.[24] His uncertain hours placed an even greater strain on their finances.

The guilt gap further shaped Carol's unemployment experience, as she lost her health insurance after her job loss, which left her feeling unable to take care of necessary health concerns. She started to have pain in her stomach and was referred to a urologist who wanted "to do a test," but she said no "because with how our insurance is, there's too much co-pay and out of pocket that would put us under." She was concerned about her health and wanted to find a job that would provide her with better health insurance and let her get the necessary tests. Not only was Carol doing most of the second shift, she would "mow someone's lawn, trying to get some money." Taking on handy jobs helped get them by, but it made it harder for Carol to search full-time.

Carol thought all this was evidence of how hard she and her husband worked to keep her family afloat (and I certainly agree that they did). Yet I also saw the disparities between what Neil and Dean did and what Carol had to do in order to get a job that left her almost maintaining a much more precarious position. We can see clearly how unemployment acts to exacerbate the already large differences between Carol and those in the middle class.

Falling Behind

Although a sizable minority of the people I met managed to move ahead or hang on after their job loss, the majority fell behind. Those in this group found work that was demonstrably not as good—either in a different occupation entirely or several steps down the ladder from where they had been—*and* that paid considerably worse than what they made before their job loss. That's if they found a job. Some of the people my research team and I caught up with one year later were still out of work, and some had decided to stop looking. There was a lot of economic variation among this group. Among the middle class, there was often both a working spouse and substantial savings remaining that meant that these folks didn't pay the same economic price for not having found an equivalent job. Among the working class, single-earner households (either those homes with single moms or those with breadwinner dads and stay-at-home moms) were more common; in most of the working-class homes, the fall was a lot harder, leaving many families in poverty or on the edge of it. The majority of working-class women (about three-quarters), working-class men (nearly three-quarters), and middle-class women (nearly two-thirds), including Tracy, Anthony, and even Joan, ended up here. Far fewer middle-class men were in this category (about a third).[25]

The working-class women who fell behind were most often the worst off after a year. Tracy's year, by most financial measures, was very difficult. She ran out of unemployment benefits before she'd found a job. Tracy (*Diverted*) had no severance and no savings to start with, lower unemployment benefits because of her lower starting salary, and no one else earning money, so her finances were very tight. Moreover, as a single mom, she did not have anyone else to rely on for help with her kids while she searched for work. She and her kids cut back on food and on her medicines and doctors' visits, and she struggled to pay basic utilities like electricity and the phone bill. Tracy's challenges reflect similar hardships in the lives of other Americans.

About 40 percent of Americans who enter poverty do so because of job loss.[26] This is, perhaps, because of perpetually low wages that make it difficult to set aside savings for the future. The Federal Reserve's Survey of Household and Economics Decisionmaking (SHED) found that about half of American families lack the buffer of a three-month rainy-day fund. Moreover, 32 percent of families said they would not be able to cope with unexpected expenses if they faced a prolonged period of financial distress.[27] Tracy had to sit down with her kids and have some tough conversations. She explained, "I'm very honest to them and they know my struggles are their struggles." While Tracy didn't like feeling her job loss made her kids grow up too fast in the past year, she needed them to understand why she was saying no so often when they asked for things.

Many families—even those that haven't experienced a job loss—can find it difficult to manage their household bills evenly over the course of the month to match the income that is coming in.[28] This is not just true of poor households; authors of the *Financial Diaries*, Jonathan Morduch and Rachel Schneider, found that even middle-income households can find balancing the ebbs and flows of income and bills challenging.[29] Tracy did get the hang of how to manage her bills; she learned to "shuffle things around." It often meant waiting until she was late one week with most of them, but as long as she wasn't late with the electric or the house payments, she could cobble together the money to pay the rest.

Once Tracy had found a routine to manage her bills, it became easier for her to search for work. Recall the work of psychologists Sendhil Mullainathan and Eldar Shafir, who study scarcity and find that people get overloaded when they have too many decisions to make.[30] After bill management became easier, Tracy was better able to concentrate on her job search. But there still weren't any advertised jobs to be found where she lived. So, Tracy got in her car, drove to all of the restaurants within what she considered a reasonable commute—to all the small mom-and-pop joints and the larger chains—walked in, and asked if they were hiring. Some were. Some weren't. Anywhere that said they would consider hiring her, Tracy sat down and filled out an application on the spot.

Tracy wanted to go back to waitressing because it was stable and she liked it better than she liked factory work. She also had more experience with it, which she hoped would lead to a job offer sooner rather than later. She took the first offer she received at a family-owned restaurant. They gave her only thirty-two hours a week, and she had to work nights and weekends, which disappointed her, since it meant less time with her kids. She was also almost twice as old as many of the other employees, who were teenagers hired during the summer season and worked after school; she felt pretty awkward around them.

But Tracy had found work. The boss seemed to really like her. The pay was pretty good—a full dollar more than she'd made at the factory, although the hours weren't full-time, and it didn't come with benefits, so she made significantly less overall and remained uninsured. She loved having her own money again—money she had earned. Her commute was good—much shorter than she'd feared it would be when she'd started driving around looking for restaurants. And even though they weren't guaranteeing full-time hours, they did guarantee she would not drop below thirty hours a week. Tracy felt confident she could make that work, and she didn't plan to look for new work. While she acknowledged the enormous financial strains and stresses of the past year, Tracy took great pride in the fact she and her family never came close to losing their home.[31] With a total annual income of about $10,000, Tracy fell in the bottom third of American households and near the bottom of that third. She certainly might have lost her home in the tumultuous year after her job loss—others I interviewed did.

Things had not returned to financial stability, however. Tracy explained, "It's always something" that "pops up" and needs to be paid. She could pay for her children's necessities again, but nothing extra. Tracy and her kids weren't back to where she'd been the last time she'd worked as a waitress, never mind where she had hoped to head when she took the factory job. After we first met, Tracy went on Medicaid through the state, but she hadn't been back to the doctor, despite numerous health problems. She felt they couldn't afford the co-pays. As for medication, she explained, "My scripts, I gotta pay cash for, so I've been looking around, trying to find the cheapest place." Tracy was buying her medications, which she hadn't always done while unemployed, but they were proving a hard expense to bear. It was not clear how long she would continue to purchase them. Her family (particularly Tracy herself) experienced hunger at times, despite their use of the SNAP program. Her once-well-stocked pantry had dwindled over the months of unemployment and had yet to be restocked. Tracy's lack of resources had shaped her search, preventing her from searching, particularly at first, and leading her to take the first job she was offered, even though it left her in a relatively precarious position.

Regina (*Diverted*) managed to find part-time temporary work. It was clerical in nature and less technical than her previous job and demanded fewer skills than she could bring to the table; it also paid less than what she'd made before she lost her job. But after two back-to-back spells of unemployment with the same employer (the factory we learned in chapter 3 that had downsized and then closed entirely), Regina was happy to find work again. The family now had nearly $10,000 in credit card debt, but they had been slowly paying down the debt. She hoped her new job would allow them to pay it down faster. Her husband had taken on additional shifts and even an extra weekend job at times, and she increased her work around the house to make his extra work hours possible. She viewed this teamwork as critical to her family's ability to weather the storm. But it had also meant her search was delayed for a long time so that she could support his longer hours. By the time she started searching, she faced skepticism from employers about the long gap on her résumé. As her son's primary caregiver, she also faced a very constrained search because she needed to find work that would provide her with some schedule flexibility. With few resources and many family demands, Regina's search led to a particularly poor reemployment outcome.

About a third of the working-class women ended up like Tracy and Regina, in part-time or temporary positions, while only about a third had found full-time work.[32] The rest were either still searching for work or had dropped out of the labor force, convinced that they would not find a job. While some were in positions that were similar to what they had held before, most were like Tracy and had ended up in positions that were a big step down from where they had been. This was particularly tough for the working-class women, because they had often started out so low on the totem pole that when they returned to even lower-wage work, they ended up making a poverty-level wage, as Tracy was doing.

Working-class men were almost as likely as working-class women to fall behind. Anthony (*Urgent*) was out of work for over a year. The technical repairman had few resources to rely on in the months after his benefits ran out. The family had already cut out their occasional pizza night out. Their church had been helping out some and subsequently started providing weekly bags of food for Anthony's family. They began visiting their local food pantry. Anthony's wife felt uncomfortable with all of the donations; they should be giving, not receiving, she'd said. But the bills piled up so fast that it was impossible to keep on top of them.

Anthony tried to develop a strategy in which he would pay bills when they were close to due—or sometimes even overdue. In their financial diary study, Morduch and Schneider note that within a given month, many households face illiquidity crises in which they don't always have money when they need it to pay bills.[33] Because he did not always have enough cash on hand, Anthony would pay some bills and delay others, juggling them to try to manage the deficit caused by his job loss (which is also what Tracy did). Yet, somehow, Anthony let the electric bill slip past due, and then he missed the second bill; by the time he realized what had happened, it was too late. He called but was told once the electric company had made a stop determination, the process had to be completed before he could ask for the power to be turned back on. The men from the company came and shut off their connection, and it took a long five days for it to be turned back on again—five days in which there was no heat and no electricity in a household with two young children and his wife's elderly aunt.

Despite searching urgently, Anthony had little luck with his job search this time around. He found one temporary job that he held very briefly—remember, it lasted only two weeks—and he may not have taken it had he understood how temporary a position it would be. He worried that his history of unemployment discouraged prospective employers who might see the gaps caused by unemployment and read a lack of industriousness (rather than a history of being in the wrong industries at the wrong times). A year into the search, Anthony decided to expand his search to jobs located almost an hour's driving time away (farther than Pennsylvania law required him to search). Finally, about eighteen months after he lost his job, Anthony found work as a technician at a new plant—a change in industries again. It was a step down from the original job loss he told me about; he was no longer part of the management team. The salary was quite a bit lower as well.

Anthony did not know if or when he would return to financial stability. When he was younger, he hoped to retire one day. After his first job loss, Anthony realized retirement might come later than he originally intended. Now, though, he didn't think retirement would be on his horizon. It wasn't just that they didn't have any savings anymore. It was also that there were so many debts and bills that had gone unpaid for so long; Anthony did not know how he would ever catch up with them all. He wondered how many years of stable employment would be necessary to dig out of the hole that so many job losses (and such little government support) had created. Looking back, he figured that each time he'd been on unemployment, it had been enough to pay only about half of his bills. The other half had gone unpaid. As someone with a history of chronic unemployment, Anthony didn't face only the cost of his most recent job loss, he also had the tolls of so many job losses and periods of unemployment weighing on him. He didn't think he could ever retire, but he worried about his body's ability to carry on; his wife worried, too. "You're overtaxing your body . . . destroying it," she said. But despite their concerns, Anthony had few choices other than to continue on.

Many of the working-class men seemed stuck in a system that did not have easy answers for them. Almost three-quarters of the working-class men with whom I reconnected were similar to Anthony; they had found jobs again, but they weren't as good as the jobs they had lost. Some were reemployed in part-time or temporary positions, and one was still looking for work.[34] And, as I mentioned at the beginning of the chapter, I was unable to reconnect with almost half of the working-class men, the largest of any of the groups, suggesting that they may have moved.[35] Several working-class men, like Anthony, experienced yet another job loss in the intervening year. My frequent coauthor, Adrianne Frech, and I have looked at national data on people's risk of chronic unemployment.[36] We find a small group of mostly men who were at great risk of chronic unemployment. These men most often came of age in areas with high unemployment rates (like so many of the working-class men in my study) and had a high school degree or less.

Although most middle-class women started their deliberate searches almost immediately, they were as likely to fall behind as they were to move ahead or just maintain. Joan (*Deliberate*) tried for six months to find something similar to her old job, but either the work was too different or the pay was too low compared to what she had earned previously. She would not take such a low-paying job, she decided. Finally, she stopped looking for research positions and reevaluated her situation. If she couldn't find work in her field, she might need to think about what other kind of work she could do. So, she stopped pursuing her beloved science career to try to begin something new.

But Joan was not interested in taking just any job; she wanted to find a new career that would be meaningful to her. She decided she wanted to work with students; she would put her master's degree and experience with the university to work in a new way. She started networking, asking friends and colleagues for advice about possible opportunities. She spoke with a former colleague and mentioned her interest in working with students; her colleague told her that she would need to get her foot in the door with a low-paying internship to gain experience. The colleague went one step further and made some phone calls to help Joan's application rise to the top of the crop. As we saw with Corey and Dean, this type of networking has been shown to be crucial for the unemployed's job searches, but not everyone has the same access to the necessary connections for finding a job.[37]

The internship seemed to go well. Joan liked working with students, even though it was different from what she'd done in the past. The pay was exceptionally low, though. At less than a fifth of her previous salary, it was lower even than some of the jobs she had first turned down in her original field. The internship ended after the expected three-month term. Joan would have to wait to see if an opening would come available now that she had the requisite experience. It took quite a while; nearly four more months would pass before she was offered a full-time job in the office where she'd interned. Finally, Joan had found a permanent full-time position; she would be reemployed, but in a very different position and at a third of her prior salary (slightly better than the internship pay).

While Joan was not able to find work in her original field, she did identify a new occupational goal and attain it (albeit making two-thirds less than she had before her job loss). Here we see both constraints and opportunities shaping Joan's path. We can see how, unlike the middle-class men, she had less ability to move her family to pursue her career goals. Unlike Corey's family, Joan and her husband never seriously considered moving so that she could find a job in the field she loved. After a year of being out of work, we talked again about why the family hadn't considered moving. Joan explained, "Unfortunately, I'm kind of stuck in the area. There haven't been many great jobs, and really there is no reason for us to move. So, I can only apply for what is available here and in the surrounding local area." Even though her work opportunities were severely limited, Joan did not view this constraint as a reason to move (remember in chapter 1, we learned that Joan and her husband had long ago decided that his job was the family's priority). This decision set a boundary around where Joan could search and what the possibilities of finding a job in the sciences would be.

Unlike the middle-class men, Joan took on a significant amount of household and childcare labor during this time period, and she often felt "depressed" around the home, going so far as to say, "Sometimes, I'm not a good person to be around." She felt cranky and irritable with her family, snapping when she normally wouldn't and losing her temper in situations where she typically would remain calm. As she explained, "I don't have as much patience, um, and so again, I need to work." Joan's move into the domestic sphere was challenging for her, and time- consuming, altering her ability to commit to her deliberate search fully, even as she recognized that returning to work would help change her mood.

Yet Joan did have access to resources many of the working-class men and women did not. Before her job loss, she and her husband had been in the top third of incomes of all families in the United States, and they'd been able to set aside quite a bit of money in savings. Unlike Neil, Joan didn't receive a severance, but she also had taken a lockstep path to the job loss, so her savings had gone untouched over the years, and they'd paid off most of their education debt. She was also able to move to her husband's health insurance plan and maintain everyone's health care needs. This was important, because at the time of her job loss, they discovered Joan had acid reflux, and she had to start medications to treat it. Her husband also continued his medications for his health condition.

Joan's search mirrored that of many of the middle-class women. Despite being the *most likely* to start looking right away, only half of the middle-class women reported achieving or settling for something slightly below their goals. Instead, the other half fell far below their initial targets; discouraged, they settled for jobs that paid significantly less and were not in fields for which they had trained. Sociologist Youngjoo Cha examined job loss and unemployment after the Great Recession and found that women experienced a significant wage penalty after losing a job—a penalty not paid by men.[38] These findings echoed those of an earlier study that found that women faced larger and more permanent wage losses after an unemployment period than men did.[39] While the middle-class women had many advantages compared to the working class, they faced many more constraints than middle-class men, and these dueling factors led to poorer outcomes for about half the middle-class women than for most middle-class men.

Some middle-class women fell even further than Joan. As the family breadwinner, Ruth (*Deliberate*) had to get back to work right away. But even with her college degree and management experience, Ruth found it hard to find full-time work. Shortly after her unemployment ran out, Ruth managed to cobble together two jobs. In one, she supervised a food-preparation cafeteria staff of eighteen employees. In the other, she worked as a food preparer on the food-service line, an entry-level job well below her expertise and training.

In chapter 5 on the guilt gap and health insurance, we learned Ruth and her family decided to purchase insurance through the ACA for her husband but not for herself; her kids went on the state plan. Sometime after our first meeting, Ruth developed kidney stones. Despite what she described as "incredible pain," she decided against seeking treatment at first, because she did not think they could afford it. Eventually, things got so bad that Ruth had to be taken to the emergency room, which turned into a very large bill that Ruth was unable to pay. Thus, we can see that living up to obligations of self-sacrifice can be hazardous; it was both for Ruth's health and her finances.

Ruth also continued to do almost all of the household labor. Although her husband's cancer was in remission, he had not taken on additional chores to help her out either during her job search or after she'd taken her two part-time jobs and continued searching for a full-time job. She explained, "I think he could do more, especially because he doesn't work, but I don't think things have progressed that much, as what we would like to see as far as men and women. There's things that he just won't do." Those things included, Ruth said, clearing his plate from the table after dinner, doing dishes, or helping with the laundry. Here we see that even as Ruth's guilt diminished, she still did not feel able to ask her husband for help; Ruth wished she could share the household burden, but she was also not willing to confront her husband about changing his behavior. Between their finances, her health, and her housework overload, Ruth didn't have time to search properly for the kind of job she wanted. In the end, she took the two poorly paid part-time jobs and hoped something else would come along. Despite searches that had been targeted and immediate, the middle-class women were much more likely than the middle-class men to find themselves falling behind at work one year later.

Taking time occasionally turned out to be a strategy that backfired. When Rodney (*Take Time*) decided to take time off before he searched for work, he felt confident he would be able to find work in his given field, as we learned in chapter 7. When we caught up with him a year later, he'd found work, but instead of a permanent position, he found two temporary ones. He'd expected to be permanently employed by now and was frustrated by the lack of opportunities. Taking time off before beginning his search was a source of disagreement between Rodney and his wife. She was working full-time in a job that required long hours. She also remained primarily responsible for the childcare and did more of the household labor. As we saw in chapter 6, men often successfully resisted taking on more labor in the household without feeling guilty. But there sometimes were marital repercussions when this happened. Daniel L. Carlson and colleagues have found that when labor isn't

shared, marital relations decline.[40] And among the long-term unemployed (as Rodney became), job search strategies can become a point
of marital tensions.[41] Frustrated with his slow job search, Rodney's wife
urged him to take a full-time computer programmer job when it was
offered to him shortly after his unemployment ran out. Rodney was
reluctant to take the full-time job. It wasn't the type of IT work he'd
wanted to do (despite the relatively good pay), so he'd negotiated to
work only thirty hours a week, as a contract employee, with the hope
that the rest of the time could be used to search for the kind of work he
really wanted. He started part-time contract work and continued his
search for a better job. After three more months of looking without finding a full-time job, his wife urged him to return to full-time hours. Rodney went to his employer and asked if he could work full-time. They said
no. Under pressure at home to contribute his "fair share," he took a second part-time position. He felt they were mostly recovered from his job
loss (they had not taken on any debt or dipped into their savings), and
their "liquid assets are further ahead than a year ago." But Rodney had
not found a job that was comparable to what he had before, and juggling
two part-time positions was certainly less than ideal.

———

Over and over again, I found evidence that the unemployment period
is one where advantages and disadvantages cumulate; one year out, we
see how the paths to job loss and then the unemployment period could
shape differences in savings, debts, and severances and how all of this
contributed to wide gulfs in experiences of financial distress. We also
see how gendered ideals about family and work shaped the guilt gap,
health care, and the second shift at home. Finally, we see how all of these
earlier differences shaped the job search and where people ended up
one year later. Successes were relatively uncommon for most, but far
more prevalent among the middle-class men, almost half of whom were
moving forward like Harold had done. About a fifth managed to almost
maintain, but again, this was more common among the middle-class
men like Neil than among others. However, most people—the

middle-class women like Joan, the working-class men like Anthony, and the working-class women like Tracy—were falling behind one year out.

Deliberate search strategies were the best way to move forward or to come close to recovering for middle-class women and working-class women and men. These more focused searches appeared to help balance out a lack of resources for some of those I met, allowing them to focus on what they wanted. Even urgent searches, at times, could lead to better outcomes, particularly when there were some other resources (like an in-demand job skill) that made the job candidate more desirable. Among the middle-class men, a variety of approaches could lead to successful outcomes, allowing the men more latitude to take time off before they started to search in earnest. Having both resources and a deliberate search strategy allowed some to move ahead, as Harold had done, as it gave them the time to discard bad possibilities and keep their options open until they found a job that put them back on the path toward success.

Yet search strategies did not balance out a lack of resources or available jobs. In fact, the middle-class men, like Neil, who took their time were more likely to either move forward or almost maintain than were the middle-class women, like Joan, who plotted such deliberate paths back to work. Moreover, a lack of resources was often the reason people found themselves searching urgently or having their searches diverted. Deliberate searches were stymied by a lack of opportunity for many middle-class women. Searching urgently for work, which was the strategy of Anthony and so many others in the working class, did not necessarily mean there was good work to be found. The working-class women, like Tracy, whose searches had been diverted by the myriad of challenges wrought by unemployment were the most likely to end up back in part-time work, close to the edge or in poverty.

In *Falling from Grace*, Katherine Newman found job loss took an emotional and psychological toll on her participants.[42] Part of the challenge was not simply the toll of the job loss but the lost belief in American meritocracy—the idea that one could go to college, gain credentials, work hard, and earn a lifetime of security and fulfillment. Their job loss represented a "broken covenant," in which that linear path was no longer guaranteed. Most of my participants no longer believed in an

American meritocracy that would lead them to a lifetime of stable employment; enough instability has been introduced into the American economy since Newman wrote her book that many people no longer expect to retire from the same job. Indeed, as discussed in chapter 3, Allison Pugh, in her study of employment insecurity, found that many workers expect work to be a "one-way honor system" in which employees devote themselves to work but their employers owe them no reciprocal return.[43]

Yet there is an important parallel between Newman's findings and mine. Some of my participants expected there to be winners in our "winner take all society," and they expected to be among them.[44] When white middle-class men, like Neil or Dean, decided they could afford to take time off to fly-fish or travel instead of immediately searching for work, it was because they expected their credentials would allow them to find work whenever they wanted it. And for many who took their time in their job search, this was true. But it was not true for all of them. So, when they found themselves ready to go back to work (but employers not ready to take them back), as happened to Rodney (and to Neil for a long time), it was a jolt to their expectations about where they stood in the social hierarchy (not as close to the top of the ladder as they had anticipated). Yet, for the most part, middle-class men correctly judged that they would find their way back close to where they'd been, and they deployed the resources they had accrued in order to achieve this goal. Thus, some men's privileges, throughout the unemployment process from the first offers of severance to their eventual return to work, allowed them to engage in a reciprocal relationship with work organizations; like most workers, they offered their devotion to work and, unlike most, in return, many of the middle-class men returned to advantaged positions.

By identifying the processes that shape the unemployment experience, we see how unemployment so thoroughly shapes one's life for a time that inequalities between groups become exacerbated and new inequalities can emerge. In the conclusion, I will explore what kinds of policy solutions might prevent these gaps from widening and create a greater safety net for all, particularly those at the bottom, like Tracy and Anthony.

Conclusion

UNCERTAINTY IN THE HEARTLAND

WHETHER DURING the Great Depression, the Great Recession, or the recession that began the 2020s, people lose jobs at alarming rates when the economy falters or craters. Yet, when we consider that in 2019—a "boom" year after a decade of economic growth—nearly 22 million workers lost their jobs through layoffs or discharges,[1] the prevalence of our unemployment problem comes sharply into view. People do not simply lose jobs during bad times; they lose them during good times as well. This book should come as a clarion cry, warning of the inadequacy of the current unemployment system to protect people from hardship even during better times.

The regularity with which people lose jobs in today's economy must be viewed alongside the findings I lay out in this book, showing the tolls job loss and unemployment take on workers and their families.[2] When viewed in this context, we can see that regardless of whether we are in the middle of a recession or not, job loss and unemployment are and will continue to be one of the most pressing labor market concerns of our lifetimes. I saw, in the lives of the people I met, the extended reach of both job loss and the unemployment period. I witnessed the personal devastation that many people experienced when the ax fell. I saw the financial hardships that were particularly devastating for the working class but that also sometimes troubled the middle class as well. I discovered a guilt gap in men's and women's responses to both their health care and their responsibilities at home, with sometimes devastating consequences for women. I saw how that guilt gap, and the resources gained over the course of the unemployment period or held in reserve from before a job loss, created different job-search strategies and job-search outcomes, and how middle-class men often had the greatest advantages at every step. Finally, I saw that one year later, the middle-class men were closer to recovery than all the others.

I found the answer to my question about what would happen when the day laborer and the high-flying executive stood side by side on the unemployment line and were joined by waitresses and nurses; the executive emerged on top.

Whether in their job loss, their finances, their health, or their household divisions of labor, most of the people I met paid some measurable price for their unemployment. Yet these tolls were not evenly distributed. There was no singular "toll," as famously titled in the Dorothea Lange photograph, but varied repercussions from job loss and unemployment. I further found that these tolls appeared to compound upon themselves, casting a long shadow on the job search process and the likelihood of its success.

Importantly, the unemployment process all too often exacerbated existing differences across gender and class. As we saw at every step of the process, the (almost entirely white) middle-class men had access to resources (both financial and cultural) that were less available to their counterparts. They benefited from severance packages, higher unemployment compensation, better savings, less guilt, health insurance, the ability to avoid household labor, time not to search, the ability to decline a "bad job," and access to better-paid jobs that were more commensurate with their past experience. This didn't mean they had a good year; as we saw in the last chapter, Neil certainly struggled and faced strains. I do not mean we should begrudge him or the other middle-class men the fact that they did not fall further. But his struggles were tempered and did not bring him anywhere near the edge of devastation as so many others. What we should do is question why so many of the resources necessary to survive the arc of the job loss, unemployment, and job search process appeared to be available primarily for the middle-class men, allowing them to bear fewer scars from their unemployment experience than the others would endure.

Too often, we think of unemployment as a uniformly bad occurrence that brings a host of negative outcomes along with it for everyone.[3] Research that focuses on the unemployed middle class may overemphasize their struggles because there isn't adequate comparison with the working class.[4] Additionally, evidence on the scarring effects of unemployment—from wages to health to job status—suggests the effects are fairly similar across class (or even, sometimes, a bit wider for those at the top).[5] But these perspectives often don't consider the differences in resources (and disadvantages) between groups to start with, nor do they consider how additional resources (and disadvantages) may cumulate during the unemployment experience.

We must think of the unemployment period as a time when people face cascading and cumulating disadvantages or advantages that, in some ways, mirror other institutional processes we see of resource accumulation over the life course. Life course scholars argue that small differences in what people have access to in their youth grow over time, leading to large differences later in life.[6] For example, we can imagine that growing up in a family with better-educated parents leads to a greater likelihood of college entrance and completion, which leads to better placement in a first job, which leads to higher wages and a better income by middle age.[7] In a similar manner, small differences in disadvantages, such as less well-educated parents, no opportunity to attend college, and a dead-end job out of high school, also accumulate over time.

Unemployment offers us a short time frame to watch this advantage accumulation process. Unemployment is not simply a lack of employment; people can be not employed for a variety of reasons, such as going to school, taking care of kids, or disability. Additionally, as we have learned, unemployment has its own unique processes—severances, length of notice, state-determined unemployment benefits, loss of health insurance, increased time for second-shift chores (or a lack of second-shift increase), and state-mandated job search requirements—that generate and exacerbate inequality differently than employment does. We saw over the course of the book how middle-class men brought more resources with them (more savings, less debt, and higher earnings) and then also accrued resources during their time out of work (severances, higher unemployment insurance benefits, the ability to maintain their health care, the ability to decline childcare responsibilities) that made it easier for them to take their desired search strategies, navigate state job search mandates, and have their search strategies lead to positions that moved them forward to jobs that were either similar or even better than those they had had before. The middle-class men were much more likely than everyone else to receive a severance when they were fired and they had higher earnings, so they also received greater weekly unemployment benefits. They were also very likely to have a dual-earning spouse. This meant that they faced far fewer financial challenges, on average, than did everyone else, as we saw in chapter 4. The middle-class men also seemed less burdened by feelings of guilt about their job loss, which translated to better health and less household work during their time unemployed. Unlike women burdened by guilt and poorer finances, the middle-class men maintained their health insurance, continued going to the doctor, and took necessary medications, and were the most likely to report improved eating habits. Middle-class men also didn't feel the need to take over all of the household or childcare chores after they lost their jobs, giving them more time to search for jobs. All of these resources allowed middle-class men the freedom either to take time off before starting a job search or to search deliberately with a clear plan of what they did and did not want in their next job. Between the search strategies and their other resources, the middle-class men started out ahead and, more often than not, ended up ahead when I caught up with them one year later. The majority in all of the other groups reported that they had fallen behind at work.

Through the unemployment experience of the working-class women, we can see how disadvantages accumulate. Unlike the middle-class men, the working-class women typically received no severances, no notice, and their unemployment benefits were the lowest of all four groups, often less than poverty-level wages. They were more likely to be single parents than anyone else in the study, raising children on their own and supporting them financially on their own, too. This meant that many working-class women were in greater financial peril from the outset of their job loss. Unlike the middle-class men whose health was maintained during this process, the working-class women bore a burden of guilt for losing their job, and they often made large sacrifices, both to their health and to their job search and leisure time. Working-class women gave up their insurance (sometimes going uninsured even while insuring the rest of the family), avoided going to the doctor's office (despite pain, illness, or physician recommendations), stopped taking necessary medications, and were the most likely to report going without food. Working-class women were the most likely to take on new household chores and report new family responsibilities that prevented them from searching for new jobs. All of these disadvantages weighed on working-class women's ability to search, leading them to be the most likely *not* to start searching for work right away, despite a desperate need to do so. One year later, these women had mostly fallen behind, finding jobs that paid significantly less and were a big step down in status compared to their previous jobs—that is, if they had managed to find full-time work at all. About a third worked only part-time, some were still unemployed, and others had stopped searching for work.

While there is much heartache and stress to go around during this process (and I hope not to diminish the strains people shared with me), we cannot understand how unemployment operates as an agent of inequality if we do not consider how unemployment outcomes differ.[8] Among the people I interviewed, at every step along the way, the process was differentiated by class and gender and race as well, although because of my small sample size, more research is needed on this topic. But my study does provide evidence of the advantages white middle-class men have—in receipt of severances, in their greater savings, in their gendered ability to prioritize their job search over tasks at home, and in their use of networks to find good work at the end of the tunnel. I additionally find evidence of several known trends: that Black and Latino workers faced greater discrimination in firing, had lower financial reserves even among the middle class, and were less likely to use social networks to find work. Given the disparities in the hardships I witnessed, current policy would benefit from considering how the currently unemployed are faring and asking what kinds of policy responses might reduce existing disparities among the unemployed.

We must also ask about the guilt gap and investigate the tolls created by cultural norms that praise women when they act in ways that are self-sacrificial. As I have told the story of the guilt gap at colleges and universities across the country, there is often large condemnation of the men—critiques of their willingness to leave wives uninsured while they protect themselves. I understand these critiques and, to a degree, can sympathize with them. But I also am concerned that such views distract us from what we should really be worried about: why women feel obligated to make such large sacrifices in the first place. For several decades now, it has been common to say that women should be able to choose whether or not they want to work. There have been many critiques of this framing of women's work and family choices. Pamela Stone, noted expert on modern motherhood, offers an incisive take on why women aren't simply "opting out" of paid work but are being pushed by the institutional constraints of demanding work organizations and the inexorable pull from home, whereas most dads still don't do as much as moms.[9] But we must continue to interrogate the ideals behind expectations of mothering—specifically those that suggest mothers should place their families at the center of their lives and do anything for them.[10] We also must ask the tough questions about whether and how these ideals may harm women or lead them to harm themselves. When women feel obligated to provide for their families out of notions of self-sacrifice, it is possible that they may do so in ways that are detrimental—or even dangerous—to themselves. And this is very worrying indeed.

In this conclusion, I ask what changes we might make to better support those who have lost work. Is it possible for us to imagine a system in which the people we've met, Neil, Joan, Anthony, and Tracy, and the others throughout the course of the book, have similar support systems through their time on unemployment? Could the waitresses, repairmen, and research scientists have outcomes more like the managers? While current labor market conditions likely mean it would not be possible for all of the unemployed to find good work again—certainly both economists and sociologists have argued there are few good jobs left for the working class[11]—it is worth asking whether we can change this system that allows so many to fall so far when they experience a period of unemployment.

What We Need

To address the inequality in the unemployment system, we need serious solutions—big and small—that address the ways that our government provides enough support for some people to flourish while others' lives fall apart. In this section, I consider five policy suggestions that, if implemented, could dramatically change the face of unemployment today.

Make Current Policies Clearer

I begin with a small policy change that could have broad impact. The unemployed need greater clarity about what they qualify for and for how long. Over and over again, I found people were unclear about their unemployment benefits as well as the scope of other state or federal benefits for which they would be eligible. They didn't understand the rules they were meant to follow, or how long they would receive unemployment, or their obligations to the state to remain on unemployment, or how much they were eligible to receive from the state. Almost half of the people I met fundamentally misunderstood some portion of the unemployment benefits program. They thought they could receive benefits longer than they could, they thought benefit extension programs would be available (they weren't), they thought that the state did not require them to take jobs unless the jobs paid a certain percentage of their wages (such a provision no longer existed), and some reported they were surprised by the size of their unemployment check, which was much smaller than they expected it to be. This sometimes caused them to misjudge their own savings because they anticipated receiving unemployment longer than they did, or it led some people to owe the state money because they had unintentionally broken the rules.

Additionally, well over half of the people I interviewed didn't understand the state and federal benefits for which they might have been eligible. Unless they lost their jobs in a large layoff, the state did not send people from multiple agencies to their workplace to explain coordinating benefits. What this means is that many people might have also been eligible to apply for the Supplemental Nutrition Assistance Program (SNAP), the state and federal Children's Health Insurance Program (CHIP), or Medicaid for themselves if they had a qualifying health condition. But what I learned was that most participants didn't apply because they did not know enough about many of the programs administered by the state and usually funded both by the federal and state governments. As Tracy explained, "I just don't know about stuff. Maybe just awareness of what's available [would be helpful]." Tracy likely qualified for state Medicaid because of her preexisting health conditions, but, as we learned in chapter 5, this is not something she knew. States (which run their unemployment programs through a mix of state and federal dollars) should not expect people to go out and search for the information about the range of assistance programs—it should be the state's responsibility to educate the public about their eligibility.

This wasn't just a problem for people who had lower levels of education. Many of the college-educated participants spoke about how they found it difficult to navigate the unemployment system. Even the better-educated participants found the array of services overwhelming and were surprised by how challenging the system was to navigate. "I guess there's assistance . . . out there for me," said Frank about the experience of job loss. "But I didn't know what it was until I needed it. And then when I needed it, I didn't know where to find it. I had a hard time navigating that. I still kinda do. So, I guess maybe educating the public [about how] we provide all this service to help you—because I think the ultimate goal is to get people back working. I mean, I want to work again." If well-educated and highly motivated Frank was this confused, it seems a good sign that the system isn't working as intended.

Yet, while a lack of government support would be shocking in places like Europe or Israel, where there is a strong expectation of government support in the wake of a job loss, in the United States, we have come to expect that the government will provide almost no services after a job loss. But there actually were services available that the unemployed were not accessing because they either did not know how to or did not know the services were available. In 2020, after the global pandemic hit, administrative barriers prevented a large number of people nationally from accessing unemployment benefits.[12] It is vital to address the faulty bureaucracy that prevents people from receiving the benefits that are actually available.

In Pennsylvania, the unemployed could have used a clearer overview of what benefits were available. An easier-to-read handbook with clearer rules and guidelines would be a significant boon. It would also be beneficial to incorporate an overview of the unemployment rules, benefits, and other government support systems into the mandatory meetings required of all the unemployed. Taking small steps to make the current policies clearer and more accessible would be an important step forward.

New Ways to Calculate Unemployment Benefits

Before her job loss, Tracy lived below the poverty line, earning just a dollar over the minimum wage. When her unemployment wages were calculated, she received about 50 percent of her prior earnings, or $154 a week for herself and her two children; there was no way to pay rent, heat the house, feed herself and her children, and pay all their bills on such a meager paycheck.

If we want to get serious about preventing the worst economic perils of unemployment, we need to consider an unemployment benefit that replaces 100 percent of the wages for those making minimum wage. While this would not prevent families like Tracy's from experiencing poverty (remember, she was already living below the poverty line despite working full-time before her job loss), it could prevent them from experiencing the incredibly sharp declines I witnessed: food scarcity, loss of basic services, homelessness, and an inability to care for one's health. It would also be an excellent first step toward reducing the cumulative effects of unemployment that I discuss at the beginning of the chapter. Single moms like Tracy who have to choose between feeding themselves or their children (and who almost always chose feeding their kids) should be given a better choice than this. As we saw with Tracy, it also became practically impossible to start searching for work while dealing with all of the emergencies that resulted from plunging this far into poverty.

Tracy and families like hers are guaranteed to be thrown further into poverty by the current way most states calculate unemployment benefits. This cannot be what FDR and Frances Perkins intended when they set up the unemployment compensation system. But it is the result of decades of massive underfunding of unemployment insurance at both the state and the federal level.[13] If the hope had been that unemployment benefits would move us away from Great Depression poverty, which Dorothea Lange called the "Toll of Uncertainty," then we have failed; the tolls are piled high for families like Tracy's. If you've read this far, I hope you will share my outrage and see the need for us to do more for Tracy and families like hers.

But Tracy's family wasn't the only one that struggled, and we need solutions for families whose more solid finances were undercut by unemployment. Unemployment is one of the fastest routes to poverty in our country,[14] but does it have to be? Latesha's family struggled quite a bit after she lost her job, even though both she and her husband had held stable middle-class jobs. But they also were supporting her mother and trying to save to put their teenage twin daughters through college in a couple of years. "Unemployment is a joke. . . . You should at least get, maybe for six months, equivalent to what you were making and then let it go down; taper it off. But going from X-amount to $300-and-something a week? My kids make more than me. Give me a fucking break." Latesha, the office administrator, was at half her original salary, now making less than her kids who worked service-industry jobs over the summer. Unemployment didn't cover the family's bills or their own college debt; it left nothing for the kids' college savings.

Pairing the 100 percent income replacement for minimum-wage workers with tiered replacement levels for everyone else for the first six months could minimize the immediate economic shock of job loss on families and communities. This would be easier to do if we thought about unemployment insurance as just that—insurance to protect workers when their jobs are lost, just as auto insurance protects us from the costs of a car accident. Fully funding the unemployment insurance program, which we have not done for decades, would go a long way to protecting the unemployed.

As it stands now, waitresses, like Tracy, and managers, like Neil, pay the same amount in federal unemployment insurance taxes, on average, because the cap is reached once someone earns $8,000 a year. We need to broaden the tax base so that someone like Neil, who receives much more money in unemployment insurance than Tracy does, pays more into it, too. Alix Gould-Werth, the director of Family Economic Security Policy at the Washington Center for Equitable Growth, proposes that we should expand the base payments for unemployment insurance by increasing it to the same level as the Social Security Index and indexing it to inflation.[15] This change would go a long way toward shoring up the federal funds for unemployment insurance.

While there has long been a debate among economists about whether more generous benefits might lengthen the amount of time before the unemployed start searching for work,[16] the best national-level data suggests there are better outcomes when benefits are more generous.[17] This would certainly align with my findings about Tracy and other diverted workers, who found that their meager benefits made it difficult to search for work. It would also align with what I found about those who searched urgently and took jobs for which they were ill prepared. They sometimes found themselves back on the unemployment line before I'd had a chance to do my initial interviews.

Moreover, some evidence suggests that more generous benefits allow for searches that lead to better matches between workers and their jobs.[18] My research certainly suggests that the current system pushed working-class men in particular, as well as some working-class women (particularly those who weren't diverted), to search for any job they could find without regard for whether it matched their skills. And it prevents others from searching at all. We remember that Anthony, a skilled electronic/computer technician, spent a year working at a grocery store because it was the first job he found. These are certainly not the desired outcomes by either the unemployed or the state. In contrast, those with greater resources were better able to mount deliberate searches, navigating state requirements, turning down jobs that weren't in their desired areas, and holding out for the jobs that they wanted.

Yet more generous unemployment insurance won't bring better outcomes for everyone. As we saw with the middle-class women in particular, sometimes there were not better jobs to be found even when the unemployed had the chance to conduct a more deliberate search. But this does not mean that more generous unemployment insurance should not be our goal. Even if people cannot find their ideal jobs, we should consider whether preventing falls into deep poverty are, at least partly, the goal of unemployment insurance. Nearly a century after we first introduced the unemployment insurance system, we must ask if our commitment to the unemployed has changed and, if not, we must seek better solutions.

Childcare Credit Expansion

In 2014, the national news across the country was focused on the job search tribulations of a woman named Shanesha Taylor.[19] She had been desperately searching for better-paying work, but she couldn't find anyone to watch her two boys while she went on an interview for what seemed to be a very good job. After failing to find childcare for her children, she decided to leave them in the car with the windows down during her interview. She was excited after the interview, thinking that she'd gotten the job. But she arrived back at her car, only to find it surrounded by the police, who had been informed that the boys were in the car alone.

Neither women nor men should have to choose between finding good-paying work and caring for their children. Instead, there is a good reason to *expand* existing childcare credit programs to those who have lost jobs in order to ensure those with child-rearing responsibilities, most often women, can continue to search for work. In chapter 6, we learned that women, much more often than men, faced strong obligations to pick up the second shift, including new childcare obligations at home. We learned many working-class women lost the childcare support they had received either from partners or from extended kin when they lost their jobs. Some like Samantha even lost their childcare credit from the state, which was a particular blow to single moms. We saw too often in chapter 7 that these increased family responsibilities prevented women, particularly working-class women, from searching for work. In chapter 8, we saw that many of the middle-class women who were able at first to avoid childcare obligations found that as their time away from work increased, so, too, did their obligations at home, which further constrained their searches.

Like others I met, Paula wished there were "free public access to really high-quality early childhood programs." As others have noted, the access to childcare can't be simply any type of childcare because parents are reluctant to use care that is of poor quality or that may not be safe.[20] Yet the childcare credits used from Temporary Assistance for Needy Families (TANF) have not always provided families (often mothers) with access to quality childcare programs.[21] We need better alternatives. Expanded access to high-quality and affordable care must be a priority. Caitlyn Collins and others have argued the patchwork system currently available in the United States is utterly inadequate.[22]

The childcare crisis during the 2020 global pandemic vividly brought to light the challenges of caring for children while attempting to work or search for a job. Multiple studies have shown that as schools and childcare centers closed under statewide mandates, women bore the brunt of the resulting increase in care work in the home; women were also more likely to quit, reduce their paid hours, or lose jobs in response to these new challenges.[23] Women of color and low-income women were not only most likely to lose work during this period, but they also bore the biggest brunt of caring challenges—not just care for children but also for the elderly (this caring demand was not seen as often among those I met, but it is one highlighted by the Covid-19 crisis).[24] As we saw earlier in this book, the twin demands of job searches (a task described both by the people I met and by unemployment expert Ofer Sharone as itself a full-time job) and childcare responsibilities are practically incompatible, prolonging searches for women who must combine the two.

Thus, my second policy suggestion is that high-quality and affordable childcare access must be expanded, nationally, and continued access to this care must be provided when women and men lose jobs. It is paradoxical to insist everyone search for work and yet ignore that job loss leads to an inability to purchase childcare for many. If the unemployed have to provide childcare rather than search for work, their ability to search for work will be greatly impeded, as we saw with the mostly working-class women in the *Diverted* search group, who were unable to start or maintain a job search because of their family responsibilities or their dive into poverty. Many of these women received little help for childcare at home and didn't have the financial ability to keep their children in childcare (either formal or informal) after they lost their jobs. This left them with little time to search for work.

These types of programs will likely impact not only people's ability to find work but also the type of work they can find. Sociologists Michelle Budig, Joya Misra, and Irene Boeckmann have found that in countries with shared societal expectations that support women's paid employment (as is generally the case in the United States), policies such as parental leave and public childcare lead to higher wages for women.[25] This suggests that public childcare could have even broader implications for the unemployed, as raised wages could mean higher unemployment benefits and a bigger financial cushion should unemployment be faced again.

Expansion of Health Care Provisions

My third policy suggestion relates to the decisions the unemployed made about their health. Those who lose jobs should have access to more affordable versions of the insurance plans offered via the Affordable Care Act (ACA). People, more often women, made devastating sacrifices to their health after a job loss. They gave up their health insurance, skipped their doctors' visits, stopped taking their needed medications, and neglected their peace of mind. These sacrifices likely have long-term effects on our economy, in terms of both worker productivity and future health care costs for these workers—costs that could be prevented if people had access to affordable coverage during the period when they are out of work.

As political scientist Jacob Hacker has noted, employers have transferred more of the "risk" of the cost of health care to employees instead of themselves carrying the burden.[26] Ruth noted this change in employment relations as she described the challenges facing those earning slightly too much to be eligible for the lower-tier levels of the ACA. She explained, "In the eighties and early nineties it was a given that you had health insurance with the job and your employer paid for it. You didn't have to pay for it. It's gotten crazy. What prompted me to even go back to school [for my master's] was my salary and the cost of insurance was crazy. Like, I was bringing home $1,100 every two weeks and my insurance for my family was almost $700 every month." Her health insurance cost Ruth almost one-third of her monthly earnings. Given such a burdensome cost, it is hard to imagine how she could afford to pay for insurance in addition to the rest of her bills after her job loss. The 2020 pandemic made the importance of affordable health insurance all the more urgent, as tens of millions of Americans lost their jobs and their health insurance along with it at a time when the globe was seized by a devastating health crisis.

The need for more affordable health insurance was one of the most popular refrains among the people I met. Although some did benefit from the introduction of the ACA, many found even the most basic plan out of reach on their very limited budgets. Seth wished we could "be like Europe and give us all free health insurance. . . . If I had the money, I would just move to Europe and start over there [chuckles]." Seth dreamed of Europe because he had his doubts that this sort of solution could be found in the United States. The ACA is clearly a first step toward expanded health care coverage. It just doesn't cover enough people at the moment, nor is it affordable enough for many of those it does cover, as we learned in chapter 5.

Much of the resentment people felt about our current health care system stemmed from the fact that they saw others as having access to free or reduced-cost health care while they did not have access to these programs. Expanding the access to health insurance could be one way to further grow support for the ACA and for the role of government in creating solutions to today's economic problems.

Rethink Incentives to Push People Back to Work

Fourth, the incentives to push people back to work as quickly as possible should be revised. Requiring that people apply for a particular number of jobs a week may force people to apply for jobs that don't match their skill set. Requiring them to take any job that they are offered may move people, like Anthony, into positions that they are overqualified for or, like Brent, into jobs that they are underqualified for. Neither of these are good outcomes and can either lead to being placed in a job that does not pay the bills or to a speedy return to unemployment (as we learned, Brent ended up taking a job in sales that he soon lost). Both situations lead to mounting debt and, often, more unemployment, which is costly for both the state and the worker. The current incentives force those without the economic resources or the knowledge necessary to navigate the rules into bad jobs for which they are not qualified and which they quickly lose. This creates churn in the system and puts some people at greater risk of chronic unemployment. Anthony's wife explained, "They need to stop essentially penalizing you for trying to get further pay and to move yourself forward." She wanted Anthony to have the same ability that Harold had—that is, to be able to receive a job offer that was less than ideal and to delay taking it to see if something better was around the corner.

Those with more resources, like Harold, whom we met again at the beginning of chapter 8 when he found a good-paying job, worked around these quick return requirements and took a more deliberate approach to finding a good and lasting job—a search strategy we should support for all workers. At first, I begrudged Harold; I thought it seemed unfair that he was able to turn down jobs he didn't want, and to delay taking offers to see how other opportunities would pan out, and not feel the despair that was so evident in Tracy's and Anthony's lives. But I came to realize that I didn't want Harold to face similar despair—I resented the system that let Harold have access to one way of being unemployed and gave Tracy and Anthony such a different set of rules to work with.

Why must workers have resources to navigate the system to get the best outcome? Everyone should have the ability to carefully look for the best kind of job one can find. Harold and others like him simply responded to the demands of the system in ways that best suited their and their families' needs. Paula, the college-educated childcare worker who didn't want to lose her home, did this, too, by only applying for jobs that would pay her well enough to keep her home. We need a system in place that allows all workers to have this option.

Of course, I did find that some folks did more than shy away from bad jobs to make sure that they found the best job they could to support their families, as Harold or Paula had done. Some, like Neil, took time off—time that Neil felt he deserved; "I'm not a person who likes charity," he told me, but unemployment wasn't charity, he reasoned; it was something he'd paid into. It is the actions of those who have taken time off—time at least partially paid for by the American public—that may make it hard for some to stomach the idea of expanding unemployment insurance for all. Perhaps this would be partly solved if the middle-class men paid more of their fair share (as I've already noted, they received much more in unemployment insurance than others but paid the same amount in federal taxes). It might also be solved with more commonsense rules—rules that mandated searching for work but that also recognized that people can't always find available work in a given week and that they can't take jobs that won't allow them to continue to pay their bills. Regardless, the actions of the few men like Neil who take time need not dictate the threshold of our generosity for everyone else.

We should also remember that part of the reason Tracy was starting so far behind Neil and so many others was because of the existing disparities in income before their job losses. Working forty hours a week and earning the most she'd made in her lifetime, Tracy lived in poverty before her job loss, which meant that even a 100 percent replacement wage would still leave her family in poverty. Addressing some of the underlying inequity in resources that people bring into the unemployment

period would help to address some of the gap in outcomes I've described in these pages. This would mean making changes to our employment system, creating better jobs for workers, so they have a better shot
of finding good work. There are many existing policy suggestions on
how to improve the quality of work and reduce job-related insecurity.[27]
There is one recommendation for creating better working-class jobs
worth highlighting here as it directly pertains to those I met. Higher
wages through the passage of new minimum-wage standards would be
a step in the right direction; it is difficult, if not impossible, for workers
like Tracy to ever financially prosper when they must make do, even
when fully employed, on wages that leave them and their families below
the poverty line.

Ultimately, we need to ask what the goals of the unemployment benefits system truly are in order to rethink how the system should be set
up. Do we simply want to move people back to work as quickly as possible, regardless of the human cost? Or do we want to create a safety net
to protect the unemployed from falling so far? If we hope to do the
latter, we need more than policy suggestions; we also need to create a
climate in which these policies can be implemented.

What We Could Be

These policy suggestions stem from a combination of my years meeting
with the unemployed, my reading of the existing policy literature, and
my belief that there can be a better way forward. This is, perhaps, a difficult charge in America, given our historical obsession with the idea
that people could better themselves simply with more hard work. As
Barack Obama noted in his presidential nomination speech to the
Democratic National Convention, it is an attitude that says to the poor
that they should "pull yourself up by your bootstraps." We are, as Max
Weber noted over a century ago, a society so committed to the importance of one's work ethic that we have long equated hard work with
morality.[28] Such an emphasis on the importance of work has led Americans, as far back as the 1800s, to look down on the unemployed, thinking
they were "lazy" and even "immoral."[29]

Some of these tensions are further imbued with deeply held beliefs about race. Some of the white participants I met thought Black Americans were more likely to unjustly access government benefits, while they (the white participants) had earned the unemployment benefits they received. Emily, a white woman, told me that she "wasn't racist" but she thought Black Americans abused the system. "Y'know they're lying," she told me. But despite this deep skepticism from some whites, research consistently finds that Black and Latino people are actually *less* likely to access the unemployment system than whites are, even when they are equally eligible.[30] Black workers, on average, receive significantly lower unemployment benefits than do white workers even when they earn similar salaries, according to economist Kathryn A. Edwards.[31] Moreover, Black and Latino workers are more likely to be employed in precarious employment that makes them *less* eligible for unemployment benefits than are whites.[32] Political scientists and sociologists consistently find that beliefs about race impinge on our ability to be generous with our shared government benefits.[33] We need to acknowledge and confront racist ideas about the use of unemployment (and other) benefits if we are to craft a better unemployment system.

And, as we have seen, we need a better system; many people need more help to weather the storm brought on by a job loss. And many, like Tracy, did not receive enough unemployment compensation to keep them and their families out of poverty, nor did they have enough resources in reserve to cover the gap between unemployment benefits and the cost of living, which prevented them from searching for good work.

Yet American beliefs in the importance of hard work and going it alone are well entrenched. Leslie McCall, a professor of political science and sociology, notes a majority of Americans today remain against government policies that could be seen as redistributive.[34] In fact, this viewpoint is so pervasive that even those who would benefit from some of the policies I've suggested might oppose them. Take Pamela, the working-class woman whose husband encouraged her to tend their large garden rather than go back to work, for example. She told me she wished the government could "help people who need help, when they need it." She could have used the help; her family moved into poverty after her job loss. But as she spoke, she reversed herself, sounding a refrain I became very familiar with over the course of my interviews. She explained, "I don't [receive] cash or anything, it's just food stamps, but I'm not saying that they should give me more money. I mean, I obviously get what I'm supposed to get." There are many contradictions here: Pamela denied receiving cash support, even though she received unemployment insurance; she also wanted more government help, then denied she needed any. If Pamela had not turned so quickly away from her own needs, she might have articulated a need for more government intervention. But she reversed course, rejecting her original thought that she would have benefited from more government aid.

But what if we did not have to turn away from this question of helping people when they need it? As Dorothea Lange showed us nearly a century ago, there is a different way to view the unemployed and our mutual obligations to each other in our society. Her photographs were never meant to be simple reflections of her times. She wanted them to be calls to action. In an interview, Lange said that the responsibility of a documentary photographer is "to the outside world," and her celebrated photographs are merely "by-products" of that external commitment.

Leslie McCall's research on American beliefs about inequality and redistribution shows us there is a possibility for a different way. While she finds little support for redistributive policies, she does discover evidence that Americans would like to find a solution that does not ask people to simply pull up their bootstraps. In fact, McCall argues that Americans became increasingly concerned about income inequality starting in the early 1990s.[35] I also found evidence of this type of sentiment among the people I met. For some, the role of the government was to step forward when people experienced an event like unemployment. Ken wanted the government to "make it easier for people who need assistance to get assistance and not have so many hoops to jump through. . . . There's people who need it who don't have a choice. Not everyone has a choice if their company closes. . . ." People like Ken saw the possibility in our mutual obligations, and we can provide these better policies if we follow their lead.

I'd like to imagine we can create a world in which Tracy does not struggle as much as she did and in which she could find her way back to better work. Tracy herself had a hard time imagining a world like that. I asked her what kind of job she would like if she could do anything she wanted, and she told me that she could grin and bear any job if it would support her and her kids. I asked her again: What if she could imagine something better than that for herself? But Tracy had not had a life that let her have such imaginings. She'd always needed to work "for the money," and that didn't allow her to indulge in some fantasy with me about what she would want to do. She told me, "I just need something that pays well. So, I don't know what my job would be. I really don't."

Tracy's dream job may remain clouded over, but what she needs from her government is not. Clearer policies, a higher unemployment benefit, a childcare credit expansion to provide care for her elementary-age daughter while she searched for work, affordable health care and access to doctors and medicines, and a new set of unemployment rules that give her more time to search for a good-paying job—and maybe even a job that paid enough to propel her out of poverty once her search ended successfully. I want to live in the America that can believe in this vision, too.

ACKNOWLEDGMENTS

THE PEOPLE who shared their unemployment stories with me are the heart of this book. Most sat down with me and my team more than once, letting us into their lives so that we could better understand our country's unemployment system. This book would not be possible without their generosity. I am grateful, beyond measure, to them all. I hope that I have done their experiences justice and that we will hear their stories as a collective call to action.

Although I say that I spent my sabbatical year enjoying the solitude of writing, in truth, I was always surrounded by the support of exceptionally talented scholars and dear friends, including my two wonderful writing groups. Jessica Halliday Hardie and Carrie Shandra read every word on every page of this book more than once (while writing their own important books), always offering insightful critiques, sharing laughter and tears, and navigating academia together. Heather Jacobson, Kristen Schultz Lee, and I have been writing, reading, and dining together for over a decade now; their feedback has shaped my work and my career. While Adrianne Frech and I do not yet have side-by-side offices with a pass-through window, we do have a tremendous collaborative partnership, now in its second decade, that provided many insights for this book; I am grateful for her generous and productive feedback on multiple portions of the book at various stages of conception. Josipa Roksa and I talked through many of the ideas in the book in our monthly chats; our friendship has been a steady support since my early graduate school days. Molly Martin provided key insights on portions of the book, and our friendship and time together provides a welcome respite from our hectic lives. My many thanks go to Léa Pessin, for her incisive comments on the book and for our walks during my final days of revising.

Many colleagues have been very generous with their time as I shared drafts, talked over ideas, asked questions about their areas of expertise, and gave talks. Generative conversations, critical feedback, encouragement, and insightful comments came from Julie Artis, Regina Baker, Jenifer Bratter, Mary Brinton, Dan Carlson, Emilio Castilla, Noelle Chesley, Caity Collins, Stephanie Coontz, Allison Daminger, Janette Dill, Kathleen Gerson, Pilar Gonalons-Pons, Jerry Jacobs, Erin Kelly, Sasha Killewald, Ellen Lamont, Michèle Lamont, Hedy Lee, Adam Lippert, Kathleen McGinn, Krista Lynn Minnotte, Olenka Mitukiewicz, Phyllis Moen, Eunsil Oh, Joanna Pepin, Allison Pugh, Leah Ruppanner, Natasha Sarkisian, Liana Sayer, Ariela Schachter, John Shandra, Lisa Wade, Adia Harvey Wingfield, Jaqlyn Wong, and Jill Yavorsky. Many thanks to the graduate students and faculty in the departments that hosted early book talks at Harvard, MIT, Washington University in St. Louis, the University of Pennsylvania, and the University of Virginia.

My deep appreciation goes to the many gender, work-family, and unemployment scholars whose work I reference in the book; your work inspires my own, and I thank you for the conversations we have had and will continue to have. Stephanie Coontz has been a champion of my work since the beginning and gave me critical advice on writing this book. Additional thanks go to Frank Anechiarico, for teaching the class that introduced me to Dorothea Lange's photographs. Jen Bratter believed in the early kernels of the idea of this book and is a wonderful mentor and friend. I am particularly grateful to Kathleen Gerson, my friend, collaborator, and mentor, who continues to cheer for me and my work.

I am deeply appreciative of the wonderful graduate and undergraduate students, many of whom worked directly on this project, either through interviews, recruitment, transcriptions, coding, reference compilation, or indirectly through work on adjacent projects. For their work either conducting interviews or recruiting at the CareerLink (or both), I thank Erica Dollhopf, Kayla Follmer, April Gunsallus, Eric LaPlant, Lydia Hayes Owens, Rachel Terman, and Tori Thomas. My deep appreciation for work on literature reviews, interview transcription, data management, and other projects goes to Maria del Rosario Castro

Bernardini, Julia Gurule, Kimmy Kim, Youngeun Lee, Sean McGinley, Ashley Niccolai, Daniel Parr, Aniruddha Ramachandra, Christen Sheroff, and Meghan Stouter. Veronica "Roni" Joyce wrote a wonderful honors thesis using this data. I have also had the honor of working with a fabulous group of gender/work/family doctoral students during this time period, including Joeun Kim, Jane Lankes, Ashley Niccolai, Sarah Patterson, Susana Quiros, and Maria del Rosario Castro Bernardini.

Meagan Levinson has an exceptionally astute editorial eye and a deep commitment to the ideas of the book and was greatly generous with her time during a period when it felt hard to find extra time to spare. It has been a joy to work with her. The entire team at Princeton University Press (PUP) has been terrific, from Christie Henry's initial phone call, to the dedicated work of Jacqueline Delaney, to Erin Davis's great work shepherding the manuscript through production, to Karen Brogno's exceptional work with the copy editing, to Jill Kramer's great proofreading, to Derek Thornton's brilliant cover design, and, finally, to all of Maria Whelan's wonderful publicity efforts. I am very appreciative of Kate Mertes's terrific index and her suggestion and compilation of the participant index. I also owe a debt of thanks to James Cook, another fabulous editor, who gave incisive feedback on the initial proposal as well as advice and valued friendship over the years. Anonymous reviewers from both PUP and Oxford University Press gave comments on the book proposal, and three anonymous PUP reviewers gave comments on the full manuscript. I hope the reviewers can see the fruits of their labors in these pages; their thoughts and suggestions resonated as I wrote, wrestled with, and revised the manuscript. I also benefited from anonymous reviews from *Gender & Society* and comments from then-editor Jo Reger. Portions of chapter 7 were previously published in *Gender & Society*, and I thank the journal and Sage Publications for their permission to reprint here.

Mark Price generously connected me to Sue Mukherjee and Randy Murphy at the Center for Workforce Information and Analysis. They connected me with the CareerLink regional directors (whose names I cannot share), who connected me with local county directors. I am very grateful for the access provided to the CareerLink centers and to the staff at those sites for their tireless work (on shoestring budgets) on behalf of the unemployed. The majority of my participants reported being impressed with the work the CareerLink staff did. While I call for change in the book, these critiques are aimed higher up—at those who underfund programs like these—and not at those doing the hard work.

At Penn State, I have been sustained by amazing women who generously shared their time, expertise, enthusiasm, support, and friendship: Mary Bellman, Michelle Frisco, Jen Glick, Corina Graif, Nancy Luke, Kate Maich, Molly Martin, Susan McHale, Léa Pessin, and Jenny van Hook. Glenn Firebaugh and Doug Teti read early drafts of my National Science Foundation (NSF) proposal, and their feedback made it stronger. Paul Whitehead generously provided employment law advice and reading recommendations. Many others in the Sociology and the Labor and Employment Relations departments and the PRI Family Demography working group provided their thoughts, enthusiasm, and support for the project, including Gary Adler, Mark Anner, Eric Baumer, Paul Clark, J. D. Daw, Gordon de Jong, Elaine Farndale, Diane Felmlee, Mark Gough, Steven Haas, Melissa Hardy, Elaine Hui, Valarie King, Stephen Matthews, John McCarthy, Hee Man Park, Jean Phillips, Sumita Raghuram, Alan Sica, and Ashton Verdery.

There are very many staff members at Penn State who do the necessary work to ensure research projects operate smoothly. I am particularly grateful to Angela Jordan, Diane Diviney, Rachel Charney, Lisa Broniszewski, Dora Hunter, and Sherry Yocum. I am also grateful to Lynn Demyan and Leslie Moore, who did a brilliant job of transcribing the vast majority of the interviews. Isabella Furth provided much appreciated, insightful, and thoughtful edits of the book proposal.

I received generous financial support for this project from many funding sources, first from a seed grant as well as developmental assistance provided by the Population Research Institute (PRI) at Penn State University, which is supported by an infrastructure grant from the Eunice Kennedy Shriver National Institute of Child Health and Human Development (NICHD) at the National Institutes of Health (NIH) (grant no. P2CHD041025), then from an award given by the American Sociological Association's Fund for the Advancement of the Discipline, and finally support from the NSF (grant no. SES-1357264). A second seed grant from

PRI and a grant from the NICHD branch of the NIH (grant no. R03HD088806-01A1) supported my work with Adrianne Frech that is presented in these pages. A sabbatical from Penn State (and the continued support from the university's then-dean, Susan Welch) were critical for the final writing phase of the book. An early-career fellowship from the Work-Family Research Network expanded my networks at an important time in my career, and I am grateful for the support, to my fellow fellows, and to Steve Sweet for running the program.

The years during which I wrote this book were filled with both great joy and sorrow in my life, as well as in the world at large. Throughout, I have been buoyed by the presence of Kaitlin and Russ Hedberg; Naomi Turbidy and Allison Cox; Chrissy Fritton; Katey Wilber; Kelly Hoffheins; Karen Winterich; Melissa Poulsen and Derek Lee; Megan Maas and Cabus Dewey; the Htet-Khins; Pearl Brandes; Amanda Paschke and Morgan Conn; Katrina Niidas Holm and Chris Holm; the Nolans; Lauren Oshman and Doug Perkins; Shibani Munshi; Carly Barner; Andy and Rachel Shelden; the Morris family; and the Vanegas-Zamora family.

My wonderful family has been with me through it all. My mom, Frankie Knapp, carried the weight of our family's world on her shoulders for much of the last decade and still manages to laugh with abandon. She takes notes on the projects I'm involved with, so she can stay up to date—thanks, Mom. Through their own scholarship and activism, Jonathan Knapp and Alexis Callender push my thinking forward. It is a gift to have siblings who are friends, as are Jon and Alex and John and Janet Damaske. I can count on John to send me gender-wage-gap gallows humor; Janet went above and beyond the call of duty, providing incisive line edits for portions of the book. Claire and Dick Damaske have celebrated my work, cheered me on, and been steady supports for all of us. My dear niece, Grace, and nephew, Noah, are treasured parts of my life. My daughter, Charlotte, was born when this project was in its nascent phases, bringing such light and joy into our lives. Thank you, my dearest girl, for understanding when the book demanded more of my time than you wanted to share and for showing continued interest in my work, reading portions of chapters, asking if the book was "nonfiction or historical fiction," making suggestions, and celebrating with me when I handed it in. Watching you grow and change has been the best part of this decade. Finally, Paul Damaske continues to be there for me and for our family every day, a steady, generous, and loving partner in my life's journey. This book would not be possible without him; thank you for co-parenting, for proofreading late into the night, and for your boundless enthusiasm for my work. I am so glad you are by my side to share both the difficult times as well as the light we find and create together. My dad, Stephen Knapp, learned that he had cancer just before I started the research for this book; he died in 2017. His absence is keenly felt, as he was always such a wonderful cheerleader for me (and for all he met). The light he created through his art and in his love for our family continues to shine in you all. Thank you.

METHODOLOGICAL APPENDIX

WHILE RESEARCHING my first book, *For the Family? How Class and Gender Shape Women's Work,* I discovered something surprising: a group of women who felt very constrained in their ability to choose whether or not to work (contrary to common parlance at the time, which suggested women were doing one or the other, rather than passing between stages).[1] These women experienced multiple job losses and great financial strains at home. The financial strains they faced at home made it impossible for them to retreat entirely from the workplace and become stay-at-home mothers (indeed, many insisted that paid work was an important part of their identity). But their employment histories and lower education levels meant they were hired into occupations that had average job tenures of six to eight months. This left them unable to steady themselves at work or to fully withdraw from the labor market; I called them "interrupted" workers. As I finished that book, I knew I needed to know more about women who experienced unemployment and how their experiences compared to men's. After my first book was complete, I began researching women and unemployment and found that even though women have somewhat similar unemployment rates to men, there was little sociological research focused on women and unemployment and almost nothing about the similarities or differences in men's and women's unemployment experiences. Indeed, in much of the research on unemployment, men's experiences remain centered while women's experiences are often set off to the side.[2]

My experience from my first book, as well as my subsequent research, led me to begin this project with a series of interlocking questions that I wanted to understand: What are the differences in the ways that men and women, across classes, experience job loss and unemployment?

More specifically, how do men and women negotiate job loss and unemployment, how does it shape their family life, and what may impede their return to work? Do women and men even make similar attempts to return to work, given their different labor force attachment levels and work-family responsibilities? Finally, how are job loss, unemployment, and job-seeking experiences further differentiated by differences in race and class? Qualitative methods are often employed to research questions like these, as in-depth interviewing is an ideal method for building theory that stems from deductive readings of the existing literature and abductive analysis of the data.[3] A life history framework (which I employed both in the development of the research questions and in the analysis) allows for the investigation of the processes through which women and men move into and out of work and how they experience job loss and unemployment. Life history analysis makes it possible to chart the ways that work and unemployment are experienced, as well as track key transition periods in workforce participation over a lifetime. Life course interviews encourage attention to pivotal turning points in a person's life pathway, such as a job loss and a period of unemployment, and allow the interviewer to trace steps leading toward the pivotal moment and leading away from it (and also allowing for the interviewer to note when such a moment is experienced as a nonevent for some, as unemployment was for Anthony, who had lost so many jobs before, even when it is experienced as a crucial moment for others, as it was for Tracy and Joan).

Selecting a Sample

This book uses data from 100 qualitative interviews with working- and middle-class men and women conducted from 2013 to 2015.[4] I've included table 1 to give readers a brief snapshot of all the participants in the study, including information about their gender, social class, marital status, number of children, and race. To determine the feasibility of the project, I began by fielding a pilot study, recruiting twenty participants from a wide range of my and others' social networks (including three participants randomly recruited via ten-digit dialing in a metropolitan area). To find people for the snowball sample, I started out small, relying on word of mouth and even randomly calling people and asking if anyone in the household had recently lost a job. Four of the pilot study participants are excluded from these analyses, as they were older than age 55 and their responses suggested they faced different challenges than younger job seekers. I received financial support first from the American Sociological Association Fund for the Advancement of the Discipline and from my own university, the Pennsylvania State University. After I concluded the pilot study, it became clear to me that the snowball design (where one person you meet introduces you to another) would not yield a large or diverse enough group of people. Although I started from a wide number of nodes (almost all of the original twenty were not connected to each other, having been recruited from a diverse network), many of the people I met in the pilot study recommended others who had lost jobs from the same companies where they had worked; I was concerned that this form of sampling would not lead to a broad range of unemployment experiences. As Mario Luis Small notes, many qualitative projects evolve over time, changing as the contours and the possibilities of the research design become clear.[5]

Then a grant from the National Science Foundation (NSF) allowed me to hire a research team and change my recruiting design. I wanted to find people through the unemployment offices—it was the one place people who had lost jobs had in common. The Pennsylvania CareerLink is a statewide clearinghouse for jobs and information for the unemployed that holds multiple weekly meetings in counties statewide. Everyone who receives unemployment benefits from the state is required to attend a meeting at the CareerLink to keep those unemployment benefits. I spoke with a regional CareerLink director to explain my research and ask if I might recruit participants from the mandatory meetings. She immediately understood why there was a need for a study like mine and agreed to allow me to recruit participants from centers in Pennsylvania. After the end of the required meeting, the person running the meeting would say someone from my team had an announcement and that people could stay to listen to it if they wanted to (making it clear that even hearing the announcement was voluntary).[6] At this

TABLE 1. Snapshot of Participants

Name*	Gender	Social class†	Married/ Partnered/Single	Number of children	Race/ Ethnicity	Bureau of Labor Statistics occupational category of most recent lost job
Alana	Female	WC	Cohabiting	4+	Asian	Sales and related
Allen	Male	MC	Married	1	White	Architecture and engineering
Anita	Female	MC	Married	1	Latina	Business and financial operations
Anthony	Male	WC	Married	2	White	Construction and extraction
Barry	Male	MC	Married	1	White	Management
Bianca	Female	MC	Married	3	White	Office and administrative support
Brandi	Female	MC	Married	1	White	Healthcare practictioner
Brent	Male	WC	Married	1	White	Computer and mathematical
Brooke	Female	MC	Married	1	White	Office and administrative support
Bruce	Male	WC	Married	1	White	Sales and related
Bryan	Male	MC	Married	4+	White	Business and financial operations
Carl	Male	MC	Married	2	White	Installation maintenance and repair
Carol	Female	WC	Married	1	White	Office and administrative support
Charles	Male	MC	Married	3	White	Sales and related
Christina	Female	MC	Single	1	Latina	Community and social service
Corey	Male	MC	Married	1	White	Architecture and engineering
Curtis	Male	WC	Married	1	White	Production
Dale	Male	WC	Single	2	Black	Installation maintenance and repair
Dana	Female	WC	Married	1	White	Transportation and material moving
Darren	Male	MC	Married	1	White	Arts design entertainment sports and media
Dawn	Female	WC	Cohabiting	1	White	Food preparation and serving related
Dean	Male	MC	Cohabiting	2	White	Computer and mathematical
Dennis	Male	WC	Married	1	White	Construction and extraction
Derek	Male	MC	Married	1	White	Computer and mathematical

Donna	Female	WC	Married	1	White	Community and social service
Edward	Male	MC	Married	1	White	Computer and mathematical
Emily	Female	WC	Married	1	White	Healthcare support
Frank	Male	MC	Married	1	White	Sales and related
George	Male	WC	Cohabiting	1	White	Transportation and material moving
Gerald	Male	MC	Married	0	Black	Arts design entertainment sports and media
Gregory	Male	WC	Single	2	White	Transportation and material moving
Harold	Male	MC	Married	2	White	Business and financial operations
Heather	Female	MC	Married	3	White	Business and financial operations
Heidi	Female	WC	Married	2	White	Healthcare support
Holly	Female	MC	Married	1	White	Healthcare practictioner
Jacob	Male	MC	Single	0	White	Sales and related
Jason	Male	MC	Single	0	White	Management
Jay	Male	WC	Married	1	White	Production
Jeff	Male	MC	Married	2	White	Production
Jerry	Male	MC	Married	3	White	Healthcare practictioner
Jesse	Male	WC	Married	1	White	Transportation and material moving
Jessica	Female	WC	Cohabiting	4+	White	Transportation and material moving
Jill	Female	MC	Cohabiting	0	White	Office and administrative support
Joan	Female	MC	Married	1	White	Life physical and social science
Jodi	Female	WC	Single	1	White	Office and administrative support
Joel	Male	WC	Married	3	White	Transportation and material moving
Joyce	Female	WC	Single	0	White	Food preparation and serving related
Julie	Female	MC	Married	2	White	Business and financial operations
Keith	Male	MC	Married	1	Latino	Arts design entertainment sports and media
Ken	Male	MC	Married	2	White	Installation maintenance and repair
Kevin	Male	MC	Single	0	White	Installation maintenance and repair
Kimberly	Female	MC	Married	2	White	Education training and library

(continued)

TABLE 1. (*continued*)

Name*	Gender	Social class†	Married/Partnered/Single	Number of children	Race/Ethnicity	Bureau of Labor Statistics occupational category of most recent lost job
Latesha	Female	WC	Married	4+	Black	Office and administrative support
Latoya	Female	MC	Married	1	Black	Business and financial operations
Lawrence	Male	WC	Cohabiting	1	White	Production
Leah	Female	WC	Married	1	White	Military specific
Leslie	Female	WC	Married	3	White	Office and administrative support
Marcus	Male	WC	Married	2	White	Building and grounds cleaning and maintenance
Martin	Male	WC	Cohabiting	2	White	Protective services
Misty	Female	WC	Single	3	White	Transportation and material moving
Monica	Female	WC	Married	2	White	Healthcare support
Natalie	Female	MC	Married	2	White	Computer and mathematical
Nathan	Male	MC	Married	0	White	Architecture and engineering
Neil	Male	MC	Married	0	White	Management
Nicole	Female	WC	Married	3	White	Life physical and social science
Noah	Male	MC	Married	1	White	Business and financial operations
Pamela	Female	WC	Married	4+	White	Food preparation and serving related
Paul	Male	WC	Married	2	White	Production
Paula	Female	MC	Single	1	White	Personal care and service
Peggy	Female	WC	Married	0	White	Office and administrative support
Phillip	Male	MC	Single	3	White	Architecture and engineering
Randall	Male	WC	Cohabiting	2	White	Construction and extraction
Regina	Female	WC	Married	2	White	Arts design entertainment sports and media
Renee	Female	MC	Single	1	White	Business and financial operations
Rhonda	Female	MC	Married	2	White	Personal care and service
Rita	Female	WC	Cohabiting	4+	White	Production

Name	Gender	Social class	Marital status	Race	Dependents	Occupation
Robin	Female	WC	Married	White	2	Installation maintenance and repair
Rodney	Male	MC	Married	White	1	Computer and mathematical
Roger	Male	WC	Single	White	0	Computer and mathematical
Ronald	Male	WC	Single	White	0	Transportation and material moving
Roy	Male	WC	Cohabiting	White	3	Production
Ruth	Female	MC	Married	White	2	Management
Samantha	Female	WC	Single	Black	2	Sales and related
Sandra	Female	MC	Married	White	1	Community and social service
Scott	Male	WC	Single	White	0	Construction and extraction
Seth	Male	WC	Married	White	1	Transportation and material moving
Stacy	Female	WC	Cohabiting	White	0	Management
Suzanne	Female	WC	Single	White	2	Building and grounds cleaning and maintenance
Tamara	Female	WC	Single	Black	1	Office and administrative support
Tiffany	Female	WC	Married	White	2	Life physical and social science
Timothy	Male	WC	Single	White	0	Production
Tony	Male	MC	Married	White	4+	Arts design entertainment sports and media
Tonya	Female	WC	Cohabiting	White	1	Food preparation and serving related
Tracy	Female	WC	Single	White	2	Production
Troy	Male	WC	Married	Black	4+	Management
Vanessa	Female	WC	Cohabiting	White	3	Healthcare support
Victoria	Female	WC	Cohabiting	White	0	Transportation and material moving
Vincent	Male	WC	Married	White	4+	Transportation and material moving
Wendy	Female	WC	Cohabiting	White	0	Food preparation and serving related
Wesley	Male	WC	Cohabiting	White	2	Construction and extraction

* Participants are listed in alphabetical order.

† Social class is based on highest occupation in household; children are dependents, age 23 and younger, living in household; race and gender are self-identified; and occupational category of last job is based on the Bureau of Labor Statistics major occupational codes (greater detail is not provided to protect participant confidentiality).

point, a member of my research team would invite people to participate in my study, letting them know they weren't obligated to do so, and also that they would receive a small monetary award ($50) if they did.[7] After the announcement, everyone who was interested in participating was invited to fill out a form that included information to determine eligibility in the study. Thus, with the support of the NSF funding and the generosity of the many CareerLink employees (who remain nameless to protect the confidentiality of the unemployed), I expanded the study design and recruited the remaining eighty-four people from the Career-Link meetings.

Pilot study results had suggested varied experiences across rural and city dwellers, so I decided to have my team recruit at CareerLink centers in five counties. The counties included one midsize city, two small cities, and two rural areas. We did not, however, visit a highly dense urban area, mostly for practical reasons. I'm a professor at Penn State, which is in central Pennsylvania—and it's a long drive from a large city like Philadelphia.

Because of the small sample size, I decided that I needed to be able to focus my attention on gender and class; therefore, I interviewed only people born between 1962 and 1987 (ages 28–52, the prime working and child-rearing years), those who worked full-time before their job loss, those who experienced an involuntary job loss during the past year, and those who did not lose a job for cause (e.g., were not fired because of their behavior at work). A theoretically informed stratified sampling design was used to achieve relatively equal distribution of participation across gender and class. Class was operationalized based on the highest occupational status in the household—if either respondents or their spouse or cohabiting partner held a professional position (in their most recent position), they were considered middle class; those with blue-collar, pink-collar, or service-work experience were considered working class.[8] Although I had originally intended to have more racial variation and the final sample varied by race, it was less racially diverse than is the national population, as were the counties from which the sample was drawn. This was a significant limitation of the sampling method that was driven by my need to restrict my travel to daylong journeys (when the research began, I had a baby, and my daughter was quite young during the years of primary data collection).

After I determined eligibility, the people who had filled out the form were contacted either by me or by a graduate student to ask them to participate in the study. While it's hard to say how many people could have signed up, of the 138 people who filled out forms and were eligible, one was excluded because of health considerations, six provided invalid/illegible phone numbers, and four were not contacted as the study had closed. This left a total of 127 people, from which eighty-four participants were recruited for a participation rate of 67 percent (the snowball sampling yielded a 100 percent response rate, as people generally only recommended those willing to participate).[9]

The participants had spent, on average, eleven weeks since their last day of work at the time of their interview (they were recruited, on average, one to three weeks prior to the interview, depending on their availability).[10] While most people completed their first interview between ten and twelve weeks after their job loss, the range was wider—from two to forty weeks. According to data from the Bureau of Labor Statistics for the years 2013 to 2015, between 22 and 28 percent of the unemployed spent less than five weeks unemployed during that time period, between 24 and 27 percent spent five to fourteen weeks unemployed, and the modal category was over twenty-seven weeks unemployed.[11] For demographic information about the participants, see table 2.

Most prior qualitative research on the unemployed has been on the long-term unemployed.[12] The valuable insight into those who are hit hardest by unemployment has shown us much about the job search process, as well as the process by which people lose hope that they will find their way back to work. But it has left largely unexplored the time period that includes people's paths to job loss, their job loss experience, and the initial changes and experiences during the unemployment process; prior research also has centered on the job-seeking strategies of the long-term unemployed, which may be, by nature, different from the experience of those unemployed for shorter durations.[13] This book centers on the early stages of unemployment while also following up with

TABLE 2. Demographic Characteristics of Sample (N = 100)

Characteristic	n
Age, mean	40
Age, range	27–51
Weeks since job loss (mean)	11
Weeks since job loss (range)	2–40
Gender	
Men	51
Women	49
Current social class	
Working class	56
Middle class	44
Race	
White	89
Black	7
Latino/a	3
Asian	1
Marital status	
Married	63
Cohabiting	17
Single	20
Has dependent children in household	
Under the age of 18	75
Under the age of 23	84

participants to investigate where they are one year later. This focus allows us to see how the unemployment system acts as an institution to shape the cumulation of disadvantage during even short periods of unemployment.

The Interviews

I put thousands of miles on my car in the years I spent conducting interviews. I drove to people's homes, their favorite diners, and coffee shops; sometimes, when people weren't sure they wanted others to know they were participating in the study, they drove to me. Some people ended up chatting for hours—the longest interview lasted almost five hours. A few people had less to say or were not used to talking about themselves, and these few interviews went only an hour or so. But most people talked for two to three hours, pouring out details of their lives. My team of research assistants conducted some interviews and did most of the recruiting at the CareerLink.

To facilitate systematic comparison across interviews, I created a detailed interview guide that included questions on household demographics, family history, education, work history, unemployment, household division of labor, future plans, and the like. Each section began with nested questions that used a life history framework to take people chronologically across each experience of interest. Questions that emphasized "who, what, and where" came first, while questions that asked "how and why" came second. This ordering allowed people to provide their interpretation of events but not to feel that their accounts of their actions had to match their stated actions. Considerable evidence suggests that people hold multiple (even inconsistent) views, but this need not mean that they are being deceptive when providing such details of their lives.[14] Instead, as I have argued, people may provide "accounts" of their lives that allow them to explain their actions in a manner that aligns with socially acceptable norms, and even update these social beliefs through their accounts, while still navigating them.[15] Probing follow-up questions were used to encourage deeper reflection and the discovery of multiple meanings. Sometimes people were long on opinion but short on relevant information from their own experience, so I worked to dig deeper and encourage more personal revelations.

The use of an open-ended interview guide meant that most key questions were answered by the people my team and I met, even if they weren't always asked. My team and I needed to know the interview guide well, skipping ahead as people answered questions and going back to ask for clarity when answers were unclear (while also respecting participants' reluctance to answer a question should that situation arise). Most of the graduate student interviewers trained in the field with me, sitting in as I conducted an interview (with Institutional Review Board approval and the permission of the participant), conducting their own interview (which I sat in on), and transcribing their first interview and reviewing it with me and the rest of the team. This "see one, do one" process allowed students to gain valuable hands-on experience and for the interviews to have greater consistency.

From 2015 to 2016, my research team and I successfully reached and followed up with fifty-eight of the eighty-four participants originally recruited from the CareerLink. Follow-up information was collected from all of the people who participated in the original pilot interviews. The follow-up interviews lasted, on average, between thirty and sixty minutes and took place over the phone. Participants received a gift card for their time. Unfortunately, twenty-six people recruited from the CareerLink could not be located to interview a second time. The follow-up interview guide included sections on their job search, their current work, their lack of work (if a job had not been found), their financial situation since we'd last met, their health, their family and household labor, and opinion questions at the end.

The Analysis

From the recorded interviews, over 5,000 pages of single-space transcribed text emerged. I inputted all interview transcripts, field notes, and other pieces of data (including an interview with a state official regarding state unemployment policies) into the qualitative software program Atlas.ti. As qualitative data analysis is something that often falls into a "black box," I attempt here to demystify the process. For the analysis, I began with a list of codes derived from the literature and then read each interview transcript, compiling a list of possible additional codes; an initial memo written after the completion of each interview also guided this process (I jotted down ideas for possible codes in the memos). I used a notebook to keep all of my working coding notes and thoughts on the project. It was divided into three parts: the first part was a list of running codes, the middle part included initial analyses of codes, and the third part included possible organizational ideas for the book. When potential codes began to be repeated and patterns emerged, I created new coding schemes (and expanded to additional notebooks). This iterative process took over a year and a half, requiring multiple readings of each transcript, as coding ideas were evaluated to determine their importance across the interview data and to discover any varia-tion in patterns.[16] After I coded something in Atlas.ti, I also entered it into my Excel master codebook, so I could keep track of the patterns that emerged across the sample. For some of the simpler codes (such as number of children in the household, spousal employment status, or parental education level), members of the research team worked on a team coding process, whereby each student separately coded a par-ticular item for all participants, and the two students then compared their notes to ensure that they had come to the same conclusion about the code to be assigned. In the case of diverging opinions, students reported the area of discrepancy to me, and we would discuss how to resolve it.

I developed and coded all of the codes used in the main analyses presented in the book. Some codes developed directly from the inter-view guide. For example, a question about whether the unemployed's spending on food had changed or not changed after job loss typically elicited one of four general responses: nothing had changed, they stopped eating out regularly, they reduced food purchases, or both eating-out and food purchases were now reduced. When people reported a reduction in food purchases, the interview guide included a follow-up question to ask for more details, which elicited additional information about the significance of these reductions to the family; this finding then led to the development of another code that indicated whether or not the participant or anyone else in the family had experienced food insecurity as a result of the job loss.

Other codes, such as the code for how participants made attempts to return to work, emerged from patterns that developed across multiple questions. In the case of attempting to return to work, the questions examined whether/when they had started their job search, their search goals, the urgency of their job search, and their perceived ability to de-cline a job. Based on the answers to this series of questions, participants were placed in the *Take Time* category if they had not started their job search yet, if they expressed no urgency about their search, if they de-scribed wanting time to enjoy themselves or think about their next steps before they started a search, and if they expected their searches to begin sometime in the next few months. Participants were placed in the *Deliberate* category if they had begun a job search soon after (or even preceding) their job loss, if they described treating their search as if it were a job, if they described themselves as being able to decline a "bad" job, if they had a clear target job in mind, and if they described a clear plan for their search. Participants were placed in the *Urgent* category if they had begun their job search immediately after their job loss, if they said they were applying to "any" job without a clear target job, and if they felt unable to decline a "bad" job. Participants were placed in the *Diverted* category if they said that they had not searched, if they tried to search but realized that they could not and had ceased all efforts to search, or if they said that they had no plans to search in the near or distant future; as long as they did not indicate that they were not searching because they wanted to take time off for themselves or to decide what they wanted to do in the future, they were considered *Diverted* searchers.

Finally, I carefully considered how to conceptualize people's feelings of financial insecurity. As Marianne Cooper demonstrated so eloquently in *Cut Adrift*, her book about families and insecurity, people with very high incomes can experience great feelings of financial insecurity.[17] My interviews made clear that unemployment heightened such feelings. Yet it was also clear that there was a tangible difference between feeling insecure, experiencing some loss of economic well-being, and experiencing insecurity in food or housing or other basic needs. People were coded as having "enough" to cover costs if they reported either unemployment alone, unemployment plus their savings, or unemployment plus their partner's earnings was enough to cover costs. Having "enough" to cover daily costs was the modal category, with 58 percent of respondents reporting they could cover their daily costs; 11 percent of respondents reported they had "barely enough" to cover their costs—included here are those who said they had given up many luxuries as well as some necessities to stay afloat. Finally, almost a third of respondents (31 percent) reported they had "not enough" to cover their daily costs. Those in this final category reported food scarcity, missed bills, loss of basic services, and an inability to pay for daily needs of their children.

Limitations

There are limitations to this study. First, the study does not match the United States in racial diversity, despite attempts to recruit a diverse population. This means Black, Latino, and Asian people were all under-represented, and further research is necessary to understand their experiences of unemployment. This is particularly important for Black and Latino workers who are likely to be at greater risk of unemployment than are white workers and who, research finds, experience unemployment differently than do whites.[18] This problem was likely exacerbated by the recruitment method, and while the theoretical sampling strategy helped to ensure more adequate representation across class, this was not possible for race. A second limitation is the geographic area. While the study included midsize and small cities as well as rural areas, there were no densely populated urban areas. Further study is necessary to explore how these findings might translate to areas with different occupational opportunities and constraints. Finally, although Bureau of Labor Statistics data suggests that the unemployed who find jobs quickly are in the minority, those who found jobs faster (in less than five weeks) were, in general, excluded by the sampling strategy. Further research is necessary to explore how these job seekers might differ from those in this study. Moreover, those who do not qualify for benefits were not included in the sampling strategy, which means that the sample, overall, is likely more privileged than those who are unemployed and not receiving benefits. This suggests that some of the unemployed may quickly face even more dire situations than those described by the working-class people interviewed for the book.

Interviewer Bias and Positionality

Questions of interviewer bias and positionality remain central to qualitative research. This is, perhaps, because quantitative research (with its reliance on numbers) can have a veneer of distance that is harder (even undesirable) to approximate with data that relies on face-to-face encounters. Yet all social scientists should face these challenges. I think the best way to address such challenges is to readily acknowledge that they exist. Within the interviews themselves, I worked hard to ensure that participants had the opportunity to tell their stories in their own words, respecting their silences, their refusals, and their verbosity. As a white woman with a PhD who has never experienced unemployment, there was much social distance between me and my many privileges and the people I met. This chasm allowed me to ask folks questions that made clear that I considered them the experts on their experiences. This interviewing technique can allow for greater insight and help bridge class divides.[19] But it also created a social dislocation between some of us that likely meant there were some divides I could not cross.

Race—both similarities and differences—also plays a role in interviews. There was a racial difference between myself and some of the participants and between some of my research team members and some participants. I do think that it is likely that some white participants looked at the color of my skin and assumed that they could say things about race (in particular, using racist language). As I note in the conclusion, some white participants openly spoke of the likelihood that people of color would abuse the use of government benefits, a racist trope that has been debunked yet remains persistent in its political uses. I am also sure that given the state of American race relations, my race likely acted as a barricade to some forms of disclosure from participants of color.[20] But I do think that the interview guide itself (which included questions about experiences of discrimination) may have extended some possibility of more open dialogue, as many participants of color spoke with me about their experiences of racial discrimination at work and even of their experiences with racist bosses and of discriminatory firings. I hope I have done justice to their decisions to share these experiences.

While there has been debate in recent years about the place of qualitative interviews within the social science canon, I firmly believe that, as sociology's only method whose central purpose is to highlight the voices of the people we meet, qualitative interviewing remains a central tool for understanding the social world and, particularly, for shedding light on the experiences of the marginalized and those whose voices would otherwise not be heard.[21]

Writing It Up

One of the most important questions to answer when we begin to write is how to protect participants' confidentiality. There have been recent calls to forgo this practice as it may promise more protection than can be given, thereby giving a "false sense of security," as Colin Jerolmack and Alexandra Murphy warn, while also diluting trust in the data.[22] Yet I fear that to practice qualitative interviewing without confidentiality would discourage the candor that is possible when participants feel confident that their stories will be protected. But the "ethical dilemma" remains, as the internet and other social media tools restrict the researcher's ability to maintain people's privacy. There are two primary ways of maintaining participant confidentiality: the alteration of participants' attributes and occupations (as Arlie Hochschild describes in *The Time Bind*) or the provision of less data (as Rachel Sherman does in *Uneasy Street*, choosing not to give physical details or descriptions of houses).[23] I have chosen the second path, agreeing with Mario Luis Small's assessment that too much change may obscure or distort, even unintentionally, the data that you mean to present.[24] But this means that I have had to be cautious with what identifying information I provide. To avoid the identification of a participant, I use pseudonyms for all proper names, and I do not describe locations with greater specificity than the state or general locale. Additionally, some participants had specialized occupations that might have easily revealed their identities; in these circumstances, I provided only generic occupational details, and I sometimes do not provide information on their new jobs (when a change of career might help with identification). I also provided physical descriptions only when such descriptions would not be particularly identifying. Moreover, because I interviewed participants across the state (from CareerLink centers in five counties in a state with dozens of counties that were within driving range for me and my team), there is, I hope, confidentiality to be found within the large number of unemployed in the state during the years I did the interviews.

I am, in general, a strong proponent of the use of numbers to describe findings (for example, to say about a fourth or about half of the participants, followed by the inclusion of the exact number from the sample). Following Howard Becker, I agree that "some" or "many" are terms that imply numeracy without actually giving a value that the reader can understand.[25] Yet I also appreciate the words of my editor, Meagan Levinson, who cautioned me that in a book for a general audience, it is worth thinking about how best to deploy numbers. Therefore, I have compromised by placing the "n" in the footnote for many of the findings discussed in the book. Please do note that for sociologists interested in these numbers, they are readily available in the footnotes throughout.

Finally, a word on generalizability. Kristen Luker writes that qualitative researchers should not be expected to achieve statistical generalizability to the population but to seek, instead, evidence that captures the many facets of the "phenomenon" that we wish to study in order to build theory.[26] Mario Luis Small argues that even as we acknowledge that statistical representation cannot be the goal of qualitative work, qualitative interviewing must be a central part of sociology because of what it can provide—a detailed case study of the question at hand.[27] Within this frame, Small argues we must also recognize that interview data provides one case study—we will always need more information to understand how it may fit into the national picture. In this, Small diverges from Glaser and Strauss, who argue that there can be "generalizability of scope" in the theory built from qualitative data.[28] I tend to think the power of interviewing is not in any one individual story but in the patterns we discern across the interviews; these patterns provide evidence of shared social experiences, social frames, and narratives. In turn, these patterns of shared social experiences, frames, and narratives can help us better understand the social phenomenon we seek to explain. For this book, I have tried, whenever possible, to include studies based on national data (including the work I do with Adrianne Frech) to help situate my findings within the broader field. I also tend to expect, as did Glaser and Strauss, that these findings may expand our understanding of the unemployment process until such a time comes for future scholars to refine, reconsider, or even refute them. Until that day, it is my hope that a carefully constructed research design may provide the foundation for a better understanding of the lived experiences of those who have experienced unemployment and for the need for better policies.

NOTES

Preface

1. Therese Thau Heyman, Sandra S. Phillips, and John Szarkowski, *Dorothea Lange: American Photographs* (San Francisco: Chronicle Books, 1994).

Introduction

1. Tracy's name and all of the names in the book are pseudonyms to protect the confidentiality of the people who participated in the research. Specific towns are left unnamed for the same reason. Small details have been omitted to further protect the confidentiality of those interviewed, but the stories of their lives are described as they told them to me. All direct quotes are in their words, and anything that is attributed to them stems directly from their own words in the interviews (e.g., if I write "she thought," it is because in the interview the person said, "I thought to myself").

2. Sarah Damaske, *For the Family? How Class and Gender Shape Women's Work* (New York: Oxford University Press, 2011).

3. For exceptions on gender comparisons, see Phyllis Moen, "Family Impacts of the 1975 Recession: Duration of Unemployment," *Journal of Marriage and Family* 41, no. 3 (1979): 561–72; Karen Davies and Johanna Esseveld, "Factory Women, Redundancy, and the Search for Work: Toward a Reconceptualisation of Employment and Unemployment," *Sociological Review* 37, no. 2 (1989): 219–52; Roberta Spalter-Roth and Cynthia Deitch, "'I Don't Feel Right Sized; I Feel Out-of-Work Sized': Gender, Race, Ethnicity, and the Unequal Costs of Displacement," *Work and Occupations* 26, no. 4 (1999): 446–82. Since I started my research, more work has been published explicitly comparing men's and women's unemployment experiences, although most others (Lane 2011; Sharone 2013) have not had gender as a central focus. Williams (2018), Rao (2020), and Norris (2016) are recent exceptions, and their findings will be considered in future chapters. Similarly, in chapter 5, I will extend Gough and Killewald's (2011) quantitative findings on household labor after a job loss. There remains, to my knowledge, a lacuna in the literature comparing gender and class differences in unemployment. See Carrie M. Lane, *A Company of One: Insecurity, Independence, and the New World of White-Collar Unemployment* (Ithaca, NY: Cornell University Press, 2011); Ofer Sharone, *Flawed System/Flawed Self: Job Searching and Unemployment Experiences* (Chicago: University of Chicago Press, 2013); Christine Williams, "The Gender of Layoffs in the Oil and Gas Industry," in *Precarious Work*, Vol. 31, ed. Arne L. Kalleberg and S. P. Vallas (Bingley, UK: Emerald Publishing, 2018), 215–41; Aliya Hamid Rao,

Crunch Time: How Married Couples Confront Unemployment (Oakland: University of California Press, 2020). Dawn R. Norris, *Job Loss, Identity, and Mental Health* (New Brunswick, NJ: Rutgers University Press, 2016); and Margaret Gough and Alexandra Killewald, "Unemployment in Families: The Case of Housework," *Journal of Marriage and Family* 73, no. 5 (2011): 1085–100.

4. Additional details are provided in the methodological appendix.

5. Of the 100 people interviewed, the majority (63) were married, with another 17 cohabiting; 20 were single. Most (84) had children under the age of 23 who lived in the household and were being supported. While we typically think of adulthood beginning at age 18, as most parents these days know, parents financially support their children long after. Since all of the children who still lived with their parents depended on their parents (rather than the other way around), I consider those under the age of 23 as dependents.

6. Of the 100 people interviewed, 56 were working class while 44 were middle class. I discuss class in depth in the methodology appendix.

7. While most people interviewed had been jobless for ten to twelve weeks, the full range extended from two to forty weeks. Generally, the distinction between the unemployed and the not employed is thought to be clear—those who are unemployed are seeking work while the not employed are not looking for work. The not employed include (among others) those who are in school, are disabled, are taking care of someone else (a child or a parent), or are otherwise engaged in an activity that prevents them from seeking work. Some people fall into the not employed category after a long period of seeking work and not finding it and giving up their job search; they are considered discouraged workers and are not counted among the unemployed, although most would take work if they could find it. Those in this study further blur the line between the employed and not employed, because some of them collected unemployment but were not actively seeking work, as we will see in later chapters. According to data from the Bureau of Labor Statistics for the years 2013 to 2015, 22 to 28 percent of the unemployed spent fewer than five weeks unemployed during those three years, between 24 and 27 percent spent five to fourteen weeks unemployed, and the modal category was over twenty-seven weeks unemployed. See Bureau of Labor Statistics, "Table A-12. Unemployed Persons by Duration of Unemployment," data retrieval: Labor Force Statistics (Current Population Survey), 2015.

8. Eduardo Bonilla-Silva, *Racism without Racists: Color-Blind Racism and the Persistence of Racial Inequality in the United States* (Plymouth, UK: Rowman & Littlefield, 2006); Devah Pager and Hana Shepherd, "The Sociology of Discrimination: Racial Discrimination in Employment, Housing, Credit, and Consumer Markets," *Annual Review of Sociology* 34, no. 1 (2008): 181–209; Louise Seamster and Victor Ray, "Against Teleology in the Study of Race: Toward the Abolition of the Progress Paradigm," *Sociological Theory* 36, no. 4 (2018): 315–42. Victor Ray, "A Theory of Racialized Organizations," *American Sociological Review* 84, no. 1 (2019): 26–53; Deadric T. Williams, "A Call to Focus on Racial Domination and Oppression: A Response to "Racial and Ethnic Inequality in Poverty and Affluence, 1959–2015.'" *Population Research and Policy Review* 38, no. 5 (2019): 655–63; Adia Harvey Wingfield, *Flatlining: Race, Work, and Health Care in the New Economy*, 1st ed. (Oakland: University of California Press, 2019).

9. Ryan Light, Vincent J. Roscigno, and Alexandra Kalev, "Racial Discrimination, Interpretation, and Legitimation at Work," *The Annals of the American Academy of Political and Social Science* 634, no. 1 (2011): 39–59.

10. Alexandra Kalev, "How You Downsize Is Who You Downsize: Biased Formalization, Accountability, and Managerial Diversity," *American Sociological Review* 79, no. 1 (2014): 109–35.

11. Dalton Conley, *Being Black, Living in the Red: Race, Wealth, and Social Policy in America* (Berkeley: University of California Press, 1999); Keeanga-Yamahtta Taylor, *Race for Profit: How Banks and the Real Estate Industry Undermined Black Homeownership* (Chapel Hill, NC: UNC Press Books, 2019).

12. Deirdre A. Royster, *Race and the Invisible Hand: How White Networks Exclude Black Men from Blue-Collar Jobs* (Berkeley: University of California Press, 2003).

13. Royster 2003; Sandra Susan Smith, *Lone Pursuit: Distrust and Defensive Individualism among the Black Poor* (New York: Russell Sage Foundation, 2007); Adia Harvey Wingfield, *No More Invisible Man: Race and Gender in Men's Work* (Philadelphia: Temple University Press, 2013).

14. Shannon Gleeson and Roberto G. Gonzales, "When Do Papers Matter? An Institutional Analysis of Undocumented Life in the United States," *International Migration* 50, no. 4 (2012): 1–19; Robert D. Mare, 2001. "Observations on the Study of Social Mobility and Inequality," in *Social Stratification: Class, Race, and Gender in Sociological Perspective*, 2nd ed., ed. David B. Grusky (Boulder, CO: Westview Press), 477–88; Mario Luis Small, "Neighborhood Institutions as Resource Brokers: Childcare Centers, Interorganizational Ties, and Resource Access among the Poor," *Social Problems* 53, no. 2 (2006): 274–92.

15. Sarah Damaske and Adrianne Frech, "The Life Course of Unemployment: The Timing, Frequency, and Level of Risk for Baby Boomers," in progress; Mark Robert Rank, Thomas A. Hirschl, and Kirk A. Foster, *Chasing the American Dream: Understanding What Shapes Our Fortunes* (New York: Oxford University Press, 2014).

16. Jennie E. Brand, "The Far-Reaching Impact of Job Loss and Unemployment," *Annual Review of Sociology* 41, no. 1 (2015): 359–75; Esteban Calvo, Christine A. Mair, and Natalia Sarkisian, "Individual Troubles, Shared Troubles: The Multiplicative Effect of Individual and Country-Level Unemployment on Life Satisfaction in 95 Nations (1981–2009)," *Social Forces* 93, no. 4 (2015): 1625–53; Markus Gangl, "Scar Effects of Unemployment: An Assessment of Institutional Complementarities," *American Sociological Review* 71, no. 6 (2006): 986–1013; Kate W. Strully, "Job Loss and Health in the U.S. Labor Market," *Demography* 46, no. 2 (2009): 221–46.

17. Carrie M. Lane, "Man Enough to Let My Wife Support Me: How Changing Models of Career and Gender Are Reshaping the Experience of Unemployment," *American Ethnologist* 36 (2009): 681–92; Katherine S. Newman, *Falling from Grace: The Experience of Downward Mobility in the American Middle Class* (New York: Free Press, 1988); Norris 2016; Sharone 2013.

18. Nicholas W. Townsend, *The Package Deal: Marriage, Work, and Fatherhood in Men's Lives* (Philadelphia: Temple University Press, 2002); William Hollingsworth Whyte, *The Organization Man* (New York: Simon and Schuster, 1956).

19. Wingfield 2013; Kevin Stainback and Donald Tomaskovic-Devey, *Documenting Desegregation: Racial and Gender Segregation in Private Sector Employment since the Civil Rights Act* (New York: Russell Sage Foundation, 2012); Ray 2019.

20. Lauren A. Rivera, *Pedigree: How Elite Students Get Elite Jobs* (Princeton, NJ: Princeton University Press, 2016).

21. Rivera 2016; Adia Harvey Wingfield, "Racializing the Glass Escalator: Reconsidering Men's Experiences with Women's Work," *Gender & Society* 23, no. 1 (2009): 5–26; Wingfield 2013; Smith 2007.

22. Annette Lareau discusses the role of class and race in shaping people's life chances, despite their inability to see such advantage, and Eduardo Bonilla-Silva discusses how an insistence on "color-blindness" reinforces the privileges that whites have access to. Bonilla-Silva 2006; Annette Lareau, *Unequal Childhoods: Class, Race, and Family Life* (Berkeley: University of California Press, 2003).

Chapter One: Job Loss in the Twenty-First Century

1. Commonly known as a "bull market," this streak represents a steady upward rise of the market from its low point in March 2009. A. Shell, "Bull Market, on Cusp of Becoming Longest in History for Stocks, Has Room to Run," *USA TODAY*, August 21, 2018.

2. Bureau of Labor Statistics, "State Employment and Unemployment (Monthly) News Release," January 24, 2020b, https://www.bls.gov/news.release/archives/laus_01242020.htm.

3. Corporate profits had averaged 6.5 percent a year since 2009, with some banks reporting nearly double that rate. Patricia Cohen, "Paychecks Lag as Profits Soar, and Prices Erode Wage Gains," *New York Times*, July 14, 2018; Bureau of Labor Statistics, "Displaced Workers Summary: 2015–17," news release, August 28, 2018b; Bureau of Labor Statistics, "Worker Displacement: 2013–15," news release, August 25, 2016; Bureau of Labor Statistics, "Worker Displacement: 2011–13," news release, August 26, 2014; Bureau of Labor Statistics, "The Employment Situation— August 2018," news release, September 7, 2018c; H. S. Farber, "Job Loss in the Great Recession: Historical Perspective from the Displaced Workers Survey, 1984–2010," NBER Working Paper No. 17040, May 2011; Bureau of Labor Statistics, "Alternative Measures of Labor Underutilization for States," Local Area Unemployment Statistics, 2018a.

4. Matissa Hollister, "Employment Stability in the U.S. Labor Market: Rhetoric versus Reality," *Annual Review of Sociology* 37, no. 1 (2011): 305–24.

5. Arne L. Kalleberg, "Precarious Work, Insecure Workers: Employment Relations in Transition," *American Sociological Review* 74, no. 1 (2009): 1–22.

6. Anat Shenker-Osorio, "Why Americans All Believe They Are 'Middle Class,'" *The Atlantic*, August 1, 2013; Emmie Martin, "70% of Americans Consider Themselves Middle Class but Only 50% Are," *CNBC.com*, June 30, 2017; Richard Reeves, interview by Hari Sreenivasan, "How the Upper Middle Class Keeps Everyone Else Out," *PBS NewsHour*, August 5, 2017.

7. Reeve Vanneman with Lynn Cannon, *The American Perception of Class* (Philadelphia: Temple University Press, 1987).

8. Philip N. Cohen, "New Data Show Change in the Class (Identity) Structure," *Family Inequality*, April 25, 2017.

9. Jennie E. Brand and Yu Xie, "Who Benefits Most from College? Evidence for Negative Selection in Heterogeneous Economic Returns to Higher Education," *American Sociological Review* 75, no. 2 (2010): 273–302.

10. Lawrence Mishel et al., *The State of Working America* (Ithaca, NY: Cornell University Press, 2012); Christine Percheski, "Opting Out? Cohort Differences in Professional Women's

Employment Rates from 1960 to 2005," *American Sociological Review* 73, no. 3 (2008): 497–517.

11. Mark D. Hayward and Bridget Gorman, "The Long Arm of Childhood: The Influence of Early Life Conditions on Men's Mortality, *Demography* 41 (2004): 87–108; Jennifer K. Montez and Mark D. Hayward, "Cumulative Childhood Adversity, Educational Attainment, and Active Life Expectancy among U.S. Adults," *Demography* 51 (2014): 413–35; Yang Yang, "Social Inequalities in Happiness in the United States, 1972 to 2004: An Age-Period-Cohort Analysis," *American Sociological Review* 73, no. 2 (2008): 204–26.

12. Richard Arum, Josipa Roksa, and Michelle Budig, "The Romance of College Attendance: Higher Education, Stratification, and Mate Selection," *Research in Social Stratification and Mobility* 26, no. 2 (2008): 107–21.

13. Arum, Roksa, and Budig, 2008; Karly Sarita Ford, "Marrying within the Alma Mater: Understanding the Role of Same-University Marriages in Educational Homogamy," *Sociological Research Online*, August 28, 2019.

14. Christine R. Schwartz, "Trends and Variation in Assortative Mating: Causes and Consequences," *Annual Review of Sociology* 39, no. 1 (2013): 451–70.

15. Sara McLanahan and Christine Percheski, "Family Structure and the Reproduction of Inequalities," *Annual Review of Sociology* 34, no. 1 (2008): 257–76; Megan M. Sweeney, "Two Decades of Family Change: The Shifting Economic Foundations of Marriage," *American Sociological Review* 67, no. 1 (February 2002): 132–47; Léa Pessin, "Changing Gender Norms and Marriage Dynamics in the United States," *Journal of Marriage and Family* 80, no. 1 (2018): 25–41.

16. Jessica McCrory Calarco, *Negotiating Opportunities: How the Middle Class Secures Advantages in School* (New York: Oxford University Press, 2018).

17. Arindrajit Dube, "The Importance of an Expanded U.S. Unemployment Insurance System during the Coronavirus Recession," *Washington Center for Equitable Growth*, March 31, 2020.

18. Alix Gould-Werth, "Fool Me Once: Investing in Unemployment Insurance Systems to Avoid the Mistakes of the Great Recession during COVID-19," *Washington Center for Equitable Growth*, April 30, 2020.

19. Pennsylvania quarterly earnings benefits charts can be found at the official Pennsylvania website, Office of Unemployment Compensation, https://www.uc.pa.gov/unemployment-benefits/Am-I-Eligible/financial-charts/Pages/default.aspx.

20. Before the Great Recession, all states offered at least twenty-six weeks of unemployment insurance (UI). Since 2011, there have been deep cuts to UI in most states. See Rick McHugh and Will Kimball, "How Low Can We Go? State Unemployment Insurance Programs Exclude Record Numbers of Jobless Workers," Briefing Paper No. 392, Economic Policy Institute, 2015; Dube, 2020.

21. Jesse Rothstein and Robert G. Valletta, "Scraping by: Income and Program Participation after the Loss of Extended Unemployment Benefits," *Journal of Policy Analysis and Management* 36, no. 4 (2017): 880–908.

22. See the Pennsylvania Work Search/Work Registration FAQs, https://www.uc.pa.gov/faq/claimant/Pages/Work-Search-Work-Registration-FAQS.aspx.

23. It may not have helped Joan if she and her husband had had an egalitarian commitment, because such couples also face bigger challenges after a job loss. See Stephen Sweet and Phyllis

Moen, "Dual Earners Preparing for Job Loss: Agency, Linked Lives, and Resilience," *Work and Occupations* 39, no. 1 (2012): 35–70.

24. Gender scholars have long argued that there isn't anything "biologically" different between men and women that teaches women to wear their hair long and men to wear theirs short (in fact, if you look around the next crowded room you are in after you read this, you will probably see that, on average, women wear their hair longer but that many women have short hair and that some men have longer hair). This is what gender scholars think of as a social difference—something that we learn to do differently and that we have to continue to do differently in order to maintain this gender difference. Gender scholars Candace West and Don Zimmerman call this "doing gender." In the frantic rush to get ourselves ready and get our kid out of bed and off to the bus on time, my husband and I share many of the same tasks—we share the jobs of helping her get dressed, of getting her breakfast, of making her snack, of helping her get out the door—and in doing so, we do what Barbara Risman has called "undoing gender." We take tasks that used to belong just to moms and we say that anyone in the household can be responsible for these tasks. But as we rush around trying to get ready before she is awake for the day, and I put on my makeup and we choose clothes that look radically different from one another (from closets that are not shared), so we also continue to "do gender" in ways emphasize our differences rather than our similarities. See Candace West and Don H. Zimmerman, "Doing Gender." *Gender & Society* 1, no. 2 (1987):125–51; Barbara J. Risman, "From Doing to Undoing: Gender as We Know It," *Gender & Society* 23, no. 1 (2009): 81–84.

25. Cecilia L. Ridgeway, *Framed by Gender: How Gender Inequality Persists in the Modern World* (New York: Oxford University Press, 2011).

26. Cecilia L. Ridgeway and Shelley J. Correll, "Unpacking the Gender System: A Theoretical Perspective on Gender Beliefs and Social Relations," *Gender & Society* 18, no. 4 (2004): 510–31; Barbara J. Risman, Maxine P. Atkinson, and Stephen P. Blackwelder, "Understanding the Juggling Act: Gendered Preferences and Social Structural Constraints," *Sociological Forum* 14, no. 2 (1999): 319–44.

27. Pamela Stone, *Opting Out? Why Women Really Quit Careers and Head Home* (Berkeley: University of California Press, 2007); Marianne Cooper, "Being the 'Go-to Guy': Fatherhood, Masculinity, and the Organization of Work in Silicon Valley," *Qualitative Sociology* 23, no. 4 (2000): 379–405.

28. Ridgeway and Correll 2004.

29. As I said above, men's unemployment was higher during the Great Recession, while women's was higher after the recession had officially ended. Lawrence Mishel, Josh Bivens, Elise Gould, and Heidi Shierholz, *The State of Working America* (Ithaca, NY: ILR Press, 2012).

30. In one of the few studies that looks at these issues, Spalter-Roth and Deitch (1999) use the 1996 Displaced Worker Survey to find that there appears to be a "queue" according to which displaced workers are hired back: This queue has white men at the front of the line while white women are disadvantaged by their gender, Black men are disadvantaged by their race with no gender advantage, Hispanic men are disadvantaged by race but do have a gender advantage, and Black and Hispanic women face both race and gender disadvantage. See also Davies and Esseveld (1989) and Moen (1983).

31. Barbara F. Reskin and Michelle L. Maroto, "What Trends? Whose Choices? Comment on England," *Gender & Society* 25, no. 1 (2011): 81–87.

32. Sarah Damaske and Adrianne Frech, "Women's Work Pathways across the Life Course," *Demography* 53, no. 2 (2016): 365–91; Phyllis Moen and Patricia Roehling, *The Career Mystique: Cracks in the American Dream* (Lanham, MD: Rowman & Littlefield, 2005).

33. Michelle J. Budig, "Male Advantage and the Gender Composition of Jobs: Who Rides the Glass Escalator?," *Social Problems* 49, no. 2 (2002): 258–77.

34. Suzanne M. Bianchi, John P. Robinson, and Melissa A. Milkie, *Changing Rhythms of American Family Life* (New York: Russell Sage Foundation, 2006).

35. Stone 2007; Youngjoo Cha, "Reinforcing Separate Spheres," *American Sociological Review* 75, no. 2 (2010): 303–29.

36. Stone 2007; Joan Williams, *Unbending Gender: Why Family and Work Conflict and What to Do about It* (New York: Oxford University Press, 2000); Damaske and Frech 2016; Tania Cabello-Hutt, "Changes in Work and Care Trajectories during the Transition to Motherhood," *Social Science Research* 90 (2020); Katherine Weisshaar and Tania Cabello-Hutt, "Labor Force Participation over the Life Course: The Long-Term Effects of Employment Trajectories on Wages and the Gendered Payoff to Employment," *Demography* 57, no. 1 (2020): 33–60.

37. Daniel L. Carlson, Amanda Jayne Miller, and Sharon Sassler, "Stalled for Whom? Change in the Division of Particular Housework Tasks and Their Consequences for Middle-to Low-Income Couples," *Socius: Sociological Research for a Dynamic World* 4 (2018): 1–17. Caitlyn Collins, *Making Motherhood Work: How Women Manage Careers and Caregiving* (Princeton, NJ: Princeton University Press, 2019); Kathleen Gerson, *The Unfinished Revolution: How a New Generation Is Reshaping Family, Work, and Gender in America* (New York: Oxford University Press, 2010); Amanda J. Miller, Daniel L. Carlson, and Sharon Sassler, "His Career, Her Job, Their Future: Cohabitors' Orientations toward Paid Work," *Journal of Family Issues* 40, no. 11 (2019): 1509–33; Joanna R. Pepin and David A. Cotter, "Separating Spheres? Diverging Trends in Youth's Gender Attitudes about Work and Family," *Journal of Marriage and Family* 80, no. 1 (2018): 7–24.

38. Damaske 2011.

39. Enobong Branch, *Opportunity Denied: Limiting Black Women to Devalued Work* (New Brunswick, NJ: Rutgers University Press, 2011); Elizabeth Higginbotham, *Too Much to Ask: Black Women in the Era of Integration* (Chapel Hill: University of North Carolina Press, 2001); Rebecca Glauber, "Race and Gender in Families and at Work," *Gender & Society* 22, no. 1 (2008): 8–30.

40. Noelle Chesley, "Stay-at-Home Fathers and Breadwinning Mothers," *Gender & Society* 25, no. 5 (2011): 642–64.

41. Damaske 2011.

42. Damaske 2011.

43. Stephanie Coontz, "Why the White Working Class Ditched Clinton," CNN, November 11, 2016.

44. Percheski 2008; Liana Christin Landivar, *Mothers at Work: Who Opts Out?* (Boulder, CO: Lynne Rienner, 2017).

45. Damaske 2011, 145.

46. Margaret K. Nelson and Joan Smith, *Working Hard and Making Do: Surviving in Small Town America* (Berkeley: University of California Press, 1999).

47. Damaske 2011; Philip N. Cohen, "Replacing Housework in the Service Economy: Gender, Class, and Race-Ethnicity in Service Spending," *Gender & Society* 12, no. 2 (1998): 219–31.

48. Arne L. Kalleberg, *Good Jobs, Bad Jobs: The Rise of Polarized and Precarious Employment Systems in the United States, 1970s–2000s* (New York: Russell Sage Foundation, 2011).

49. Silke Aisenbrey and Anette Fasang, "The Interplay of Work and Family Trajectories over the Life Course: Germany and the United States in Comparison," *American Journal of Sociology* 122, no. 5 (2017): 1448–84.

50. M. J. Hill et al., *Men Out of Work: A Study of Unemployment in Three English Towns* (Cambridge: Cambridge University Press, 1973).

51. Carl Hulse, "Jobless Aid Fuels Partisan Divide over Next Pandemic Rescue Package," *New York Times*, May 7, 2020.

52. Baron William Henry Beveridge, *Unemployment: A Problem of Industry* (London: Longmans, Green, 1912).

53. Raj Chetty, "Moral Hazard versus Liquidity and Optimal Unemployment Insurance," *Journal of Political Economy* 116, no. 2 (2008): 173–234; Ammar Farooq, Adriana D. Kugler, and Umberto Muratori. 2020. "Do Unemployment Insurance Benefits Improve Match Quality? Evidence from Recent U.S. Recessions," NBER Working Paper No. 27574, 2020.

54. Victor Tan Chen, *Cut Loose: Jobless and Hopeless in an Unfair Economy* (Oakland: University of California Press, 2015).

55. Chen 2015; Sharone 2013; Townsend 2002.

56. Carla Shows and Naomi Gerstel, "Fathering, Class, and Gender: A Comparison of Physicians and Emergency Medical Technicians," *Gender & Society* 23, no. 2 (2009): 161–87.

57. Gokce Basbug and Ofer Sharone, "The Emotional Toll of Long-Term Unemployment: Examining the Interaction Effects of Gender and Marital Status," *RSF: The Russell Sage Foundation Journal of the Social Sciences* 3, no. 3 (2017): 222–44.

58. Aliya Hamid Rao, "Stand by Your Man: Wives' Emotion Work during Men's Unemployment," *Journal of Marriage and Family* 79, no. 3 (2017): 636–56.

59. Andrea E. Zuelke et al., "The Association between Unemployment and Depression-Results from the Population-Based LIFE-Adult-Study," *Journal of Affective Disorders* 235 (2018): 399–406; Newman 1988.

60. Brand 2015; Chen 2015.

Chapter Two: The Paths to Job Loss

1. Life course scholars have long argued that what happens early in one's life can have a lasting influence later in one's life (Elder 1998; Dannefer 2003). My first book also followed this frame (Damaske 2011). This may be particularly true for job loss and unemployment, where one job loss may beget another or where the particular timing of a job loss may have lasting implications across the life course. There are also gendered dimensions to these timings, as men and women may have different access to jobs and to different family responsibilities, which may further shape the paths they take (Moen 2001). See G. H. Elder Jr., "The Life Course as

Developmental Theory," *Child Development* 69, no. 1 (1998): 1–12; Dale Dannefer, "Cumulative Advantage/Disadvantage and the Life Course: Cross-Fertilizing Age and Social Science Theory," *Journals of Gerontology Series B: Psychological Sciences and Social Sciences* 58, no. 6 (2003): S327–37; Phyllis Moen, "The Gendered Life Course," in *Handbook of Aging and the Social Sciences*, ed. L. George and R. Binstock (San Diego: Academic Press, 2001), 179–96.

2. Most of the unemployment literature remains focused on cross-sectional data rather than on longitudinal approaches to job loss. There are some important exceptions, although they tend to examine the lasting effects of job loss rather than the processes that led people to their job loss in the first place. For long-term effects of job loss, see David Dooley, Joann Prause, and Kathleen Ham-Rowbottom, "Underemployment and Depression: Longitudinal Relationships," *Journal of Health and Social Behavior* 41, no. 4 (2000): 421–36. For a discussion of the effects of multiple job displacement, which comes closer to a life course approach but still does not quite capture one, see Ann Huff Stevens, "Persistent Effects of Job Displacement: The Importance of Multiple Job Losses," *Journal of Labor Economics* 15, no. 1 (1997): 165–88.

3. National Center for Education Statistics, "Fast Facts: Teacher Characteristics and Trends," 2020.

4. Bureau of Labor Statistics, "Nursing Assistants and Orderlies," *Occupational Outlook Handbook*, accessed April 10, 2020.

5. Dan Clawson and Naomi Gerstel, *Unequal Time: Gender, Class, and Family in Employment Schedules* (New York: Russell Sage Foundation, 2014).

6. Kate W. Strully, "Job Loss and Health in the U.S. Labor Market," *Demography* 46, no. 2 (2009): 221–46.

7. Jennie E. Brand, "The Effects of Job Displacement on Job Quality: Findings from the Wisconsin Longitudinal Study," *Research in Social Stratification and Mobility* 24, no. 3 (2006): 275–98; Henry S. Farber, "What Do We Know about Job Loss in the United States? Evidence from the Displaced Workers Survey, 1984–2004," *Economic Perspectives* 29, no. 2 (2005): 13–29; Michael Hout, Asaf Levanon, and Erin Cumberworth, "Job Loss and Unemployment," in *The Great Recession* (New York: Russell Sage Foundation, 2011), 59–81.

8. Kalleberg 2011.

9. Susan J. Lambert and Julia R. Henly, "Frontline Managers Matter: Labour Flexibility Practices and Sustained Employment in U.S. Retail Jobs," in *Are Bad Jobs Inevitable? Trends, Determinants, and Responses to Job Quality in the Twenty-First Century* (New York: Macmillan International Higher Education, 2012), 143–59; Susan J., Lambert, Anna Haley-Lock, and Julia R. Henly, "Schedule Flexibility in Hourly Jobs: Unanticipated Consequences and Promising Directions," *Community, Work & Family* 15, no. 3 (2012): 293–315; Daniel Schneider and Kristen Harknett, "Consequences of Routine Work-Schedule Instability for Worker Health and Well-Being," *American Sociological Review* 84, no. 1 (2019): 82–114.

10. Building on Moen and Roehling's "lockstep lives" concept, in which they argue that in times past, workers could expect to work for a small number of companies over the course of their career, I borrow their term to refer to those who have had had three or fewer employers over their work history and had experienced no more than two job losses—the vast majority of the lockstep workers had experienced only this first one. See Phyllis Moen and Patricia Roehling, *The Career Mystique: Cracks in the American Dream* (Lanham, MD: Rowman & Littlefield, 2005).

11. Eight middle-class women (n = 18), ten working-class women (n = 31), eight middle-class men (n = 26), and six working-class men (n = 25) took the lockstep path.

12. This term is used to encapsulate workers who experience multiple transitions with different employers. See Sarah E. Patterson, Sarah Damaske, and Christen Sheroff, "Gender and the MBA: Differences in Career Trajectories, Institutional Support, and Outcomes," *Gender & Society* 31, no. 3 (2017): 310–32.

13. Eight middle-class women (n = 18), 15 working-class women (n = 31), ten middle-class men (n = 26), and eight working-class men (n = 25).

14. Two middle-class women (n = 18), seven working-class women (n = 31), eight middle-class men (n = 26), 11 working-class men (n = 25).

15. Damaske and Frech, in progress.

16. Jennie E. Brand and Sarah A. Burgard, "Job Displacement and Social Participation over the Lifecourse: Findings for a Cohort of Joiners," *Social Forces* 87, no. 1 (2008): 211–42.

17. Patterson, Damaske, and Sheroff 2017.

18. Peter Marsden, Arne L. Kalleberg, and Cynthia R. Cook. 1993. "Gender Differences in Organizational Commitment: Influences of Work Positions and Family Roles," *Work and Occupations* 20, no. 3 (1993): 368–90.

19. Alfonso Sousa-Poza and Andrés A. Sousa-Poza, "The Effect of Job Satisfaction on Labor Turnover by Gender: An Analysis for Switzerland," *Journal of Socio-Economics* 36, no. 6 (2007): 895–913.

20. Jonathan F. Pingle, "The Relocation Decisions of Working Couples," FEDS Working Paper No. 2006-33, 2006.

21. Elizabeth Anne Whitaker, "Moving On to Stay Put," in *Beyond the Cubicle: Job Insecurity, Intimacy, and the Flexible Self* (New York: Oxford University Press, 2016), 203–28.

22. Alison L. Booth and Marco Francesconi, "Job Mobility in 1990s Britain: Does Gender Matter?," *Research in Labor Economics* 19 (2000):173–89.

23. Bureau of Labor Statistics, "Number of Jobs, Labor Market Experience, and Earnings Growth: Results from a National Longitudinal Survey," news release, August 22, 2019c.

24. U.S. Department of Labor, "Family and Medical Leave (FMLA)," accessed August 22, 2019, https://www.dol.gov/general/topic/benefits-leave/fmla.

25. U.S. Equal Employment Opportunity Commission, "Facts about Pregnancy Discrimination," accessed September 16, 2019, https://www.eeoc.gov/eeoc/publications/fs-preg.cfm; Reginald A. Byron and Vincent J. Roscigno, "Relational Power, Legitimation, and Pregnancy Discrimination," *Gender & Society* 28, no. 3 (2014): 435–62.

26. This observation echoed what my colleagues and I found in our MBA study; see Patterson, Damaske, and Sheroff 2017.

27. Townsend 2002.

28. Cooper 2000.

29. Brand 2015.

30. Allison J. Pugh, *The Tumbleweed Society: Working and Caring in an Age of Insecurity* (New York: Oxford University Press, 2015); Adrianne Frech, Jane Lankes, and Sarah Damaske, "The Myth of Men's Stable, Continuous Labor Force Attachment: Multi-trajectories of U.S. Baby-Boomer Men's Employment," in progress.

31. Damaske and Frech, in progress.

32. When we look at only the full-time workers and compare men and women, we confirm that men are significantly at higher risk than women of experiencing high levels of unemployment from their midtwenties until middle age.

33. These analyzes use what the U.S. Bureau of Labor Statistics calls the "major occupation categories." Looking at these categories, I saw in that in eight of them, women made up no more than one-fifth of the workers (and often far fewer), and in two additional categories they made up less than one-third. In eight other categories, men made up none of the workers (that's right—*no* men worked in eight of the categories where women were represented); and in two more categories, men made up barely a third. In other words, even in my small sample, men's and women's occupations rarely overlapped. Smith (2001) had similar findings. Vicki Smith, *Crossing the Great Divide: Worker Risk and Opportunity in the New Economy* (Ithaca, NY: Cornell University Press, 2002).

34. Mishel et al. 2012; Hout, Levanon, and Cumberworth 2011.

35. Paula England, "The Gender Revolution: Uneven and Stalled," *Gender & Society* 24, no. 2 (2010): 149–66.

36. Devah Pager, *Marked: Race, Crime, and Finding Work in an Era of Mass Incarceration* (Chicago: University of Chicago Press, 2008); Ray 2019, 27; Rivera 2016; Royster 2003; Donald Tomaskovic-Devey, Melvin Thomas, and Kecia Johnson, "Race and the Accumulation of Human Capital across the Career: A Theoretical Model and Fixed-Effects Application," *American Journal of Sociology* 111, no 1 (2005): 58–89.

37. Brand 2015; Amon Emeka, "Where Race Matters Most: Measuring the Strength of Association between Race and Unemployment across the 50 United States," *Social Indicators Research* 136, no. 2 (2018): 557–73.

Chapter Three: The Ax Falls

1. William J. Baumol, Alan S. Blinder, and Edward N. Wolff. *Downsizing in America: Reality, Causes, and Consequences* (New York: Russell Sage Foundation, 2003).

2. Some, but not all, of these terms can also refer to those fired "for cause." See the Bureau of Labor Statistics Glossary, https://www.bls.gov/bls/glossary.htm.

3. Kalleberg 2011.

4. Jacob Hacker, *The Great Risk Shift: Why American Jobs, Families, Health Care, and Retirement Aren't Secure—and How We Can Fight Back* (New York: Oxford University Press, 2006).

5. Kalleberg 2011; Heather Boushey, *Finding Time: The Economics of Work-Life-Conflict* (Cambridge, MA: Harvard University Press, 2016).

6. Ofer Sharone (2013) argues that in America, after an initial period of frustration, many of the long-term unemployed come to blame themselves for being out of work.

7. Katherine Newman also found evidence that severances eased hurt feelings, although she did not have cross-class and gender data to examine. Newman 1988.

8. Newman 1988; Sharone 2013; Lane 2011; Norris 2016.

9. For a great introductory discussion of this issue, see Boushey 2016.

10. Kalleberg 2011.

11. Heather Boushey and Sarah Jane Glynn, *There Are Significant Business Costs to Replacing Employees* (Washington, DC: Center for American Progress, 2012).

12. Rosemary Batt and Alexander J. S. Colvin, "An Employment Systems Approach to Turnover: Human Resources Practices, Quits, Dismissals, and Performance," *Academy of Management Journal* 54, no. 4 (2011): 695–717.

13. You may wonder, if firing people is so expensive, why haven't companies caught on and started trying to reduce costs in other ways? A review article written only a few years ago says professors in business schools until very recently relied on outdated assumptions that firing people was always good for business and only started questioning this logic very recently. See Tae-youn Park and Jason D. Shaw, "Turnover Rates and Organizational Performance: A Meta-Analysis," *Journal of Applied Psychology* 98, no. 2 (2013): 268–309; Deepak K. Datta et al., "Causes and Effects of Employee Downsizing: A Review and Synthesis," *Journal of Management* 36, no. 1 (2010): 281–348.

14. "Compare Your Country: Employment Protection Legislation," n.d.

15. Montana's Wrongful Discharge from Employment Act gives employees—after they meet a threshold requirement—just cause protection, although it also has limits on their recoverable damages. American Law Institute, *Restatement of the Law, Second, Contracts 2d*. Rev. and enl. (Washington, DC: American Law Institute, 2015).

16. Directorate General Employment, Social Affairs, and Equal Opportunities, *Termination of Employment Relationships: Legal Situation in the Member States of the European Union* (Brussels: European Commission, 2006).

17. The Federal Worker Adjustment and Retraining Notification Act does require that employers inform employees of impending mass layoffs (i.e., fifty or more people to lose a job from a single location), but there are so many loopholes to this law (including natural disasters, as many employees learned during the Covid-19 pandemic layoffs) that they protect few workers. See U.S Department of Labor, "WARN Act Compliance Assistance," accessed July 16, 2020 https://www.dol.gov/agencies/eta/layoffs/warn.

18. Norris 2016.

19. Stainback and Tomaskovic-Devey 2012.

20. Sherry N. Mong and Vincent J. Roscigno, "African American Men and the Experience of Employment Discrimination," *Qualitative Sociology* 33, no. 1 (2010): 1–21; Light, Roscigno, and Kalev 2011.

21. Vincent J. Roscigno, Lisa M. Williams, and Reginald A. Byron, "Workplace Racial Discrimination and Middle Class Vulnerability," *American Behavioral Scientist* 56, no. 5 (2012): 696–710.

22. Louwanda Evans, *Cabin Pressure: African American Pilots, Flight Attendants, and Emotional Labor* (Lanham, MD: Rowman & Littlefield, 2013); Louwanda Evans and Wendy Leo Moore, "Impossible Burdens: White Institutions, Emotional Labor, and Micro-Resistance," *Social Problems* 62, no. 3 (2015): 439–54.

23. George Wilson and Vincent Roscigno, "End of an Era? Managerial Losses of African American and Latinos in the Public Sector," *Social Science Research* 54 (2015): 36–49.

24. Hedwig Lee and Kristin Turney, "Investigating the Relationship between Perceived Discrimination, Social Status, and Mental Health," *Society and Mental Health* 2, no. 1 (2015): 1–20.

25. Kalev 2014.

26. Pugh 2015.

27. Sharone 2013: 13.

28. Smith 2001.

29. Steven H. Lopez and Lora A. Phillips, "Unemployed: White-Collar Job Searching after the Great Recession," *Work and Occupations* 46, no. 4 (2019): 470–510.

30. Among the 100 participants in my study, 17 of the 26 middle-class men were offered a severance, five of the 18 middle-class women, seven of the 31 working-class women, and none of the 25 working-class men.

31. Age Discrimination in Employment Act of 1967, Pub. L. 90-202; see https://www.eeoc .gov/statutes/age-discrimination-employment-act-1967.

32. Elisabeth Buchwald, "Airbnb Will Give Laid-off Employees 14 Weeks Base Pay and Health Insurance, but Millions of Other Laid-off Workers Are Not So Lucky," *MarketWatch*, May 7, 2020; Keith J. Kelly, "Wired Magazine Blasts Condé Nast's 'Meager or Nonexistent' Severance Packages," *New York Post*, May 19, 2020; Glenn Jordan, "Recent Layoffs Raise Questions about Severance, Notification," *Press Herald*, May 4, 2020.

33. Steven Greenhouse, *The Big Squeeze: Tough Times for the American Worker* (New York: Alfred A. Knopf, 2008), 38.

34. Hacker 2006.

35. Williams 2018.

Chapter Four: Insecurity after the Job Loss

1. Van Horn and his colleagues reported that 42 percent of the currently unemployed reported a major lifestyle change and 34 percent reported a minor lifestyle change. The numbers for the long-term unemployed were even bleaker, with 54 percent reporting a major change and 29 percent reporting a minor change. Unfortunately, the survey did not specify what these changes would have been; people were asked only to indicate whether they had undergone a major or minor lifestyle change or no change. Carl Van Horn, Cliff Zukin, and Allison Kopicki, *Left Behind: The Long-Term Unemployed Struggle in an Improving Economy* (New Brunswick, NJ: John J. Heldrich Center for Workforce Development, 2014).

2. Of 100 interviewees, 11 reported having barely enough, 31 not enough, and 58 enough to pay their daily bills.

3. Rakesh Kochhar, "The American Middle Class Is Stable in Size but Losing Ground Financially to Upper-Income Families," Pew Research Center, September 6, 2018.

4. Jeff Hayes and Heidi Hartmann, *Women and Men Living on the Edge: Economic Insecurity after the Great Recession* (Washington, DC: Institute for Women's Policy Research/Rockefeller Survey of Economic Security, 2011).

5. See Sharone 2013. We don't see the financial challenges each group faces in Sharone's book, however, which makes it hard to gauge the difference between the two.

6. Kathryn Edin and H. Luke Shaefer, *$2.00 a Day: Living on Almost Nothing in America* (New York: Houghton Mifflin Harcourt, 2015).

7. Newman 1988; Lane 2011; Basbug and Sharone 2017.

8. Lane 2011: 103.

9. Basbug and Sharone 2017.

10. Rao 2020.

11. Bruce Western et al., "Economic Insecurity and Social Stratification," *Annual Review of Sociology* 38, no. 1 (2012): 341–59.

12. Stephanie Riegg Cellini, Signe-Mary McKernan, and Caroline Ratcliffe, "The Dynamics of Poverty in the United States: A Review of Data, Methods, and Findings," *Journal of Policy Analysis and Management* 27, no. 3 (2008): 577–605.

13. National Employment Law Project, "Maintaining Fair Weekly Benefits Amounts," *Unemployment Insurance Policy Advocate's Toolkit*, accessed September 4, 2020.

14. Among the 100 interviewees, 19 working-class women and 11 working-class men reported having barely enough or not enough money to pay bills, while only 12 working-class women and 14 working-class men reported having enough. In contrast, 20 middle-class men and 12 middle-class women reported having enough, while only six middle-class men and six middle-class women reported having barely enough or not enough.

15. United States Department of Agriculture, Center for Nutrition Policy and Promotion, "Official USDA Food Plans: Cost of Food at Home at Four Levels, U.S. Average, December 2013," January 2014.

16. Andrew Cherlin argues that, increasingly, marriages appear to be attainable only for those in the middle class with money and resources. Andrew J. Cherlin, *The Marriage-Go-Round: The State of Marriage and the Family in America Today* (New York: Vintage, 2010); Pessin 2018.

17. Kathryn Edin and Timothy Jon Nelson, *Doing the Best I Can: Fatherhood in the Inner City* (Berkeley: University of California Press, 2013).

18. Damaske 2011.

19. James Heckman, "Shadow Prices, Market Wages, and Labor Supply," *Econometrica* 42 (1974): 679–94.

20. Damaske 2011; Stone 2007.

21. Paula England et al., "Do Highly Paid, Highly Skilled Women Experience the Largest Motherhood Penalty?" *American Sociological Review* 81, no. 6 (2016): 1161–89.

22. Damaske and Frech 2016. See also Alexandra Killewald and Xiaolin Zhuo, "U.S. Mothers' Long-Term Employment Patterns," *Demography* 56, no. 1 (2019): 285–320.

23. Sarah Bowen, Joslyn Brenton, and Sinikka Elliott, *Pressure Cooker: Why Home Cooking Won't Solve Our Problems and What We Can Do about It* (New York: Oxford University Press, 2019).

24. Emmanuel Saez and Gabriel Zucman, "Wealth Inequality in the United States since 1913: Evidence from Capitalized Income Tax Data," *Quarterly Journal of Economics* 131, no. 2 (2016): 519–78.

25. Chinhui Juhn and Kevin Murphy, "Wage Inequality and Family Labor Supply," *Journal of Labor Economics* 15 (1997): 72–97. Francine D. Blau and Lawrence M. Kahn, "Changes in the Labor Supply Behavior of Married Women: 1980–2000," *Journal of Labor Economics* 25, no. 3 (2007): 393–438; Leslie McCall and Christine Percheski, "Income Inequality: New Trends and Research Directions," *Annual Review of Sociology* 36, no. 1 (2010): 329–47.

26. Among my 100 interviews, 20 (of 26) middle-class men and 12 (of 18) middle-class women reported having enough money to cover daily costs.

27. Elizabeth Warren and Amelia Warren Tyagi, *The Two-Income Trap: Why Middle-Class Mothers and Fathers Are Going Broke* (New York: Basic Books, 2003).

28. Allison Pugh (2015) also found that upper-middle-class men were better able to rebound from job loss or employment insecurity than their working-class peers. This is supported by new findings from my work with Adrianne Frech and Jane Lankes (in progress).

29. In some ways, this is similar to what Aliya Rao (2020) found, but Joan and Neil and their families had different reactions to their search strategies (which I describe in detail in chapter 7).

30. There are a remarkable number of investment websites touting this rule of thumb. Fidelity, a leading financial broker, is one example; see https://www.fidelity.com/mymoneybasics/50-15-5-saving-spending-rule.

31. Federal Reserve System, *Report on the Economic Well-Being of U.S. Households in 2018*, Board of Governors of the Federal Reserve System, May 2019; Moritz Kuhn, Moritz Schularick, and Ulrike I. Steins, "Income and Wealth Inequality in America, 1949–2016," preprint, 2018, Federal Reserve Bank of Minneapolis.

32. Pew Charitable Trusts, "Pursuing the American Dream: Economic Mobility across Generations," July 2012.

33. Melvin L. Oliver and Thomas M. Shapiro, *Black Wealth/White Wealth: A New Perspective on Racial Inequality* (New York: Routledge, 1995); Taylor 2019.

34. Marianne Cooper, *Cut Adrift: Families in Insecure Times* (Oakland: University of California Press, 2014).

35. Oliver and Shapiro 1995.

36. Natalia Sarkisian and Naomi Gerstel, "Kin Support among Blacks and Whites: Race and Family Organization," *American Sociological Review* 69, no. 6 (2004): 812–37.

37. Sarah Patterson, "Adult Children's Help to Parents" (unpublished dissertation, Pennsylvania State University, 2017).

38. Fenaba R. Addo, Jason N. Houle, and Daniel Simon, "Young, Black, and (Still) in the Red: Parental Wealth, Race, and Student Loan Debt," *Race and Social Problems* 8, no. 1 (2016): 64–76.

39. Warren and Tyagi 2003.

40. There are many reasons that Black and white Americans have different levels of wealth in this country; differing family responsibilities are just one of many. Predatory lending policies, redlining practices, and many other discriminatory practices also contribute to this unequal distribution. Whites with college and noncollege degrees have substantially more savings even than Black and Hispanic people with college degrees. In comparison to the college-educated whites (who had average savings of $375,000 in 2013), college-educated Black Americans had a median net worth of not quite $37,000, and Black Americans without a college degree had a net worth of just over $10,000. Nearly one in five Black families had no savings whatsoever, according to Federal Reserve data; see Lisa J. Detting et al., "Recent Trends in Wealth-Holding by Race and Ethnicity: Evidence from the Survey of Consumer Finances." *FEDS Notes*, September 27, 2017. See also Oliver and Shapiro 1995; Taylor 2019.

41. Chen 2015; Brand 2015.

42. Jennie E. Brand and Juli Simon Thomas, "Job Displacement among Single Mothers: Effects on Children's Outcomes in Young Adulthood," *American Journal of Sociology* 119, no. 4 (2014): 955–1001.

43. Norris 2016.

44. Chen 2015; Sharone 2013.

45. Damaske 2011.

46. Adrianne Frech and Sarah Damaske, "The Relationships between Mothers' Work Pathways and Physical and Mental Health," *Journal of Health and Social Behavior* 53, no. 4 (2012): 396–412.

47. Research has found that women, those with a high school degree or less, and people of color are also less likely to be eligible for unemployment and to receive less compensation when they are eligible. Our safety net isn't what Perkins and FDR had hoped it would be, and it covers far fewer people today than it did when it was first implemented. See Rachel West et al., *Strengthening Unemployment Protections in America: Modernizing Unemployment Insurance and Establishing a Jobseeker's Allowance* (Washington, DC: Center for American Progress, 2016).

48. Gould-Werth 2020.

49. Martha May, "The Historical Problem of the Family Wage: The Ford Motor Company and the Five Dollar Day," *Feminist Studies* 8, no. 2 (1982): 399–424.

50. Nick Wing and Arthur Delaney, "Tom Corbett, Pennsylvania Governor: Drug Users Boosting Unemployment Rate (UPDATE)," *HuffPost*, December 6, 2017.

51. May 1982.

52. Technically speaking, employers, not workers, pay both the state and federal unemployment tax, but most economists agree that this regressive tax is passed from the employer to the employee in the form of lowered wages, thus making it a tax that workers indirectly pay. About 80 percent of workers are estimated to pay this tax, although far fewer than half (some estimate around 30 percent) of the unemployed are eligible to receive benefits. See Chad Stone and William Chen, "Introduction to Unemployment Insurance," *Center on Budget and Policy Priorities*, July 30, 2014.

Chapter Five: The Guilt Gap and Health

1. Kaiser Family Foundation, "Key Facts about the Uninsured Population," December 13, 2019.

2. Centers for Disease Control and Prevention, "*QuickStats*: Percentage of Persons in Families Having Problems Paying Medical Bills in the Past 12 Months, by Age Group—National Health Interview Survey, 2011–2017," *Morbidity and Mortality Weekly Report* 68, no. 14 (2019): 334.

3. Bureau of Labor Statistics, "Employee Benefits in the United States—March 2019," news release, September 19, 2019a.

4. Commonwealth Fund, "Three Quarters of Those Who Have Lost Jobs and Health Insurance Are Skipping Needed Medicine and Health Care; Many Struggling with Medical Debt," news release, August 24, 2011.

5. Adam Sonfield, Jennifer Froster, Ruth Dawson, and Laura Lindberg, "COVID-19 Job Losses Threaten Insurance Coverage and Access to Reproductive Health Care for Millions," *Health Affairs Blog*, August 3, 2020.

6. Commonwealth Fund 2011.

7. Of the 100 interviewees, six middle-class women saw no change to their health insurance, ten lost their health insurance, and two did not indicate. Of the working-class women, 14 of them saw no change to their health insurance (many of whom were not insured), 13 lost their health insurance, and four did not indicate. Among middle-class men, 11 saw no change to their health insurance, 13 lost their health insurance, and three did not indicate. Seven working-class men saw no change to their health insurance, 17 lost their health insurance, and one did not indicate.

8. My finding was that six of 13 middle-class men, seven of 10 middle-class women, ten of 17 working-class men, and eight of 13 working-class women who lost their insurance remained uninsured.

9. Zero of 26 middle-class men, six of 18 middle-class women, four of 25 working-class men, and 19 of 31 working-class women reported untreated health conditions or going without necessary medications for themselves. Two of 26 middle-class men, zero of 18 middle-class women, nine of 25 working-class men, and zero of 31 working-class women reported their spouse or children went with untreated health or necessary medications.

10. Michael T. French et al., "Key Provisions of the Patient Protection and Affordable Care Act (ACA): A Systematic Review and Presentation of Early Research Findings," *Health Services Research* 51, no. 5 (2016): 1735–71.

11. Medicaid, 2014. *FY 2013 Number of Children Ever Enrolled in Medicaid and Chip.* Accessed October 7, 2020.

12. Author's calculation based on the number of children enrolled (see footnote 11) and the number of children living in the state. For the number of children in the state for 2013, see Kids Count Data Center, "Population—Children (Ages 0–19) by Race and Age Group in Pennsylvania," accessed September 4, 2020, https://datacenter.kidscount.org/data/tables/9015 -population—children-ages-0-19-by-race-and-age-group?loc=40&loct=2#detailed/2/any/false /870,573,869,36,868,867,133/3008,3655,2318,4929,2320,2321,2322/18038,18039.

13. Hacker 2006; Jonathan Morduch and Rachel Schneider, *The Financial Diaries: How American Families Cope in a World of Uncertainty* (Princeton, NJ: Princeton University Press, 2017).

14. Hacker 2006.

15. Morduch and Schneider 2017.

16. Morduch and Schneider 2017.

17. Centers for Disease Control and Prevention 2019.

18. Commonwealth Fund 2011.

19. Newman 1988.

20. Mirra Komarovsky, *The Unemployed Man and His Family: The Effect of Unemployment upon the Status of the Man in Fifty-Nine Families* (1940; repr., New York: Octagon Books, 1971).

21. Townsend 2002; Cooper 2000.

22. Lane 2011.

23. Ellen Goodman, "Guilt Gap," *Washington Post*, May 12, 1990.

24. Sharon Hays (1996: 104) uses this term similarly to describe how mothers, but not fathers, spend more time "worrying" about children; she further notes that mothers are aware of this gap in parenting worry.

25. Seven of 10 middle-class women who lost insurance remained uninsured.

26. Eight of 13 working-class women who lost insurance remained uninsured.

27. The one-in-four-women statistic is from the Migraine Research Foundation, https://migraineresearchfoundation.org/about-migraine/migraine-facts/.

28. This finding was for 25 of the 49 women interviewed: six of 18 middle-class women, 19 of 31 working-class women, no middle-class men (n = 26), and four of 25 working-class men.

29. Harriet Beecher Stowe and Catharine Esther Beecher, *American Woman's Home* (New Brunswick, NJ: Rutgers University Press, 2002).

30. Chris Bobel, *Paradox of Natural Mothering* (Philadelphia: Temple University Press, 2010); Dawn Marie Dow, *Mothering While Black: Boundaries and Burdens of Middle-Class Parenthood* (Oakland: University of California Press, 2019); Sharon Hays, *The Cultural Contradictions of Motherhood* (New Haven, CT: Yale University Press, 1996); Stone 2007; Pamela Stone and Meg Lovejoy, *Opting Back In: What Really Happens When Mothers Go Back to Work* (Oakland: University of California Press, 2019); Nancy Folbre, *The Invisible Heart: Economics and Family Values* (New York: New Press, 2001); Damaske 2011.

31. Folbre 2001.

32. Jean-Anne Sutherland, "Mothering, Guilt, and Shame," *Sociology Compass* 4, no. 5 (2010): 310–21.

33. Damaske 2011.

34. Caitlyn Collins, "Is Maternal Guilt a Cross-National Experience?," *Qualitative Sociology* (2020).

35. Riché J. Daniel Barnes, *Raising the Race: Black Career Women Redefine Marriage, Motherhood, and Community* (New Brunswick, NJ: Rutgers University Press, 2015).

36. In this way, Joan's language echoes the "for the family" language I found women used in my first book, which was a way of talking about work choices that privileged their families' needs rather than their own priorities (even though their own work and family opportunities and constraints had shaped their decisions). See Damaske 2011.

37. Of those interviewed, four of 51 men did not seek care for themselves; 11 of 51 men had a spouse or child who went without medical treatment; 16 of 30 men remained uninsured.

38. Among the 13 middle-class men who lost insurance, seven switched to their wives' plans or purchased insurance through COBRA or the ACA.

39. None of the middle- or working-class women interviewed (n = 49) did the same. Of the middle-class men (n = 26), one man reported his spouse went without care and one reported both spouse and children did. Of the working-class men (n = 25), six reported their spouses went without care and three reported both spouse and children did.

40. Four of the 51 men interviewed.

41. Of 51 men, 11 reported that their wives or children had untreated medical conditions or had gone without medications.

42. Hayes and Hartmann 2011.

43. Of the 49 women, 14 described themselves as eating less and/or experiencing food insecurity, while five of 51 men reported the same.

44. Vanessa is actually the exception to what social scientists more commonly find, which is that poverty most often leads to obesity among mothers. See Molly A. Martin and Adam M. Lippert, "Feeding Her Children, but Risking Her Health: The Intersection of Gender, Household Food Insecurity, and Obesity," *Social Science & Medicine* 74, no. 11 (2012): 1754–64.

45. Twelve of 49 women were eating more junk food, but only seven of 51 men.

46. Rachel Pechey et al., "Socioeconomic Differences in Purchases of More vs. Less Healthy Foods and Beverages: Analysis of over 25,000 British Households in 2010," *Social Science & Medicine* 92 (2013): 22–26.

47. Martin and Lippert 2012.

48. Of the men, nine reported that they were eating healthier, but only four women said they were.

49. Liana C. Sayer, "Trends in Housework," in *Dividing the Domestic: Men, Women, and Household Work in Cross-National Perspective*, ed. Judith Treas and Sonja Drobnič (Stanford, CA: Stanford University Press 2010), 19–38.

50. About two-fifths of the women (7 middle-class women and 12 working-class women) and about a quarter of the men (7 each in the middle class and the working class).

51. Sarah A. Burgard, "The Needs of Others: Gender and Sleep Interruptions for Caregivers," *Social Forces* 89, no. 4 (2011): 1189–215; David J. Maume, Anthony R. Bardo, and Rachel A. Sebastian, "Gender Differences in Sleep Disruption among Retail Food Workers," *American Sociological Review* 74, no. 6 (2009): 989–1007.

52. Nathaniel F. Watson et al., "Recommended Amount of Sleep for a Healthy Adult: A Joint Consensus Statement of the American Academy of Sleep Medicine and Sleep Research Society," *Journal of Clinical Sleep Medicine* 11, no. 6 (2015): 591–92.

53. Read, Jen'nan Ghazal and Bridget K. Gorman. 2010. "Gender and Health Inequality." *Annual Review of Sociology* 36:371–86.

54. Debra Umberson, "Gender, Marital Status, and the Social Control of Health Behavior," *Social Science & Medicine* 34, no. 8 (1992): 907–17; Corinne Reczek et al., "Diet and Exercise in Parenthood: A Social Control Perspective," *Journal of Marriage and Family* 76, no. 5 (2014): 1047–62; Corinne Reczek et al., "Healthcare Work in Marriage: How Gay, Lesbian, and Heterosexual Spouses Encourage and Coerce Medical Care," *Journal of Health and Social Behavior* 59, no. 4 (2018): 554–68.

55. Chloe E. Bird and Patricia P. Rieker, *Gender and Health: The Effects of Constrained Choices and Social Policies* (New York: Cambridge University Press, 2008); Pechey et al. 2013.

Chapter Six: The Guilt Gap and the Second Shift

1. Carlson, Miller, and Sassler 2018.

2. Natalia Sarkisian and Naomi Gerstel, "Marriage: The Good, the Bad, and the Greedy," *Contexts* 5, no. 4 (2006): 16–21.

3. Liana C. Sayer, "Gender, Time, and Inequality: Trends in Women's and Men's Paid Work, Unpaid Work, and Free Time," *Social Forces* 84, no. 1 (2005): 285–303.

4. Gough and Killewald. 2011.

5. Gough and Killewald. 2011.

6. Rao 2020.

7. Margaret Gough, "Gender Differences in Time in Child Care during Unemployment," *SocArXiv*, January 23, 2019.

8. The breakdown is 37 men and 36 women. Although 80 people were married or cohabiting, only 73 provided detailed information about their household and/or childcare chores. Also, not all couples had children; some kids lived with single moms like Tracy.

9. Sayer 2005; Suzanne M. Bianchi et al., "Housework: Who Did, Does, or Will Do It, and How Much Does It Matter?," *Social Forces* 91, no. 1 (2012): 55–63.

10. Carlson, Miller, and Sassler 2018; Scott Coltrane, "Research on Household Labor: Modeling and Measuring the Social Embeddedness of Routine Family Work," *Journal of Marriage and Family* 62, no. 4 (2000): 1208–33; Mylène Lachance-Grzela and Geneviève Bouchard, "Why Do Women Do the Lion's Share of Housework? A Decade of Research," *Sex Roles* 63, no. 11 (2010): 767–80.

11. Routine tasks included cooking, doing the dishes, laundry, or cleaning the house. Non-routine tasks included yardwork, bill paying, and car repair.

12. Of my interviewees, 12 of 15 middle-class women and 15 of 24 working-class women increased their routine household work (the three middle-class women and six working-class women who did not reported already doing all of the routine household tasks). In contrast, 11 of 20 middle-class men and 9 of 16 working-class men increased their routine household work (none of the men previously had done all of the work, so nine middle-class men and seven working-class men either continued to share the tasks or let their wives do most of the labor).

13. Out of 32 middle- and working-class women who were partnered with children in the household, 12 were solely responsible for childcare after their job loss and 13 more said they were primarily responsible with their husbands' help; only five said that the childcare was shared equally, and two women reported their husbands were primarily responsible for their stepdaughters' care. In stark contrast, only one of the 35 middle- and working-class men who were partnered with children in the household were solely responsible for childcare after their job loss, and only two more said they were primarily responsible with some help from their wives; 16 men reported equally sharing childcare with their wives and 16 said that their wives remained in charge of the childcare.

14. A. W. Geiger, "Sharing Chores a Key to Good Marriage, Say Most Married Adults," Pew Research Center, November 30, 2016.

15. Bianchi, Robinson, and Milkie 2006.

16. Bianchi et al. 2012.

17. Bianchi et al. 2012.

18. Gerson 2010.

19. Gerson 2010; Collins 2019; Leah Ruppanner, *Motherlands: How States in the U.S. Push Mothers Out of Employment* (Philadelphia, PA: Temple University Press, 2020).

20. Alexandra Killewald and Margaret Gough, "Does Specialization Explain Marriage Penalties and Premiums?" *American Sociological Review* 78, no. 3 (2013): 477–502.

21. Killewald has further found that only a small proportion of women use their greater earnings to buy out their labor. See Alexandra Killewald, "Opting Out and Buying Out: Wives' Earnings and Housework Time," *Journal of Marriage and Family* 73, no. 2 (2011): 459–71.

22. Daniel Schneider, "Market Earnings and Household Work: New Tests of Gender Performance Theory," *Journal of Marriage and Family* 73, no. 4 (2011): 845–60.

23. Jennifer L. Hook, "Women's Housework: New Tests of Time and Money," *Journal of Marriage and Family* 79, no. 1 (2017): 179–98.

24. Gough and Killewald 2011.

25. Hook 2017; Gough and Killewald 2011.

26. Killewald and Gough 2011, 1001.

27. One of the most prominent theories suggests that if men aren't masculine enough— either by outearning their wives or by working in a male-dominated field—they will refuse to do "their share" of household labor (even if, as we've seen, that share is considerably less than women's). While there continues to be a lot of debate about this among academics, there is some good evidence that men who work in female-dominated fields don't do as much around the home as men in gender-balanced or male-dominated occupations. For a discussion, see Daniel Schneider, "Gender Deviance and Household Work: The Role of Occupation," *American Journal of Sociology* 117, no. 4 (2012): 1029–72.

28. While I did not control for sexuality, only people who identified as heterosexual signed up and participated in the study. This is likely, at least partially, due to the geographic area in which the study was conducted. I am not aware of research on whether LGBTQ workers report less access to unemployment benefits than their heterosexual counterparts, but it may be that they were less likely to receive benefits as well. This is an open question deserving of future research.

29. Sutherland 2010.

30. Kathleen L. McGinn and Eunsil Oh, "Gender, Social Class, and Women's Employment," *Current Opinion in Psychology* 18 (2017): 84–88; Bobel 2010.

31. Hays 1996.

32. See Mary Blair-Loy, *Competing Devotions: Career and Family among Women Executives* (Cambridge, MA: Harvard University Press, 2003); Hays 1996; Stone and Lovejoy 2019.

33. Dow 2019.

34. Dow 2019, 165.

35. Liana C. Sayer and Leigh Fine, "Racial-Ethnic Differences in U.S. Married Women's and Men's Housework," *Social Indicators Research* 101, no. 2 (2011): 259–65.

36. Arlie Russell Hochschild, *The Second Shift: Working Parents and the Revolution at Home* (New York: Viking, 1989).

37. Sara Raley, Suzanne M. Bianchi, and Wendy Wang, "When Do Fathers Care? Mothers' Economic Contribution and Fathers' Involvement in Child Care," *American Journal of Sociology* 117, no. 5 (2012): 1422–59; Allison Daminger, "The Cognitive Dimension of Household Labor," *American Sociological Review* 84, no. 4 (2019): 609–33; Cadhla McDonnell, Nancy Luke, and Susan E. Short, "Happy Moms, Happier Dads: Gendered Caregiving and Parents' Affect," *Journal of Family Issues* 40, no. 17 (2019): 2553–81.

38. McDonnell, Luke, and Short 2019.

39. Damaske and Frech 2016; Landivar 2017; Percheski 2008.

40. Amanda J. Miller and Daniel L. Carlson, "Great Expectations? Working- and Middle-Class Cohabitors' Expected and Actual Divisions of Housework," *Journal of Marriage and Family* 78, no. 2 (2016): 346–63.

41. Sharon Sassler and Amanda Miller, *Cohabitation Nation: Gender, Class, and the Remaking of Relationships* (Berkeley: University of California Press, 2017).

42. Esther De Ruijter, Judith K. Treas, and Philip N. Cohen, "Outsourcing the Gender Factory: Living Arrangements and Service Expenditures on Female and Male Tasks," *Social Forces* 84, no. 1 (2005): 305–22.

43. McGinn and Oh 2017.

44. In doing so, I build on original work done by Scott and Lyman (1968) on this topic. I argue accounts are often used to reframe cultural schemas, changing them somewhat to fit new ways of doing gender, giving men and women more leeway, but also reinforcing the original framework because it does not tear it down. See Damaske (2011); Marvin Scott and Stanford Lyman, "Accounts," *American Sociological Review* 33 (1968): 46–61.

45. It's important to note that there is a long history of feminist scholarship that considers why the important work done in the home has been devalued and ignored (and why women themselves use such language). For an introduction, I recommend Paula England and Nancy Folbre, "The Cost of Caring," *Annals of the American Academy of Political and Social Science* 561 (1999): 39–51.

46. Scott Coltrane, "Parenting in Transition," in *Mothers and Children: Feminist Analyses and Personal Narratives*, ed. Susan E. Chase and Mary F. Rogers (New Brunswick, NJ: Rutgers University Press, 2001), 103–7.

47. Chesley 2011.

48. Karen Christopher, "Extensive Mothering: Employed Mothers' Constructions of the Good Mother," *Gender & Society* 26, no. 1 (2012): 73–96.

49. Myra Marx Ferree, "Family and Job for Working-Class Women: Gender and Class Systems Seen from Below," in *Families and Work*, ed. Naomi Gerstel and Harriet E. Gross (Philadelphia: Temple University Press, 1987), 289–301; Anita Ilta Garey, *Weaving Work and Motherhood* (Philadelphia: Temple University Press, 1999).

50. Jennifer Sherman, *Those Who Work, Those Who Don't: Poverty, Morality, and Family in Rural America* (Minneapolis: University of Minnesota Press, 2009).

51. Sherman 2009.

52. Maria Charles and David B. Grusky, *Occupational Ghettos: The Worldwide Segregation of Women and Men* (Stanford, CA: Stanford University Press, 2004); Paula England, "Reassessing the Uneven Gender Revolution and Its Slowdown," *Gender & Society* 25, no. 1 (2011): 113–23.

53. Mike Rose, *The Mind at Work: Valuing the Intelligence of the American Worker* (New York: Viking, 2004); Damaske 2011.

54. Miller and Carlson 2016.

55. Sassler and Miller 2017.

56. Damaske 2011.

57. Six of 18 middle-class and 15 of 24 working-class women reported being the only ones who did routine household labor, while three middle- and four working-class women reported they were primarily responsible for routine tasks, but husbands helped out a little bit. Six

middle- and two working-class women reported the tasks were shared equally. None of the women reported that their spouses were primarily responsible. Please note that the total number of reports of division of childcare are lower than the total reports for division of household labor because some of the households with married or cohabiting partners did not have children.

58. Naomi Gerstel, "The Third Shift: Gender, Employment, and Care Work outside the Home," *Qualitative Sociology* 23 (2000): 467–83.

59. Elizabeth Miklya Legerski and Marie Cornwall, "Working-Class Job Loss, Gender, and the Negotiation of Household Labor," *Gender & Society* 24, no. 4 (2010): 447–74.

60. Sassler and Miller 2017.

61. Shows and Gerstel 2009.

62. Sherman 2009.

63. Of the men interviewed, 15 middle-class men and 12 working-class men reported equally sharing the workload, while four middle- and four working-class men said their wives remained solely or primarily responsible for the work. Two middle-class men (but no working-class men) reported being mostly responsible at home with some help from wives.

64. Karen Christopher (2012) argues that outsourcing childcare continues to be an important part of maintaining "intensive mothering norms" for married middle-class mothers, who participate in "extensive mothering" through their management of the delegated childcare, but not for single mothers, who are most often working class and less tied to intensive mothering norms.

65. Julia R. Henly and Susan Lambert, "Nonstandard Work and Child-Care Needs of Low-Income Parents," in *Work, Family, Health, and Well-Being*, ed. S. M. Bianchi, L. M. Casper, and B. R. King (Mahwah, NJ: Lawrence Erlbaum Associates, 2005), 473–92.

66. Francine Deutsch, *Halving It All: How Equally Shared Parenting Works* (Cambridge, MA: Harvard University Press, 1999).

Chapter Seven: Attempting to Return to Work

1. Matthias Pollmann-Schult and Felix Büchel, "Unemployment Benefits, Unemployment Duration, and Subsequent Job Quality: Evidence from West Germany," *Acta Sociologica* 48, no. 1 (2005): 21–39; Farooq, Kugler, and Muratori 2020.

2. Marco Caliendo, Konstantinos Tatsiramos, and Arne Uhlendorff, "Benefit Duration, Unemployment Duration, and Job Match Quality: A Regression-Discontinuity Approach." *Journal of Applied Econometrics* 28, no. 4 (2013): 604–27.

3. Corina Boar and Simon Mongey, "Dynamic Trade-Offs and Labor Supply under the CARES Act," NBER Working Paper No. 27727, 2020; Guido Matias Cortes and Eliza Forsythe, "Impacts of the COVID-19 Pandemic and the CARES Act on Earnings and Inequality," Social Science Research Network, Working Paper No. 3689187, 2020.

4. Chetty 2008.

5. Mary Gatta (2014) lays out how this works in the state of New Jersey. See Gatta, *All I Want Is a Job! Unemployed Women Navigating the Public Workforce System* (Stanford, CA: Stanford University Press, 2014). See also Chen 2015.

6. Sarah Damaske, "Job Loss and Attempts to Return to Work: Complicating Inequalities across Gender and Class," *Gender & Society* 34, no. 1 (2020): 7–30

7. As with the sample as a whole, the search groups were largely similar in age. The *Deliberate* group's average age was 41, the *Take Time* group's average age was 40, the *Urgent* group's average age was 40, and the *Diverted* group's average age was 38.5.

8. In this way, these job seekers were the most like those noted in other studies of the unemployed middle class found in research by Sharone (2013) and Lane (2011).

9. This search approach was used by 14 middle-class women (n = 18).

10. Moen and Roehling 2005; Townsend 2002; Newman 1988.

11. The *Take Time* group included 12 middle-class men (n = 26).

12. On an urgent search were 15 working-class men (n = 25).

13. Eight working-class women (n = 31).

14. Gatta 2014.

15. *Diverted* searchers included 11 working-class women (n = 31).

16. The 11 working-class women were out of 16 total in the *Diverted* group.

17. Fourteen of the 18 middle-class women; 12 of 26 middle-class men; seven of 31 working-class women; four of 25 working-class men. Two working-class men did not fall into any of the search categories, as they were seasonally unemployed from their companies and not searching for work, as they expected to be rehired, as they were annually, when their company's busy season commenced.

18. Rao 2020.

19. Erin L. Kelly and Phyllis Moen, "Rethinking the Clockwork of Work: Why Schedule Control May Pay Off at Work and at Home," *Advances in Developing Human Resources* 9, no. 4 (2007): 487–506.

20. Hays 1996.

21. Damaske 2011.

22. Katherine Weisshaar, "From Opt Out to Blocked Out: The Challenges for Labor Market Re-Entry after Family-Related Employment Lapses," *American Sociological Review* 83, no. 1 (2018): 34–60; Youngjoo Cha, "Job Mobility and the Great Recession: Wage Consequences by Gender and Parenthood," *Sociological Science* 1 (2014): 159.

23. Sharone 2013.

24. Lane 2011.

25. Louise Kapp Howe, *Pink Collar Workers: Inside the World of Women's Work* (New York: Putnam, 1977).

26. Sociologists Janette Dill and Melissa Hodges argue that health care jobs have become some of the best work that working-class women can find, as "blue-collar jobs" once were for working-class men. See Janette Dill and Melissa J. Hodges, "Is Healthcare the New Manufacturing? Industry, Gender, and 'Good Jobs' for Low- and Middle-Skill Workers," *Social Science Research* 84 (2019): 102350.

27. Lane 2011; Sharone 2013.

28. In this group were 12 middle-class men (n = 26), zero middle-class women (n = 18), three working-class men (n = 25), and five working-class women (n = 31).

29. Whyte 1956; Moen and Roehling 2005; Townsend 2002.

30. Lareau 2003.

31. The breakdown was 15 of 25 working-class men and eight of 31 working-class women, and two of 26 middle-class men and zero of 18 middle-class women.

32. Sharone 2013.

33. This finding echoes Allison Pugh's (2015) qualitative research and my own research looking at national patterns with Adrianne Frech and Jane Lankes (in progress).

34. See Basbug and Sharone (2017) for a discussion of the costs of long-term unemployment on middle-class men.

35. Eleven working-class women, four middle-class women, and one working-class man were *Diverted* searchers.

36. Sendhil Mullainathan and Eldar Shafir, *Scarcity: Why Having Too Little Means So Much* (New York: Macmillan, 2013).

37. Sharone 2013; Lane 2011.

38. Morduch and Schneider 2017.

39. Joya Misra and Marta Murray-Close, "The Gender Wage Gap in the United States and Cross Nationally." *Sociology Compass* 8, no. 11 (2014): 1281–95.

40. Leslie McCall, *Complex Inequality: Gender, Class, and Race in the New Economy* (New York: Routledge, 2001); Francine D. Blau and Lawrence M. Kahn, "The Gender Wage Gap: Extent, Trends, and Explanations," *Journal of Economic Literature* 55, no. 3 (2017): 789–865.

41. The Bureau of Labor Statistics provides this information. Married-couple families are defined as "opposite-sex married couples residing together and any of their family members residing in the household." See Bureau of Labor Statistics 2019.

42. Legerski and Cornwall 2010.

43. Bureau of Labor Statistics, Mid–Atlantic Information Office, "Women's Earnings in Pennsylvania—2018," December 9, 2019.

44. Breakdown is 20 middle-class men ($n = 26$) and 12 middle-class women ($n = 18$).

45. Nineteen of the working-class women ($n = 31$) and 11 of the working-class men ($n = 25$).

46. Shelley J. Correll, "Constraints into Preferences: Gender, Status, and Emerging Career Aspirations," *American Sociological Review* 69, no. 1 (2004): 93–113; Cecilia L. Ridgeway, "Interaction and the Conservation of Gender Inequality: Considering Employment," *American Sociological Review* 62, no. 2 (1997): 218–35.

47. Sherman 2009.

48. Eighty percent ($n = 80$) were partnered or married, and 84 percent ($n = 84$) had a child age 23 or younger who lived in their household and depended on their income. In research on families, children's ages are often listed as under age 5 or under age 18. I included children up to age 23 if they were living at home because I am primarily interested in their financial dependence on the respondent (although no one had a child living at home age 23 or younger who was not a financial dependent).

49. They worked part-time ($n = 3$) or not at all ($n = 6$).

50. Ferree 1987.

51. Ottessa Moshfegh, *My Year of Rest and Relaxation* (New York: Penguin Books, 2019); Irene Bloemraad et al., "Membership without Social Citizenship? Deservingness and Redistribution as Grounds for Equality," *Daedalus* 148, no. 3 (2019): 73–104.

52. Lareau 2003. This is seen in some of the more recent work by Jessica Calarco (2018) on middle-class students in the classroom.

Chapter Eight: One Year Later

1. Gangl 2006; Van Horn, Zukin, and Kopicki 2014.

2. Middle-class men were overrepresented in this group, as ten of the 17 people whose jobs were similar or better one year later were middle-class men. Three middle-class women, four working-class men, and none of the working-class women found similar or better work.

3. More details about the coding of this and other key variables are available in the methodological appendix.

4. Three middle-class women (of 15), six working-class women (of 23), and four middle-class men (of 22). I was not able to follow up with everyone. Due to this, the size of each group is smaller than in previous chapters. This chapter includes information for 22 middle-class men (of 26 originally), 15 middle-class women (of 18 originally), 14 working-class men (of the original 25), and 23 working-class women (of the original 31).

5. Seventeen of the 23 working-class women.

6. Nine of the 14 working-class men.

7. Nine of the 15 middle-class women.

8. Of the 25 working-class men, 11 of them were not available for a follow-up interview, and we did not have any follow-up job information for them. My research team and I had much better luck reaching everyone else; I did not have updated job information for three of 18 middle-class women, eight of 31 working-class women, and four of 26 middle-class men.

9. The data for this chapter, then, is based on the people with whom we did follow-up interviews and also includes some information from those who had found jobs by the time we interviewed them. (Although a minority, some of the people we interviewed found work and were about to start or had started work at the time of the interview. This was most common among the snowball sample, but a few of those recruited through the CareerLink had recently found work before the interview.)

10. Gangl 2006; Cristobal Young, "Losing a Job: The Nonpecuniary Cost of Unemployment in the United States," *Social Forces* 91, no. 2 (2012): 609–34. It's important to note that when there are large losses to income, they were found among those with higher incomes—which makes sense, as they have the most to lose.

11. Lori G. Kletzer, "Job Displacement," *Journal of Economic Perspectives* 12, no. 1 (1998): 115–36; K. A. Dixon and Carl E. Van Horn, "The Disposable Worker: Living in a Job-Loss Economy," *Heldrich Work Trends* 6, no. 2 (2003).

12. Frech, Lankes, and Damaske, in progress.

13. Of the 100 people I interviewed, 17 participants were "moving ahead," including ten middle-class men, three middle-class women, and four working-class men.

14. Cooper 2014.

15. Lane 2011.

16. Jerry A. Jacobs and Kathleen Gerson, *The Time Divide: Work, Family, and Gender Inequality* (Cambridge, MA: Harvard University Press, 2004).

17. There are many great books on how job seekers go about searching for jobs—see, for example, Sharone (2013) and Lane (2011).

18. Henry S. Farber, John Haltiwanger, and Katharine G. Abraham, "The Changing Face of Job Loss in the United States, 1981–1995," *Brookings Papers on Economic Activity: Microeconomics*; Brand 2006.

19. Rakesh Kochhar and Richard Fry, "America's 'Middle' Holds Its Ground after the Great Recession," Pew Research Center, February 4, 2015. While Pew has updated this research, this post is based on data from the time period when the interviews were conducted.

20. Basbug and Sharone 2017.

21. Wingfield 2013.

22. Sarah Damaske, "Brown Suits Need Not Apply: The Intersection of Race, Gender, and Class in Institutional Network Building," *Sociological Forum* 24, no. 2 (2009): 402–24.

23. Sharone 2013.

24. Henly and Lambert 2005.

25. The tally: middle-class women (nine of 15); working-class women (17 of 23); middle-class men (eight of 22); working-class men (ten of 14).

26. Cellini, McKernan, and Ratcliffe 2008.

27. As reported by Morduch and Schneider (2017).

28. Morduch and Schneider 2017.

29. Morduch and Schneider 2017.

30. Mullainathan and Shafir 2013.

31. Eviction is a serious problem for low-income women, particularly for single mothers like Tracy, and can make people more at risk for job loss. It is likely that job loss also increases their risk of eviction. Matthew Desmond and Carl Gershenson, "Housing and Employment Insecurity among the Working Poor," *Social Problems* 63, no. 1 (2016): 46–67.

32. These figures are across all three groups. Nine were working full-time, nine were working part-time, three continued to search for work and were unemployed, and two had dropped out of the labor force entirely. I could not contact eight of the original 31 working-class women.

33. Morduch and Schneider 2017.

34. Nine were employed full-time, four were in part-time or temporary work, and one was unemployed. Only four had moved ahead, and ten were falling behind. I could not contact 11 of the original 25 working-class men.

35. Eleven of the 25 working-class men may have moved.

36. Damaske and Frech, in progress.

37. Lane 2009; Sharone 2013; Wingfield 2013.

38. Cha 2014.

39. Gangl 2006.

40. Daniel L. Carlson, Sarah Hanson, and Andrea Fitzroy, "The Division of Child Care, Sexual Intimacy, and Relationship Quality in Couples," *Gender & Society* 30, no. 3 (2016): 442–66.

41. Basbug and Sharone 2017.

42. Newman 1988.

43. Pugh 2015.

44. Robert H. Frank and Philip J. Cook, *The Winner-Take-All Society: Why the Few at the Top Get So Much More than the Rest of Us* (New York: Random House, 2010).

Conclusion

1. Bureau of Labor Statistics, "Job Openings and Labor Turnover (JOLT) Survey," news release, January 2020a.

2. Hollister 2011; Kalleberg 2011.

3. Lane 2011; Sharone 2013; Gangl 2006; Young 2012.

4. Lane 2011; Sharone 2013.

5. Gangl 2006; Young 2012.

6. Glen H. Elder Jr., "The Life Course Paradigm: Social Change and Individual Development," in *Examining Lives in Context: Perspectives on the Ecology of Human Development* (Washington, DC: American Psychological Association, 1995), 101–40; Dannefer 2003.

7. This is similar to the process that I identify with Adrianne Frech. See Adrianne Frech and Sarah Damaske, "Men's Income Trajectories and Physical and Mental Health at Midlife," *American Journal of Sociology* 124, no. 5 (2019): 1372–412.

8. There is certainly very good research on who is most likely to be at risk of unemployment and on the lasting income and wealth effects of chronic unemployment. See David B. Grusky, Bruce Western, and Christopher Wimer, "The Consequences of the Great Recession," in *The Great Recession* (New York: Russell Sage Foundation, 2011), 2–20; Hout, Levanon, and Cumberworth 2011.

9. Stone 2007.

10. Damaske 2011; Sutherland 2010.

11. Hacker 2006; Kalleberg 2011.

12. Gould-Werth 2020.

13. Gould-Werth 2020.

14. Cellini, McKernan, and Ratcliffe 2008.

15. Gould-Werth 2020.

16. Sjoberg finds no evidence of this among seventeen OCED countries. Ola Sjöberg. "Unemployment and Unemployment Benefits in the OECD 1960–1990: An Empirical Test of Neo-Classical Economic Theory." *Work, Employment, and Society* 14, no. 1 (2000): 51–76.

17. Pollmann-Schult and Büchel 2005; Nick Bunker, "Unemployment Insurance Might Increase Unemployment, but Only Slightly," *Washington Center for Equitable Growth*, April 13, 2016.

18. Pollmann-Schult and Büchel 2005.

19. Shaila Dewan, "A Job Seeker's Desperate Choice," *New York Times*, June 21, 2014.

20. Collins 2019.

21. Sharon Hays, *Flat Broke with Children: Women in the Age of Welfare Reform* (New York: Oxford University Press, 2003).

22. Collins 2019.

23. Alison Andrew et al., *How Are Mothers and Fathers Balancing Work and Family under Lockdown?* (London: Institute for Fiscal Studies, 2020); Daniel L. Carlson, Richard Petts, and Joanna R. Pepin, "US Couples' Divisions of Housework and Childcare during COVID-19 Pandemic," *SocArXiv*, May 6, 2020; Caitlyn Collins et al., "COVID-19 and the Gender Gap in Work Hours," *Gender, Work & Organization* (2020): 1–12; Alix Gould-Werth and Raksha Kopparam, "How the Coronavirus Pandemic Is Harming Family Well-Being for US Low-Wage Workers," *Washington Center for Equitable Growth*, April 1, 2020; Brian Heilman, María Rosario Castro

Bernardini, and Kimberly Pfeifer, *Caring under COVID-19: How the Pandemic Is—and Is Not—Changing Unpaid Care and Domestic Work Responsibilities in the United States* (Boston: Oxfam and Washington, DC: Promundo-US, 2020); "Understanding Coronavirus in America: Understanding America Study," *USC Dornsife Center for Economic and Social Research*, accessed June 27, 2020, https://covid19pulse.usc.edu/.

24. Heather Boushey and Carmen Sanchez Cumming, "Coronavirus Recession Deepens U.S. Job Losses in April Especially among Low-Wage Workers and Women," *Washington Center for Equitable Growth*, May 8, 2020; Heilman, Bernardini, and Pfeifer 2020.

25. Michelle J. Budig, Joya Misra, and Irene Boeckmann, "The Motherhood Penalty in Cross-National Perspective: The Importance of Work–Family Policies and Cultural Attitudes," *Social Politics: International Studies in Gender, State & Society* 19, no. 2 (2012): 163–93.

26. Hacker 2006.

27. See Lambert and Henly (2012). Work-family scholars Julia Henly and Susan Lambert have long explored the challenges for working-class families, particularly those headed by women, in jobs that do not provide enough hours or that change hours at the last minute. The passage of the Schedules That Work Act, a proposal that would allow employees the "right to request a flexible, predictable, or stable schedule," would also do much to improve the quality of their work and address some of the concerns they have raised—issues that also align with many of the challenges faced by the people I met.

28. Max Weber, *The Protestant Ethic and the Spirit of Capitalism* (New York: Routledge, 2013).

29. May 1982.

30. Alix Gould-Werth and H. Luke Schaefer, "Unemployment Insurance Participation by Education and by Race and Ethnicity," *Monthly Labor Review* (October 2012): 28–41.

31. This is because Black unemployed workers are more likely than white unemployed workers to live in states that give less generous unemployment benefits. But as Kathryn Edwards notes, many scholars agree that state generosity to workers is likely shaped by the racial makeup of the state workforce; states are less generous when Black people make up a larger portion of the population. Edwards, "The Racial Disparity in Unemployment Benefits," *The RAND Blog*, July 15, 2020.

32. Liz Ben-Ishai, Rick McHugh, and Claire McKenna, "Out of Sync: How Unemployment Insurance Rules Fail Workers with Volatile Job Schedules," *National Employment Law Project*, August 4, 2015. Studies find that workers of color are more likely to have these volatile schedules; see, for example, Clawson and Gerstel 2014.

33. Bloemraad et al. 2019.

34. Leslie McCall, *The Undeserving Rich: American Beliefs about Inequality, Opportunity, and Redistribution.* (Cambridge: Cambridge University Press, 2013).

35. McCall 2013.

Methodological Appendix

1. Damaske 2011.

2. While Carrie Lane's *A Company of One* (2011) importantly considers gender (and this book hopes to build on her analyses), only 30 percent of her sample interviews were women. The sample in Ofer Sharone's *Flawed System/Flawed Self* was closer to parity, but the role of

gender was not interrogated fully within its pages. In fact, both books depicted the unemployed as men on their covers. Both Marianne Cooper's *Cut Adrift* (2014) and Allison Pugh's *The Tumbleweed Society* (2015) importantly center women in their studies of job insecurity, although both have a broader focus than unemployment. Aliya Rao's *Crunch Time* (2020) is a crucial exception and welcome addition to these studies; she interviewed both unemployed men and women and their spouses (although in elite circumstances). I hope to build on all of these contributions in this book.

3. Barney. G. Glaser and Anselm L. Strauss, *The Discovery of Grounded Theory: Strategies for Qualitative Research* (Chicago: Aldine, 1967); Stone 2007; Kathleen Gerson and Sarah Damaske, *The Science and Art of Qualitative Interviewing* (New York: Oxford University Press, 2020). See also Stefan Timmermans and Iddo Tavory, "Theory Construction in Qualitative Research: From Grounded Theory to Abductive Analysis," *Sociological Theory* 30, no. 3 (2012): 167–86.

4. For additional thoughts on how I approach qualitative interviewing, please see my book with Kathleen Gerson (Gerson and Damaske 2020).

5. Mario Luis Small, *Someone to Talk To* (New York: Oxford University Press, 2017).

6. We discussed the implications of recruiting from these meetings very carefully. Since participation in the meetings was mandated by the state, we decided that my team and I could not recruit until the meetings were concluded.

7. It is standard practice in social science research for people to receive a small monetary compensation for participating in a study. This research study was reviewed and approved by the Pennsylvania State University's Institutional Review Board, which oversees all research conducted on human subjects at Penn State. Everyone who participated received a statement explaining the study and its goals and was told that there was no obligation to participate in the study; people could choose not to answer any questions they didn't want to answer, and they could end their participation at any time.

8. I used a similar process in my first book (Damaske 2011). While detailed occupational status remains a particularly important way of identifying the importance of occupation for class, it is not practical to have numerous categories with a small sample size that is also considering variation according to gender and other factors. Nevertheless, this approach does inform my thinking about class. See Kim A. Weeden and David B. Grusky, "The Case for a New Class Map," *American Journal of Sociology* 111, no. 1 (2005): 141–212.

9. It is not possible to calculate how many people did not fill out the form who may have been eligible for the study.

10. Generally, the distinction between the unemployed and the not employed is thought to be clear—those who are unemployed are seeking work, while the not employed are not. Those in this study blur this line, because they collected unemployment even though some were not actively seeking work.

11. Bureau of Labor Statistics 2015.

12. Lane (2011), Sharone (2013), Newman (1988), Norris (2016), and Rao (2020) all interviewed participants at closer to six months or longer (nearly 40 percent of Sharone's participants had been unemployed for over a year) rather than eleven weeks.

13. Newman (1988) does consider the job loss, and Mary Gatta (2014), in her ethnography of a state career center, does focus on this time period, showing how these centers often push working-class women to take any job (even one that won't provide for their families).

14. See Gerson and Damaske (2020).

15. Damaske 2011.

16. Glaser and Strauss 1967.

17. Cooper 2014.

18. Brand 2015; Smith 2007.

19. I did something similar in my first book; see the appendix of Damaske (2011). See also Collins (2019).

20. Natasha Warikoo has an important discussion of this challenge in the appendix of her book. See Warikoo, *The Diversity Bargain: And Other Dilemmas of Race, Admissions, and Meritocracy at Elite Universities* (Chicago: University of Chicago Press, 2016).

21. See Gerson and Damaske (2020).

22. Colin Jerolmack and Alexandra K. Murphy, "The Ethical Dilemmas and Social Scientific Trade-Offs of Masking in Ethnography," *Sociological Methods & Research* 48, no. 4 (2019): 801–27.

23. A third, the creation of composite characters, has largely fallen out of practice. Arlie Russell Hochschild, *The Time Bind: When Work Becomes Home and Home Becomes Work* (New York: Metropolitan Books, 1997); Rachel Sherman, *Uneasy Street: The Anxieties of Affluence* (Princeton, NJ: Princeton University Press, 2019).

24. Small 2017.

25. Howard S. Becker, "Field Work Evidence," in *Sociological Work: Method and Substance* (New Brunswick, NJ: Transaction Books, 1970), 39–62.

26. Kristin Luker, *Salsa Dancing into the Social Sciences: Research in an Age of Info-Glut* (Cambridge, MA: Harvard University Press, 2008).

27. Mario Luis Small, "'How Many Cases Do I Need?' On Science and the Logic of Case Selection in Field-Based Research," *Ethnography* 10, no. 1 (2009): 5–38.

28. Glaser and Strauss 1967.

BIBLIOGRAPHY

Addo, Fenaba R., Jason N. Houle, and Daniel Simon. 2016. "Young, Black, and (Still) in the Red: Parental Wealth, Race, and Student Loan Debt." *Race and Social Problems* 8(1): 64–76.

Aisenbrey, Silke, and Anette Fasang. 2017. "The Interplay of Work and Family Trajectories over the Life Course: Germany and the United States in Comparison." *American Journal of Sociology* 122(5): 1448–84.

American Law Institute. 2015. *Restatement of the Law, Second, Contracts 2d*. Rev. and enl. Washington, DC: American Law Institute.

Andrew, Alison, Sarah Cattan, Monica Costa Dias, Christine Farquharson, Lucy Kraftman, Sonya Krutikova, Angus Phimister, and Almudena Sevilla. 2020. *How Are Mothers and Fathers Balancing Work and Family under Lockdown?* London: Institute for Fiscal Studies

Armstrong, Elizabeth A., and Laura T. Hamilton. 2013. *Paying for the Party*. Cambridge, MA: Harvard University Press.

Arum, Richard, Josipa Roksa, and Michelle Budig. 2008. "The Romance of College Attendance: Higher Education, Stratification, and Mate Selection." *Research in Social Stratification and Mobility* 26(2): 107–21.

Barnes, Riché J. Daniel. 2015. *Raising the Race: Black Career Women Redefine Marriage, Motherhood, and Community*. New Brunswick, NJ: Rutgers University Press.

Basbug, Gokce, and Ofer Sharone. 2017. "The Emotional Toll of Long-Term Unemployment: Examining the Interaction Effects of Gender and Marital Status." *RSF: The Russell Sage Foundation Journal of the Social Sciences* 3(3): 222–44.

Batt, Rosemary, and Alexander J. S. Colvin. 2011. "An Employment Systems Approach to Turnover: Human Resources Practices, Quits, Dismissals, and Performance." *Academy of Management Journal* 54(4): 695–717.

Baumol, William J., Alan S. Blinder, and Edward N. Wolff. 2003. *Downsizing in America: Reality, Causes, and Consequences*. New York: Russell Sage Foundation.

Becker, Howard S. 1970. "Field Work Evidence." In *Sociological Work: Method and Substance*, 39–62. New Brunswick, NJ: Transaction Books.

Ben-Ishai, Liz, Rick McHugh, and Claire McKenna. 2015. "Out of Sync: How Unemployment Insurance Rules Fail Workers with Volatile Job Schedules." *National Employment Law Project*, August 4.

Beveridge, Baron William Henry. 1912. *Unemployment: A Problem of Industry*. London: Longmans, Green.

Bianchi, Suzanne M., John P. Robinson, and Melissa A. Milkie. 2006. *Changing Rhythms of American Family Life*. New York: Russell Sage Foundation.

Bianchi, Suzanne M., Liana C. Sayer, Melissa A. Milkie, and John P. Robinson. 2012. "House-work: Who Did, Does, or Will Do It, and How Much Does It Matter?" *Social Forces* 91(1): 55–63.

Bird, Chloe E., and Patricia P. Rieker. 2008. *Gender and Health: The Effects of Constrained Choices and Social Policies.* New York: Cambridge University Press.

Blair-Loy, Mary. 2003. *Competing Devotions: Career and Family among Women Executives.* Cambridge, MA.: Harvard University Press.

Blau, Francine D., and Lawrence M. Kahn. 2007. "Changes in the Labor Supply Behavior of Married Women: 1980–2000." *Journal of Labor Economics* 25(3): 393–438.

———. 2017. "The Gender Wage Gap: Extent, Trends, and Explanations." *Journal of Economic Literature* 55(3): 789–865.

Bloemraad, Irene, Will Kymlicka, Michèle Lamont, and Leanne Son Hing. 2019. "Membership without Social Citizenship? Deservingness and Redistribution as Grounds for Equality." *Daedalus* 148(3): 73–104.

Boar, Corina, and Simon Mongey. 2020. "Dynamic Trade-Offs and Labor Supply under the CARES Act." NBER Working Paper No. 27727.

Bobel, Chris. 2010. *Paradox of Natural Mothering.* Philadelphia: Temple University Press.

Bonilla-Silva, Eduardo. 2006. *Racism without Racists: Color-Blind Racism and the Persistence of Racial Inequality in the United States.* Plymouth, UK: Rowman & Littlefield.

Booth, Alison L., and Marco Francesconi. 2000. "Job Mobility in 1990s Britain: Does Gender Matter?" *Research in Labor Economics* 19:173–89.

Boushey, Heather. 2016. *Finding Time: The Economics of Work-Life-Conflict.* Cambridge, MA: Harvard University Press.

Boushey, Heather, and Sarah Jane Glynn. 2012. *There Are Significant Business Costs to Replacing Employees.* Washington, DC: Center for American Progress.

Boushey, Heather, and Carmen Sanchez Cumming. 2020. "Coronavirus Recession Deep-ens U.S. Job Losses in April Especially among Low-Wage Workers and Women." Washington Center for Equitable Growth, May 8.

Bowen, Sarah, Joslyn Brenton, and Sinikka Elliott. 2019. *Pressure Cooker: Why Home Cooking Won't Solve Our Problems and What We Can Do about It.* New York: Oxford University Press.

Branch, Enobong. 2011. *Opportunity Denied: Limiting Black Women to Devalued Work.* New Brunswick, NJ: Rutgers University Press.

Brand, Jennie E. 2006. "The Effects of Job Displacement on Job Quality: Findings from the Wis-consin Longitudinal Study." *Research in Social Stratification and Mobility* 24(3): 275–98.

———. 2015. "The Far-Reaching Impact of Job Loss and Unemployment." *Annual Review of Sociology* 41(1): 359–75.

Brand, Jennie E., and Sarah A. Burgard. 2008. "Job Displacement and Social Participation over the Lifecourse: Findings for a Cohort of Joiners." *Social Forces* 87(1): 211–42.

Brand, Jennie E., and Juli Simon Thomas. 2014. "Job Displacement among Single Mothers: Effects on Children's Outcomes in Young Adulthood." *American Journal of Sociology* 119(4): 955–1001.

Brand, Jennie E., and Yu Xie. 2010. "Who Benefits Most from College? Evidence for Negative Selection in Heterogeneous Economic Returns to Higher Education." *American Sociological Review* 75(2): 273–302.

Bricker, Jesse, Lisa J. Dettling, Alice Henriques, Joanne W. Hsu, Lindsay Jacobs, Kevin B. Moore, Sarah Pack, John Sabelhaus, Jeffrey Thompson, and Richard A. Windle. 2017. "Changes in U.S. Family Finances from 2013 to 2016: Evidence from the Survey of Consumer Finances." *Federal Reserve Bulletin* 103(3): 1–41.

Buchwald, Elisabeth. 2020. "Airbnb Will Give Laid-off Employees 14 Weeks Base Pay and Health Insurance, but Millions of Other Laid-off Workers Are Not So Lucky." *Market-Watch*, May 7.

Budig, Michelle J. 2002. "Male Advantage and the Gender Composition of Jobs: Who Rides the Glass Escalator?" *Social Problems* 49(2): 258–77.

Budig, Michelle J., Joya Misra, and Irene Boeckmann. 2012. "The Motherhood Penalty in Cross-National Perspective: The Importance of Work–Family Policies and Cultural Attitudes." *Social Politics* 19(2): 163–93.

Bunker, Nick. 2016. "Unemployment Insurance Might Increase Unemployment, but Only Slightly." Washington Center for Equitable Growth, April 13.

Bureau of Labor Statistics. 2014. "Worker Displacement: 2011–13." News release, August 26. https://www.bls.gov/news.release/archives/disp_08262014.pdf.

———. 2015. "Table A-12. Unemployed Persons by Duration of Unemployment." Data Retrieval: Labor Force Statistics (Current Population Survey). Last modified February 19, 2020. https://www.bls.gov/webapps/legacy/cpsatab12.htm/Table-A-12-Unemployed-persons-by-duration-of-unemployment.

———. 2016. "Worker Displacement: 2013–15." News release, August 25. https://www.bls.gov/news.release/archives/disp_08252016.pdf.

———. 2018a. "Alternative Measures of Labor Underutilization for States." Local Area Unemployment Statistics. Accessed September 6, 2018. https://www.bls.gov/lau/stalt.htm.

———. 2018b. "Displaced Workers Summary: 2015–17." News release, August 28. https://www.bls.gov/news.release/archives/disp_08282018.htm.

———. 2018c. "The Employment Situation—August 2018." News release, September 7. https://www.bls.gov/news.release/archives/empsit_09072018.pdf.

———. 2019a. "Employee Benefits in the United States—March 2019." News release, September 19. https://www.bls.gov/news.release/pdf/ebs2.pdf.

———. 2019b. "Employment Characteristics of Families Summary." News release, April 18. https://www.bls.gov/news.release/archives/famee_04182019.pdf.

———. 2019c. "Number of Jobs, Labor Market Experience, and Earnings Growth: Results from a National Longitudinal Survey." News release, August 22.

———. 2019d. "Nursing Assistants and Orderlies." *Occupational Outlook Handbook*. Accessed August 20, 2019. https://www.bls.gov/ooh/healthcare/nursing-assistants.htm.

———. 2020a. "Job Openings and Labor Turnover (JOLT) Survey." News release, January.

———. 2020b. "State Employment and Unemployment (Monthly) News Release." January 24. https://www.bls.gov/news.release/archives/laus_01242020.htm.

Bureau of Labor Statistics, Mid–Atlantic Information Office. 2019. "Women's Earnings in Pennsylvania—2018." December 9. https://www.bls.gov/regions/mid-atlantic/news-release/womensearnings_pennsylvania.htm#wepac1_2018.

Burgard, Sarah A. 2011. "The Needs of Others: Gender and Sleep Interruptions for Caregivers." *Social Forces* 89(4): 1189–215.

Byrd, Ayana. 2019. "LISTEN: Code Switch Dives into Story Behind the 'Welfare Queen.'" *Colorlines*, June 10.

Byron, Reginald A., and Vincent J. Roscigno. 2014. "Relational Power, Legitimation, and Pregnancy Discrimination." *Gender & Society* 28(3): 435–62.

Cabello-Hutt, Tania. 2020. "Changes in Work and Care Trajectories during the Transition to Motherhood." *Social Science Research* 90 (August): 102439.

Calarco, Jessica McCrory. 2018. *Negotiating Opportunities: How the Middle Class Secures Advantages in School*. New York: Oxford University Press.

Caliendo, Marco, Konstantinos Tatsiramos, and Arne Uhlendorff. 2013. "Benefit Duration, Unemployment Duration, and Job Match Quality: A Regression-Discontinuity Approach." *Journal of Applied Econometrics* 28(4): 604–27.

Calvo, Esteban, Christine A. Mair, and Natalia Sarkisian. 2015. "Individual Troubles, Shared Troubles: The Multiplicative Effect of Individual and Country-Level Unemployment on Life Satisfaction in 95 Nations (1981–2009)." *Social Forces* 93(4): 1625–53

Carlson, Daniel. In progress. "Are All Egalitarian Relations Created Equal? Routine Housework Task Sharing and Relationship Quality in Egalitarian Couples."

Carlson, Daniel L., Sarah Hanson, and Andrea Fitzroy. 2016. "The Division of Child Care, Sexual Intimacy, and Relationship Quality in Couples." *Gender & Society* 30(3): 442–66.

Carlson, Daniel L., Amanda Jayne Miller, and Sharon Sassler. 2018. "Stalled for Whom? Change in the Division of Particular Housework Tasks and Their Consequences for Middle-to Low-Income Couples." *Socius: Sociological Research for a Dynamic World* 4:1–17.

Carlson, Daniel L., Richard Petts, and Joanna R. Pepin. 2020. "U.S. Couples' Divisions of Housework and Childcare during COVID-19 Pandemic." *SocArXiv*, May 6.

Cellini, Stephanie Riegg, Signe-Mary McKernan, and Caroline Ratcliffe. 2008. "The Dynamics of Poverty in the United States: A Review of Data, Methods, and Findings." *Journal of Policy Analysis and Management* 27(3): 577–605.

Centers for Disease Control and Prevention. 2019. "*QuickStats*: Percentage of Persons in Families Having Problems Paying Medical Bills in the Past 12 Months, by Age Group—National Health Interview Survey, 2011–2017." *Morbidity and Mortality Weekly Report* 68(14): 334. http://dx.doi.org/10.15585/mmwr.mm6814a6.

Cha, Youngjoo. 2010. "Reinforcing Separate Spheres." *American Sociological Review* 75(2): 303–29.

———. 2014. "Job Mobility and the Great Recession: Wage Consequences by Gender and Parenthood." *Sociological Science* 1:159.

Charles, Maria, and David B. Grusky. 2004. *Occupational Ghettos: The Worldwide Segregation of Women and Men*. Stanford, CA: Stanford University Press.

Chen, Victor Tan. 2015. *Cut Loose: Jobless and Hopeless in an Unfair Economy*. Oakland: University of California Press.

Cherlin, Andrew J. 2010. *The Marriage-Go-Round: The State of Marriage and the Family in America Today*. New York: Vintage.

Chesley, Noelle. 2011. "Stay-at-Home Fathers and Breadwinning Mothers." *Gender & Society* 25(5): 642–64.

Chetty, Raj. 2008. "Moral Hazard versus Liquidity and Optimal Unemployment Insurance." *Journal of Political Economy* 116(2): 173–234.

Chikhale, Nisha. 2018. "Household Insecurity Matters for U.S. Economic Growth and Stability." Washington Center for Equitable Growth, May 16.

Christopher, Karen. 2012. "Extensive Mothering: Employed Mothers' Constructions of the Good Mother." *Gender & Society* 26(1): 73–96.

Clawson, Dan, and Naomi Gerstel. 2014. *Unequal Time: Gender, Class, and Family in Employment Schedules*. New York: Russell Sage Foundation.

Cohen, Patricia. 2018. "Paychecks Lag as Profits Soar, and Prices Erode Wage Gains." *New York Times*, July 14.

———. 2019. "Companies Cut Back, but Consumers Party On, Driving the Economy." *New York Times*, November 4.

Cohen, Philip N. 1998. "Replacing Housework in the Service Economy: Gender, Class, and Race-Ethnicity in Service Spending." *Gender & Society* 12(2): 219–31.

———. 2017. "New Data Show Change in the Class (Identity) Structure." *Family Inequality*, April 25.

Collins, Caitlyn. 2019. *Making Motherhood Work: How Women Manage Careers and Caregiving*. Princeton, NJ: Princeton University Press.

———. 2020. "Is Maternal Guilt a Cross-National Experience?" *Qualitative Sociology*.

Collins, Caitlyn, Liana Christin Landivar, Leah Ruppanner, and William J. Scarborough. 2020. "COVID-19 and the Gender Gap in Work Hours." *Gender, Work & Organization*: 1–12.

Coltrane, Scott. 2000. "Research on Household Labor: Modeling and Measuring the Social Embeddedness of Routine Family Work." *Journal of Marriage and Family* 62(4): 1208–33.

———. 2001. "Parenting in Transition." In *Mothers and Children: Feminist Analyses and Personal Narratives*, ed. Susan E. Chase and Mary F. Rogers, 103–7. New Brunswick, NJ: Rutgers University Press.

Commonwealth Fund. 2011. "*Three Quarters of Those Who Have Lost Jobs and Health Insurance Are Skipping Needed Medicine and Health Care; Many Struggling with Medical Debt.*" 2011. News Release, August 24.

Compare Your Country. N.d. "Compare Your Country: Employment and Protection Legislation." Accessed November 13, 2019. https://www1.compareyourcountry.org/employment -protection-legislation/en/0/178/datatable/.

Conley, Dalton. 1999. *Being Black, Living in the Red: Race, Wealth, and Social Policy in America*. Berkeley: University of California Press.

Coontz, Stephanie. 2016. "Why the White Working Class Ditched Clinton." CNN, November 11.

Cooper, Marianne. 2000. "Being the 'Go-to Guy': Fatherhood, Masculinity, and the Organization of Work in Silicon Valley." *Qualitative Sociology* 23(4): 379–405.

———. 2014. *Cut Adrift: Families in Insecure Times*. Oakland: University of California Press.

Correll, Shelley J. 2004. "Constraints into Preferences: Gender, Status, and Emerging Career Aspirations." *American Sociological Review* 69(1): 93–113.

Cortes, Guido Matias, and Eliza Forsythe. 2020. "Impacts of the COVID-19 Pandemic and the CARES Act on Earnings and Inequality." Social Science Research Network, Working Paper No. 3689187.

Cotter, David, Joan M. Hermsen, and Reeve Vanneman. 2011. "The End of the Gender Revolution? Gender Role Attitudes from 1977 to 2008." *American Journal of Sociology* 117(1): 259–89.

Damaske, Sarah. 2009. "Brown Suits Need Not Apply: The Intersection of Race, Gender, and Class in Institutional Network Building." *Sociological Forum* 24 (2): 402–24.

———. 2011. *For the Family? How Class and Gender Shape Women's Work.* New York: Oxford University Press.

———. 2020. "Job Loss and Attempts to Return to Work: Complicating Inequalities across Gender and Class." *Gender & Society* 34(1): 7–30.

Damaske, Sarah, and Adrianne Frech. In progress. "Unemployment Trajectories across the Life Course Gender, Economic Context, and Work-Family Responsibilities." Unpublished working paper.

Damaske, Sarah, and Adrianne Frech. 2016. "Women's Work Pathways across the Life Course." *Demography* 53(2): 365–91.

Daminger, Allison. 2019. "The Cognitive Dimension of Household Labor." *American Sociological Review* 84(4): 609–33.

Dannefer, Dale. 2003. "Cumulative Advantage/Disadvantage and the Life Course: Cross-Fertilizing Age and Social Science Theory." *Journals of Gerontology Series B: Psychological Sciences and Social Sciences* 58(6): S327–37.

Datta, Deepak K., James P. Guthrie, Dynah Basuil, and Alankrita Pandey. 2010. "Causes and Effects of Employee Downsizing: A Review and Synthesis." *Journal of Management* 36(1): 281–348.

Davies, Karen, and Johanna Esseveld. 1989. "Factory Women, Redundancy, and the Search for Work: Toward a Reconceptualisation of Employment and Unemployment." *Sociological Review* 37(2): 219–52.

De Ruijter, Esther, Judith K. Treas, and Philip N. Cohen. 2005. "Outsourcing the Gender Factory: Living Arrangements and Service Expenditures on Female and Male Tasks." *Social Forces* 84(1): 305–22.

Desmond, Matthew. 2018. "Americans Want to Believe Jobs Are the Solution to Poverty. They're Not." *New York Times*, September 11.

Desmond, Matthew, and Carl Gershenson. 2016. "Housing and Employment Insecurity among the Working Poor." *Social Problems* 63(1): 46–67.

Detting, Lisa J., Joanne W. Hsu, Lindsay Jacobs, Kevin B. Moore, Jeffrey P. Thompson, and Elizabeth Llanes. 2017. "Recent Trends in Wealth-Holding by Race and Ethnicity: Evidence from the Survey of Consumer Finances." *FEDS Notes*, September 27.

Deutsch, Francine. 1999. *Halving It All: How Equally Shared Parenting Works.* Cambridge, MA: Harvard University Press.

Dewan, Shaila. 2014. "A Job Seeker's Desperate Choice." *New York Times*, June 21.

Dill, Janette, and Melissa J. Hodges. 2019. "Is Healthcare the New Manufacturing? Industry, Gender, and 'Good Jobs' for Low- and Middle-Skill Workers." *Social Science Research* 84:102350.

Directorate General Employment, Social Affairs, and Equal Opportunities. 2006. *Termination of Employment Relationships: Legal Situation in the Member States of the European Union.* Brussels: European Commission.

Dixon, K. A., and Carl E. Van Horn. 2003. "The Disposable Worker: Living in a Job-Loss Economy." *Heldrich Work Trends* 6(2): 1–28.

Dooley, David, Joann Prause, and Kathleen Ham-Rowbottom. 2000. Underemployment and Depression: Longitudinal Relationships. *Journal of Health and Social Behavior* 41(4): 421–36.

Dow, Dawn Marie. 2019. *Mothering While Black: Boundaries and Burdens of Middle-Class Parenthood*. Oakland: University of California Press.

Dube, Arindrajit. 2020. "The Importance of an Expanded U.S. Unemployment Insurance System during the Coronavirus Recession." Washington Center for Equitable Growth, March 31.

Edin, Kathryn, and Maria Kefalas. 2005. *Promises I Can Keep: Why Poor Women Put Motherhood before Marriage*. Berkeley: University of California Press.

Edin, Kathryn, and Laura Lein. 1997. *Making Ends Meet: How Single Mothers Survive Welfare and Low-Wage Work*. New York: Russell Sage Foundation.

Edin, Kathryn, and Timothy Jon Nelson. 2013. *Doing the Best I Can: Fatherhood in the Inner City*. Berkeley: University of California Press.

Edin, Kathryn, and H. Luke Shaefer. 2015. *$2.00 a Day: Living on Almost Nothing in America*. New York: Houghton Mifflin Harcourt.

Edwards, Kathryn A. 2020. "The Racial Disparity in Unemployment Benefits." *The RAND Blog*, July 15.

Elder, Glen H., Jr. 1995. "The Life Course Paradigm: Social Change and Individual Development." In *Examining Lives in Context: Perspectives on the Ecology of Human Development*, 101–40. Washington, DC: American Psychological Association.

———. 1998. "The Life Course as Developmental Theory." *Child Development* 69(1): 1–12.

Elkins, Kathleen. 2018. "Here's How Much Money Americans Have in Savings at Every Income Level." *CNBC.com*, September 27.

Emeka, Amon. 2018. "Where Race Matters Most: Measuring the Strength of Association between Race and Unemployment across the 50 United States." *Social Indicators Research* 136(2): 557–73.

Employee Benefits Security Administration. 2015. "FAQs on COBRA Continuation Health Coverage." *U.S. Department of Labor*. Accessed November 13, 2019. https://www.dol.gov/sites/dolgov/files/legacy-files/ebsa/about-ebsa/our-activities/resource-center/faqs/cobra-continuation-health-coverage-consumer.pdf.

England, Paula. 2010. "The Gender Revolution: Uneven and Stalled." *Gender & Society* 24(2): 149–66.

England, Paula. 2011. "Reassessing the Uneven Gender Revolution and Its Slowdown." *Gender & Society* 25(1): 113–23.

England, Paula, Jonathan Bearak, Michelle J. Budig, and Melissa J. Hodges. 2016. "Do Highly Paid, Highly Skilled Women Experience the Largest Motherhood Penalty?" *American Sociological Review* 81(6): 1161–89.

England, Paula, and Nancy Folbre. 1999. "The Cost of Caring." *The Annals of the American Academy of Political and Social Science* 561:39–51.

Evans, Louwanda. 2013. *Cabin Pressure: African American Pilots, Flight Attendants, and Emotional Labor*. Lanham, MD: Rowman & Littlefield.

Evans, Louwanda, and Wendy Leo Moore. 2015. "Impossible Burdens: White Institutions, Emotional Labor, and Micro-Resistance." *Social Problems* 62(3): 439–54.

Farber, H. S. 2011. "Job Loss in the Great Recession: Historical Perspective from the Displaced Workers Survey, 1984–2010." NBER Working Paper No. 17040, May.

Farber, Henry S. 2005. "What Do We Know about Job Loss in the United States? Evidence from the Displaced Workers Survey, 1984–2004." *Economic Perspectives* 29(2): 13–29.

Farber, Henry S., John Haltiwanger, and Katharine G. Abraham. 1997. "The Changing Face of Job Loss in the United States, 1981–1995." *Brookings Papers on Economic Activity: Microeconomics*, 55–142.

Farooq, Ammar, Adriana D. Kugler, and Umberto Muratori. 2020. "Do Unemployment Insurance Benefits Improve Match Quality? Evidence from Recent U.S. Recessions." NBER Working Paper No. 27574.

Fauser, Sophia. 2019. "Time Availability and Housework: The Effect of Unemployment on Couples' Hours of Household Labor." *Social Science Research* 83:102304.

Federal Reserve System. 2019. *Report on the Economic Well-Being of U.S. Households in 2018.* Board of Governors of the Federal Reserve System, May.

Ferree, Myra Marx. 1987. "Family and Job for Working-Class Women: Gender and Class Systems Seen from Below." In *Families and Work*, ed. N. Gerstel and H. E. Gross, 289–301. Philadelphia: Temple University Press.

Folbre, Nancy. 2001. *The Invisible Heart: Economics and Family Values.* New York: New Press.

Ford, Karly Sarita. 2019. "Marrying within the Alma Mater: Understanding the Role of Same-University Marriages in Educational Homogamy." *Sociological Research Online*, August 28.

Frank, Robert H., and Philip J. Cook. 2010. *The Winner-Take-All Society: Why the Few at the Top Get So Much More than the Rest of Us.* New York: Random House.

Frech, Adrianne, and Sarah Damaske. 2012. "The Relationships between Mothers' Work Pathways and Physical and Mental Health." *Journal of Health and Social Behavior* 53(4): 396–412.

———. 2019. "Men's Income Trajectories and Physical and Mental Health at Midlife." *American Journal of Sociology* 124(5): 1372–412.

Frech, Adrianne, Jane Lankes, and Sarah Damaske. In progress. "The Myth of Men's Stable, Continuous Labor Force Attachment: Multi-trajectories of U.S. Baby-Boomer Men's Employment."

French, Michael T., Jenny Homer, Gulcin Gumus, and Lucas Hickling. 2016. "Key Provisions of the Patient Protection and Affordable Care Act (ACA): A Systematic Review and Presentation of Early Research Findings." *Health Services Research* 51(5): 1735–71.

Gangl, Markus. 2006. "Scar Effects of Unemployment: An Assessment of Institutional Complementarities." *American Sociological Review* 71(6): 986–1013.

Garey, Anita Ilta. 1999. *Weaving Work and Motherhood.* Philadelphia: Temple University Press.

Gatta, Mary. 2014. *All I Want Is a Job!: Unemployed Women Navigating the Public Workforce System.* Stanford, CA: Stanford University Press.

Geiger, A. W. 2016. "Sharing Chores a Key to Good Marriage, Say Most Married Adults." Pew Research Center, November 30.

Gerson, Kathleen. 2010. *The Unfinished Revolution: How a New Generation Is Reshaping Family, Work, and Gender in America.* New York: Oxford University Press.

Gerson, Kathleen, and Sarah Damaske. 2020. *The Art and Science of Qualitative Interviewing*. New York: Oxford University Press.

Gerstel, Naomi. 2000. "The Third Shift: Gender, Employment, and Care Work outside the Home." *Qualitative Sociology* 23:467–83.

Glaser, Barney G., and Anselm L. Strauss. 1967. *The Discovery of Grounded Theory: Strategies for Qualitative Research*. Chicago: Aldine.

Glauber, Rebecca. 2008. "Race and Gender in Families and at Work." *Gender & Society* 22(1): 8–30.

Gleeson, Shannon, and Roberto G. Gonzales. 2012. "When Do Papers Matter? An Institutional Analysis of Undocumented Life in the United States." *International Migration* 50(4): 1–19.

Goldstein, Amy. 2018. *Janesville: An American Story*. New York: Simon and Schuster.

Goodman, Ellen. 1990. "Guilt Gap." *Washington Post*, May 12.

Gough, Margaret. 2019. "Gender Differences in Time in Child Care during Unemployment." *SocArXiv*, January 23.

Gough, Margaret, and Alexandra Killewald. 2011. "Unemployment in Families: The Case of Housework." *Journal of Marriage and Family* 73(5): 1085–1100.

Gould-Werth, Alix. 2020. "Fool Me Once: Investing in Unemployment Insurance Systems to Avoid the Mistakes of the Great Recession during COVID-19." Washington Center for Equitable Growth, April 30.

Gould-Werth, Alix, and Raksha Kopparam. 2020. "How the Coronavirus Pandemic Is Harming Family Well-Being for U.S. Low-Wage Workers." Washington Center for Equitable Growth, April 1.

Gould-Werth, Alix, and H. Luke Schaefer. 2012. "Unemployment Insurance Participation by Education and by Race and Ethnicity." *Monthly Labor Review* (October): 28–41.

Greenhouse, Steven. 2008. *The Big Squeeze: Tough Times for the American Worker*. New York: Alfred A. Knopf.

Grusky, David B., Bruce Western, and Christopher Wimer. 2011. "The Consequences of the Great Recession." In *The Great Recession*, 2–20. New York: Russell Sage Foundation.

Hacker, Jacob. 2006. *The Great Risk Shift: Why American Jobs, Families, Health Care, and Retirement Aren't Secure—and How We Can Fight Back*. New York: Oxford University Press.

Hayes, Jeff, and Heidi Hartmann. 2011. *Women and Men Living on the Edge: Economic Insecurity after the Great Recession*. Washington, DC: Institute for Women's Policy Research.

Hays, Sharon. 1996. *The Cultural Contradictions of Motherhood*. New Haven, CT: Yale University Press.

———. 2003. *Flat Broke with Children: Women in the Age of Welfare Reform*. New York: Oxford University Press.

Hayward, Mark D., and Bridget Gorman. 2004. "The Long Arm of Childhood: The Influence of Early Life Conditions on Men's Mortality." *Demography* 41:87–108.

Heckman, James. 1974. "Shadow Prices, Market Wages, and Labor Supply." *Econometrica* 42:679–94.

Heilman, Brian, María Rosario Castro Bernardini, and Kimberly Pfeifer. 2020. *Caring under COVID-19: How the Pandemic Is—and Is Not—Changing Unpaid Care and Domestic Work Responsibilities in the United States*. Boston: Oxfam and Washington, DC: Promundo-US.

Henly, Julia R., and Susan Lambert. 2005. "Nonstandard Work and Child-Care Needs of Low-Income Parents." In *Work, Family, Health, and Well-Being*, ed. S. M. Bianchi, L. M. Casper, and B. R. King, 473–92. Mahwah, NJ: Lawrence Erlbaum Associates.

Heyman, Therese Thau, Sandra S. Phillips, and John Szarkowski. 1994. *Dorothea Lange: American Photographs*. San Francisco: Chronicle Books.

Higginbotham, Elizabeth. 2001. *Too Much to Ask: Black Women in the Era of Integration*. Chapel Hill: University of North Carolina Press.

Hill, M. J., R. M. Harrison, A. V. Sargeant, and V. Talbot. 1973. *Men Out of Work: A Study of Unemployment in Three English Towns*. Cambridge: Cambridge University Press.

Hochschild, Arlie Russell. 1989. *The Second Shift: Working Parents and the Revolution at Home*. New York: Viking.

———. 1997. *The Time Bind: When Work Becomes Home and Home Becomes Work*. New York: Metropolitan Books.

Hollister, Matissa. 2011. "Employment Stability in the U.S. Labor Market: Rhetoric versus Reality." *Annual Review of Sociology* 37(1): 305–24.

Hook, Jennifer L. 2017. "Women's Housework: New Tests of Time and Money." *Journal of Marriage and Family* 79(1): 179–98.

Hout, Michael, Asaf Levanon, and Erin Cumberworth. 2011. "Job Loss and Unemployment." In *The Great Recession*, 59–81. New York: Russell Sage Foundation.

Howe, Louise Kapp. 1977. *Pink Collar Workers: Inside the World of Women's Work*. New York: Putnam.

Hulse, Carl. 2020. "Jobless Aid Fuels Partisan Divide over Next Pandemic Rescue Package." *New York Times*, May 7.

Ishizuka, Patrick. 2019. "Social Class, Gender, and Contemporary Parenting Standards in the United States: Evidence from a National Survey Experiment." *Social Forces* 98(1): 31–58.

Jacobs, Elisabeth. 2015. "The Declining Labor Force Participation Rate: Causes, Consequences, and the Path Forward." Washington Center for Equitable Growth, July 15.

Jacobs, Jerry A., and Kathleen Gerson. 2004. *The Time Divide: Work, Family, and Gender Inequality*. Cambridge, MA: Harvard University Press.

Jerolmack, Colin, and Alexandra K. Murphy. 2019. "The Ethical Dilemmas and Social Scientific Trade-Offs of Masking in Ethnography." *Sociological Methods & Research* 48(4): 801–27.

Jordan, Glenn. 2020. "Recent Layoffs Raise Questions about Severance, Notification." *Press Herald*, May 4.

Juhn, Chinhui, and Kevin Murphy. 1997. "Wage Inequality and Family Labor Supply." *Journal of Labor Economics* 15:72–97.

Kaiser Family Foundation. 2019. "Key Facts about the Uninsured Population," December 13. https://www.kff.org/uninsured/fact-sheet/key-facts-about-the-uninsured-population/.

Kalev, Alexandra. 2014. "How You Downsize Is Who You Downsize: Biased Formalization, Accountability, and Managerial Diversity." *American Sociological Review* 79(1): 109–35.

Kalleberg, Arne L. 2009. "Precarious Work, Insecure Workers: Employment Relations in Transition." *American Sociological Review* 74(1): 1–22.

———. 2011. *Good Jobs, Bad Jobs: The Rise of Polarized and Precarious Employment Systems in the United States, 1970s–2000s*. New York: Russell Sage Foundation.

Kelly, Erin L., and Phyllis Moen. 2007. "Rethinking the Clockwork of Work: Why Schedule Control May Pay Off at Work and at Home." *Advances in Developing Human Resources* 9(4): 487–506.

Kelly, Keith J. 2020. "Wired Magazine Blasts Condé Nast's 'Meager or Nonexistent' Severance Packages." *New York Post*, May 19.

Killewald, Alexandra. 2011. "Opting Out and Buying Out: Wives' Earnings and Housework Time." *Journal of Marriage and Family* 73(2): 459–71.

Killewald, Alexandra, and Margaret Gough. 2013. "Does Specialization Explain Marriage Penalties and Premiums?" *American Sociological Review* 78(3): 477–502.

Killewald, Alexandra, and Xiaolin Zhuo. 2019. "U.S. Mothers' Long-Term Employment Patterns." *Demography* 56(1): 285–320.

Kletzer, Lori G. 1998. "Job Displacement." *Journal of Economic Perspectives* 12(1): 115–36.

Kochhar, Rakesh. 2018. "The American Middle Class Is Stable in Size but Losing Ground Financially to Upper-Income Families." Pew Research Center, September 6.

Kochhar, Rakesh, and Richard Fry. 2015. "America's 'Middle' Holds Its Ground after the Great Recession." Pew Research Center, February 4.

Komarovsky, Mirra. 1940 [1971]. *The Unemployed Man and His Family: The Effect of Unemployment upon the Status of the Man in Fifty-Nine Families*. New York: Octagon Books.

Kuhn, Moritz, Moritz Schularick, and Ulrike I. Steins. 2018. "Income and Wealth Inequality in America, 1949–2016." Preprint. Federal Reserve Bank of Minneapolis.

Lachance-Grzela, Mylène, and Geneviève Bouchard. 2010. "Why Do Women Do the Lion's Share of Housework? A Decade of Research." *Sex Roles* 63(11): 767–80.

Lambert, Susan J., Anna Haley-Lock, and Julia R. Henly. 2012. "Schedule Flexibility in Hourly Jobs: Unanticipated Consequences and Promising Directions." *Community, Work & Family* 15(3): 293–315.

Lambert, Susan J., and Julia R. Henly. 2012. "Frontline Managers Matter: Labour Flexibility Practices and Sustained Employment in U.S. Retail Jobs." In *Are Bad Jobs Inevitable? Trends, Determinants, and Responses to Job Quality in the Twenty-First Century*, 143–59. New York: Macmillan International Higher Education.

Landivar, Liana Christin. 2017. *Mothers at Work: Who Opts Out?* Boulder, CO: Lynne Rienner.

Lane, Carrie M. 2009. "Man Enough to Let My Wife Support Me: How Changing Models of Career and Gender Are Reshaping the Experience of Unemployment." *American Ethnologist* 36: 681–92.

———. 2011. *A Company of One: Insecurity, Independence, and the New World of White-Collar Unemployment*. Ithaca, NY: Cornell University Press.

Lareau, Annette. 2003. *Unequal Childhoods: Class, Race, and Family Life*. Berkeley: University of California Press.

Lee, Hedwig, and Kristin Turney. 2015. "Investigating the Relationship between Perceived Discrimination, Social Status, and Mental Health." *Society and Mental Health* 2(1): 1–20.

Legerski, Elizabeth Miklya, and Marie Cornwall. 2010. "Working-Class Job Loss, Gender, and the Negotiation of Household Labor." *Gender & Society* 24(4): 447–74.

Light, Ryan, Vincent J. Roscigno, and Alexandra Kalev. 2011. "Racial Discrimination, Interpretation, and Legitimation at Work." *The Annals of the American Academy of Political and Social Science* 634(1): 39–59.

Lopez, Steven H., and Lora A. Phillips. 2019. "Unemployed: White-Collar Job Searching after the Great Recession." *Work and Occupations* 46(4): 470–510.

Luker, Kristin. 2008. *Salsa Dancing into the Social Sciences: Research in an Age of Info-Glut.* Cambridge, MA: Harvard University Press.

Mare, Robert D. 2001. "Observations on the Study of Social Mobility and Inequality." In *Social Stratification: Class, Race, and Gender in Sociological Perspective,* 2nd ed., ed. David B. Grusky, 477–88. Boulder, CO: Westview Press.

Marsden, Peter, Arne L. Kalleberg, and Cynthia R. Cook. 1993. "Gender Differences in Organizational Commitment: Influences of Work Positions and Family Roles." *Work and Occupations* 20(3): 368–90.

Martin, Emmie. 2017. "70% of Americans Consider Themselves Middle Class but Only 50% Are." CNBC.com, June 30.

Martin, Molly A., and Adam M. Lippert. 2012. "Feeding Her Children, but Risking Her Health: The Intersection of Gender, Household Food Insecurity, and Obesity." *Social Science & Medicine* 74(11): 1754–64.

Maume, David J., Anthony R. Bardo, and Rachel A. Sebastian. 2009. "Gender Differences in Sleep Disruption among Retail Food Workers." *American Sociological Review* 74(6): 989–1007.

May, Martha. 1982. "The Historical Problem of the Family Wage: The Ford Motor Company and the Five Dollar Day." *Feminist Studies* 8(2): 399–424.

McCall, Leslie. 2001. *Complex Inequality: Gender, Class, and Race in the New Economy.* New York: Routledge.

———. 2013. *The Undeserving Rich: American Beliefs about Inequality, Opportunity, and Redistribution.* Cambridge: Cambridge University Press.

McCall, Leslie, and Christine Percheski. 2010. "Income Inequality: New Trends and Research Directions." *Annual Review of Sociology* 36(1): 329–47.

McDonnell, Cadhla, Nancy Luke, and Susan E. Short. 2019. "Happy Moms, Happier Dads: Gendered Caregiving and Parents' Affect." *Journal of Family Issues* 40(17): 2553–81.

McGinn, Kathleen L., and Eunsil Oh. 2017. "Gender, Social Class, and Women's Employment." *Current Opinion in Psychology* 18:84–88.

McHugh, Rick, and Will Kimball. 2015. "How Low Can We Go? State Unemployment Insurance Programs Exclude Record Numbers of Jobless Workers." Briefing Paper No. 392. Economic Policy Institute.

McLanahan, Sara, and Christine Percheski. 2008. "Family Structure and the Reproduction of Inequalities." *Annual Review of Sociology* 34 (1): 257–76.

Mederer, Helen J. 1999. "Surviving the Demise of a Way of Life: Stress and Resilience in Northeastern Commercial Fishing Families." In *The Dynamics of Resilient Families,* edited by Hamilton McCubbin, Elizabeth A. Thompson, Anne I. Thompson, and Jo A. Futrell, 135–63. Thousand Oaks, CA: Sage Publications.

Medicaid. 2014. *FY 2013 Number of Children Ever Enrolled in Medicaid and Chip.* Accessed October 7, 2020. https://www.medicaid.gov/sites/default/files/2019-12/fy-2013-childrens-ever-enrolled-report.pdf.

Miller, Amanda J., and Daniel L. Carlson. 2016. "Great Expectations? Working- and Middle-Class Cohabitors' Expected and Actual Divisions of Housework." *Journal of Marriage and Family* 78(2): 346–63.

Miller, Amanda J., Daniel L. Carlson, and Sharon Sassler. 2019. "His Career, Her Job, Their Future: Cohabitors' Orientations toward Paid Work." *Journal of Family Issues* 40(11): 1509–1533.

Miller, Claire Cain. 2019."Women Did Everything Right. Then Work Got 'Greedy.'" *New York Times*, April 26.

Mishel, Lawrence, Jared Bernstein, and Heidi Shierholz. 2009. *The State of Working America 2008–2009*. Ithaca, NY: ILR Press.

Mishel, Lawrence, Josh Bivens, Elise Gould, and Heidi Shierholz. 2012. *The State of Working America*. Ithaca, NY: Cornell University Press.

Misra, Joya, and Marta Murray-Close. 2014. "The Gender Wage Gap in the United States and Cross Nationally." *Sociology Compass* 8(11): 1281–95.

Moen, Phyllis. 1979. "Family Impacts of the 1975 Recession: Duration of Unemployment." *Journal of Marriage and Family* 41(3): 561–72.

———. 1983. "Unemployment, Public Policy, and Families: Forecasts for the 1980s." *Journal of Marriage and the Family* 751–60.

———. 2001. "The Gendered Life Course." In *Handbook of Aging and the Social Sciences*, edited by L. George and R. Binstock, 179–96. San Diego: Academic Press.

Moen, Phyllis, and Patricia Roehling. 2005. *The Career Mystique: Cracks in the American Dream*. Lanham, MD: Rowman & Littlefield.

Mong, Sherry N., and Vincent J. Roscigno. 2010. "African American Men and the Experience of Employment Discrimination." *Qualitative Sociology* 33(1): 1–21.

Montez, Jennifer K., and Mark D. Hayward. 2014. "Cumulative Childhood Adversity, Educational Attainment, and Active Life Expectancy among U.S. Adults." *Demography* 51:413–35.

Morduch, Jonathan, and Rachel Schneider. 2017. *The Financial Diaries: How American Families Cope in a World of Uncertainty*. Princeton, NJ: Princeton University Press.

Moshfegh, Ottessa. 2019. *My Year of Rest and Relaxation*. New York: Penguin Books.

Mosley, Tonya. 2019. "Freaking Out about the Next Recession? Don't Put Your Money under the Mattress Just Yet." *New York Times*, October 19.

Mullainathan, Sendhil, and Eldar Shafir. 2013. *Scarcity: Why Having Too Little Means So Much*. New York: Macmillan.

National Bureau of Economic Research. 2010. "U.S. Business Cycle Expansions and Contractions." Accessed June 17, 2019. https://www-nber-org.proxy.mul.missouri.edu/cycles/cyclesmain.html.

National Center for Education Statistics. 2020. "Fast Facts: Teacher Characteristics and Trends." Retrieved October 6, 2020. https://nces.ed.gov/fastfacts/display.asp?id=28.

National Employment Law Project, "Maintaining Fair Weekly Benefits Amounts," *Unemployment Insurance Policy Advocate's Toolkit*, accessed September 4, 2020, https://www.nelp.org/wp-content/uploads/1C-Maintaining-Fair-Weekly-Benefits-Amounts.pdf.

Nelson, Margaret K., and Joan Smith. 1999. *Working Hard and Making Do: Surviving in Small Town America*. Berkeley: University of California Press.

Newman, Katherine S. 1988. *Falling from Grace: The Experience of Downward Mobility in the American Middle Class*. New York: Free Press.

Norris, Dawn R. 2016. *Job Loss, Identity, and Mental Health*. New Brunswick, NJ: Rutgers University Press.

Oliver, Melvin L., and Thomas M. Shapiro. 1995. *Black Wealth/White Wealth: A New Perspective on Racial Inequality*. New York: Routledge.

Pager, Devah. 2008. *Marked: Race, Crime, and Finding Work in an Era of Mass Incarceration*. Chicago: University of Chicago Press.

Pager, Devah, and Hana Shepherd. 2008. "The Sociology of Discrimination: Racial Discrimination in Employment, Housing, Credit, and Consumer Markets." *Annual Review of Sociology* 34(1): 181–209.

Park, Tae-youn, and Jason D. Shaw. 2013. "Turnover Rates and Organizational Performance: A Meta-Analysis." *Journal of Applied Psychology* 98(2): 268–309.

Patterson, Sarah. 2017. "Adult Children's Help to Parents." Unpublished dissertation. Pennsylvania State University.

Patterson, Sarah E., Sarah Damaske, and Christen Sheroff. 2017. "Gender and the MBA: Differences in Career Trajectories, Institutional Support, and Outcomes." *Gender & Society* 31(3): 310–32.

Pechey, Rachel, Susan A. Jebb, Michael P. Kelly, Eva Almiron-Roig, Susana Conde, Ryota Nakamura, Ian Shemilt, Marc Suhrcke, and Theresa M. Marteau. 2013. "Socioeconomic Differences in Purchases of More vs. Less Healthy Foods and Beverages: Analysis of over 25,000 British Households in 2010." *Social Science & Medicine* 92:22–26.

Pepin, Joanna R., and David A. Cotter. 2018. "Separating Spheres? Diverging Trends in Youth's Gender Attitudes about Work and Family." *Journal of Marriage and Family* 80(1): 7–24.

Percheski, Christine. 2008. "Opting Out? Cohort Differences in Professional Women's Employment Rates from 1960 to 2005." *American Sociological Review* 73(3): 497–517.

Pessin, Léa. 2018. "Changing Gender Norms and Marriage Dynamics in the United States." *Journal of Marriage and Family* 80(1): 25–41.

Pew Charitable Trusts. 2012. "Pursuing the American Dream: Economic Mobility across Generations," July.

Pingle, Jonathan F. 2006. "The Relocation Decisions of Working Couples." FEDS Working Paper No. 2006-33.

Pollmann-Schult, Matthias, and Felix Büchel. 2005. "Unemployment Benefits, Unemployment Duration, and Subsequent Job Quality: Evidence from West Germany." *Acta Sociologica* 48(1): 21–39.

Pugh, Allison J. 2015. *The Tumbleweed Society: Working and Caring in an Age of Insecurity*. New York: Oxford University Press.

Raley, Sara, Suzanne M. Bianchi, and Wendy Wang. 2012. "When Do Fathers Care? Mothers' Economic Contribution and Fathers' Involvement in Child Care." *American Journal of Sociology* 117(5): 1422–59.

Rank, Mark Robert, Thomas A. Hirschl, and Kirk A. Foster. 2014. *Chasing the American Dream: Understanding What Shapes Our Fortunes*. New York: Oxford University Press.

Rao, Aliya Hamid. 2017. "Stand by Your Man: Wives' Emotion Work during Men's Unemployment." *Journal of Marriage and Family* 79(3): 636–56.

———. 2020. *Crunch Time: How Married Couples Confront Unemployment*. Oakland: University of California Press.

Ray, Victor. 2019. "A Theory of Racialized Organizations." *American Sociological Review* 84(1): 26–53.

Read, Jen'nan Ghazal, and Bridget K. Gorman. 2010. "Gender and Health Inequality." *Annual Review of Sociology* 36:371–86.

Reczek, Corinne, Mieke Beth Thomeer, Amy C. Lodge, Debra Umberson, and Megan Underhill. 2014. "Diet and Exercise in Parenthood: A Social Control Perspective." *Journal of Marriage and Family* 76(5): 1047–62.

Reczek, Corinne, Lauren Gebhardt-Kram, Alexandra Kissling, and Debra Umberson. 2018. "Healthcare Work in Marriage: How Gay, Lesbian, and Heterosexual Spouses Encourage and Coerce Medical Care." *Journal of Health and Social Behavior* 59(4): 554–68.

Reeves, Richard, interview by Hari Sreenivasan. 2017. "How the Upper Middle Class Keeps Everyone Else Out." *PBS NewsHour*, August 5.

Reskin, Barbara F., and Michelle L. Maroto. 2011. "What Trends? Whose Choices? Comment on England." *Gender & Society* 25(1): 81–87.

Ridgeway, Cecilia L. 1997. "Interaction and the Conservation of Gender Inequality: Considering Employment." *American Sociological Review* 62(2): 218–35.

———. 2011. *Framed by Gender: How Gender Inequality Persists in the Modern World*. New York: Oxford University Press.

Ridgeway, Cecilia L., and Shelley J. Correll. 2004. "Unpacking the Gender System: A Theoretical Perspective on Gender Beliefs and Social Relations." *Gender & Society* 18(4): 510–31.

Risman, Barbara J. 2009. "From Doing to Undoing: Gender as We Know It." *Gender & Society* 23(1): 81–84.

Risman, Barbara J., Maxine P. Atkinson, and Stephen P. Blackwelder. 1999. "Understanding the Juggling Act: Gendered Preferences and Social Structural Constraints." *Sociological Forum* 14(2): 319–44.

Rivera, Lauren A. 2016. *Pedigree: How Elite Students Get Elite Jobs*. Princeton, NJ: Princeton University Press.

Roscigno, Vincent J., Lisa M. Williams, and Reginald A. Byron. 2012. "Workplace Racial Discrimination and Middle Class Vulnerability." *American Behavioral Scientist* 56(5): 696–710.

Rose, Mike. 2004. *The Mind at Work: Valuing the Intelligence of the American Worker*. New York: Viking.

Rothstein, Jesse, and Robert G. Valletta. 2017. "Scraping by: Income and Program Participation after the Loss of Extended Unemployment Benefits." *Journal of Policy Analysis and Management* 36(4): 880–908.

Royster, Deirdre A. 2003. *Race and the Invisible Hand: How White Networks Exclude Black Men from Blue-Collar Jobs*. Berkeley: University of California Press.

Ruppanner, Leah. 2020. *Motherlands: How States in the U.S. Push Mothers Out of Employment*. Philadelphia, PA: Temple University Press.

Saez, Emmanuel, and Gabriel Zucman. 2016. "Wealth Inequality in the United States since 1913: Evidence from Capitalized Income Tax Data." *Quarterly Journal of Economics* 131(2): 519–78.

Sarkisian, Natalia, and Naomi Gerstel. 2004. "Kin Support among Blacks and Whites: Race and Family Organization." *American Sociological Review* 69(6): 812–37.

———. 2006. "Marriage: The Good, the Bad, and the Greedy." *Contexts* 5(4): 16–21.

———. 2008. "Till Marriage Do Us Part: Adult Children's Relationships with Their Parents." *Journal of Marriage and Family* 70(2): 360–376.

Sassler, Sharon, and Amanda Miller. 2017. *Cohabitation Nation: Gender, Class, and the Remaking of Relationships.* Berkeley: University of California Press.

Sayer, Liana C. 2005. "Gender, Time, and Inequality: Trends in Women's and Men's Paid Work, Unpaid Work, and Free Time." *Social Forces* 84(1): 285–303.

———. 2010. "Trends in Housework." In *Dividing the Domestic: Men, Women, and Household Work in Cross-National Perspective*, ed. Judith Treas and Sonja Drobnič, 19–38. Stanford, CA: Stanford University Press.

Sayer, Liana C., and Leigh Fine. 2011. "Racial-Ethnic Differences in U.S. Married Women's and Men's Housework." *Social Indicators Research* 101(2): 259–65.

Schneider, Daniel. 2011. "Market Earnings and Household Work: New Tests of Gender Performance Theory." *Journal of Marriage and Family* 73(4): 845–60.

———. 2012. "Gender Deviance and Household Work: The Role of Occupation." *American Journal of Sociology* 117(4): 1029–72.

Schneider, Daniel, and Kristen Harknett. 2019. "Consequences of Routine Work-Schedule Instability for Worker Health and Well-Being." *American Sociological Review* 84(1): 82–114.

Schwartz, Christine R. 2013. "Trends and Variation in Assortative Mating: Causes and Consequences." *Annual Review of Sociology* 39(1): 451–70.

Scott, Marvin, and Stanford Lyman. 1968. "Accounts." *American Sociological Review* 33:46–61.

Seamster, Louise, and Victor Ray. 2018. "Against Teleology in the Study of Race: Toward the Abolition of the Progress Paradigm." *Sociological Theory* 36(4): 315–42.

Sharone, Ofer. 2013. *Flawed System/Flawed Self: Job Searching and Unemployment* Experiences. Chicago: University of Chicago Press.

Shell, A. 2018. "Bull Market, on Cusp of Becoming Longest in History for Stocks, Has Room to Run." *USA TODAY*, August 21.

Shenker-Osorio, Anat. 2013. "Why Americans All Believe They Are 'Middle Class.'" *The Atlantic*, August 1.

Sherman, Jennifer. 2009. *Those Who Work, Those Who Don't: Poverty, Morality, and Family in Rural America.* Minneapolis: University of Minnesota Press.

Sherman, Rachel. 2019. *Uneasy Street: The Anxieties of Affluence.* Princeton, NJ: Princeton University Press.

Shows, Carla, and Naomi Gerstel. 2009. "Fathering, Class, and Gender: A Comparison of Physicians and Emergency Medical Technicians." *Gender & Society* 23(2): 161–87.

Sjöberg, Ola. 2000. "Unemployment and Unemployment Benefits in the OECD 1960–1990: An Empirical Test of Neo-Classical Economic Theory." *Work, Employment, and Society* 14(1): 51–76.

Small, Mario Luis. 2006. "Neighborhood Institutions as Resource Brokers: Childcare Centers, Interorganizational Ties, and Resource Access among the Poor." *Social Problems* 53(2): 274–92.

———. 2009. "'How Many Cases Do I Need?': On Science and the Logic of Case Selection in Field-Based Research." *Ethnography* 10(1): 5–38.

————. 2017. *Someone to Talk To*. New York: Oxford University Press.

Smith, Sandra Susan. 2007. *Lone Pursuit: Distrust and Defensive Individualism among the Black Poor*. New York: Russell Sage Foundation.

Smith, Vicki. 2002. *Crossing the Great Divide: Worker Risk and Opportunity in the New Economy*. Ithaca, NY: Cornell University Press.

Sonfield, Adam, Jennifer Froster, Ruth Dawson, and Laura Lindberg. "COVID-19 Job Losses Threaten Insurance Coverage and Access to Reproductive Health Care for Millions." *Health Affairs Blog*, August 3, 2020. https://www.healthaffairs.org/do/10.1377/hblog20200728 .779022/full/.

Sousa-Poza, Alfonso, and Andrés A. Sousa-Poza. 2007. "The Effect of Job Satisfaction on Labor Turnover by Gender: An Analysis for Switzerland." *Journal of Socio-Economics* 36(6): 895–913.

Spalter-Roth, Roberta, and Cynthia Deitch. 1999. "'I Don't Feel Right Sized; I Feel Out-of-Work Sized': Gender, Race, Ethnicity, and the Unequal Costs of Displacement." *Work and Occupations* 26(4): 446–82.

Stainback, Kevin, and Donald Tomaskovic-Devey. 2012. *Documenting Desegregation: Racial and Gender Segregation in Private Sector Employment since the Civil Rights Act*. New York: Russell Sage Foundation.

Stevens, Ann Huff. 1997. "Persistent Effects of Job Displacement: The Importance of Multiple Job Losses." *Journal of Labor Economics* 15(1): 165–88.

Stone, Chad, and William Chen. 2014. "Introduction to Unemployment Insurance." *Center on Budget and Policy Priorities*, July 30.

Stone, Pamela. 2007. *Opting Out? Why Women Really Quit Careers and Head Home*. Berkeley: University of California Press.

Stone, Pamela, and Meg Lovejoy. 2019. *Opting Back In: What Really Happens When Mothers Go Back to Work*. Oakland: University of California Press.

Stowe, Harriet Beecher, and Catharine Esther Beecher. 2002. *American Woman's Home*. New Brunswick, NJ: Rutgers University Press.

Strully, Kate W. 2009. "Job Loss and Health in the U.S. Labor Market." *Demography* 46(2): 221–46.

Sutherland, Jean-Anne. 2010. "Mothering, Guilt, and Shame." *Sociology Compass* 4(5): 310–21.

Sweeney, Megan M. 2002. "Two Decades of Family Change: The Shifting Economic Foundations of Marriage." *American Sociological Review* 67, no. 1 (February): 132–47.

Sweet, Stephen, and Phyllis Moen. 2012. "Dual Earners Preparing for Job Loss: Agency, Linked Lives, and Resilience." *Work and Occupations* 39 (1): 35–70.

Taylor, Keeanga-Yamahtta. 2019. *Race for Profit: How Banks and the Real Estate Industry Undermined Black Homeownership*. Chapel Hill, NC: UNC Press Books.

Timmermans, Stefan, and Iddo Tavory. 2012. "Theory Construction in Qualitative Research: From Grounded Theory to Abductive Analysis." *Sociological Theory* 30(3): 167–86.

Tomaskovic-Devey, Donald, Melvin Thomas, and Kecia Johnson. 2005. "Race and the Accumulation of Human Capital across the Career: A Theoretical Model and Fixed-Effects Application." *American Journal of Sociology* 111(1): 58–89.

Townsend, Nicholas W. 2002. *The Package Deal: Marriage, Work, and Fatherhood in Men's Lives*. Philadelphia: Temple University Press.

Umberson, Debra. 1992. "Gender, Marital Status, and the Social Control of Health Behavior." *Social Science & Medicine* 34(8): 907–917.

United States Department of Agriculture, Center for Nutrition Policy and Promotion. 2014. "Official USDA Food Plans: Cost of Food at Home at Four Levels, U.S. Average, December 2013." January. https://fns-prod.azureedge.net/sites/default/files/usda_food_plans_cost_of_food/CostofFoodDec2013.pdf.

U.S. Department of Labor. N.d. "Continuation of Health Coverage (COBRA)." Accessed October 7, 2020. https://www.dol.gov/general/topic/health-plans/cobra.

Van Horn, Carl, Cliff Zukin, and Allison Kopicki. 2014. *Left Behind: The Long-Term Unemployed Struggle in an Improving Economy*. New Brunswick, NJ: John J. Heldrich Center for Workforce Development.

Vanneman, Reeve, with Lynn Cannon. 1987. *The American Perception of Class*. Philadelphia: Temple University Press.

Warikoo, Natasha K. 2016. *The Diversity Bargain: And Other Dilemmas of Race, Admissions, and Meritocracy at Elite Universities*. Chicago: University of Chicago Press.

Warren, Elizabeth, and Amelia Warren Tyagi. 2003. *The Two-Income Trap: Why Middle-Class Mothers and Fathers Are Going Broke*. New York: Basic Books.

Watson, Nathaniel F., M. Safwan Badr, Gregory Belenky, Donald L. Bliwise, Orfeu M. Buxton, Daniel Buysse, David F. Dinges, James Gangwisch, Michael A. Grandner, Clete Kushida et al. 2015. "Recommended Amount of Sleep for a Healthy Adult: A Joint Consensus Statement of the American Academy of Sleep Medicine and Sleep Research Society." *Journal of Clinical Sleep Medicine* 11(06): 591–92.

Weber, Max. 2013. *The Protestant Ethic and the Spirit of Capitalism*. New York: Routledge.

Weeden, Kim A., and David B. Grusky. 2005. "The Case for a New Class Map." *American Journal of Sociology* 111(1): 141–212.

Weisshaar, Katherine. 2018. "From Opt Out to Blocked Out: The Challenges for Labor Market Re-Entry after Family-Related Employment Lapses." *American Sociological Review* 83: 34–60.

Weisshaar, Katherine, and Tania Cabello-Hutt. 2020. "Labor Force Participation over the Life Course: The Long-Term Effects of Employment Trajectories on Wages and the Gendered Payoff to Employment." *Demography* 57(1): 33–60.

West, Candace, and Don H. Zimmerman. 1987. "Doing Gender." *Gender & Society* 1(2): 125–51.

West, Rachel, Indivar Dutta-Gupta, Kali Grant, Melissa Boteach, Claire McKenna, and Judy Conti. 2016. *Strengthening Unemployment Protections in America: Modernizing Unemployment Insurance and Establishing a Jobseeker's Allowance*. Washington, DC: Center for American Progress.

Western, Bruce, Deirdre Bloome, Benjamin Sosnaud, and Laura Tach. 2012. "Economic Insecurity and Social Stratification." *Annual Review of Sociology* 38(1): 341–59.

Whitaker, Elizabeth Anne. 2016. "Moving On to Stay Put." In *Beyond the Cubicle: Job Insecurity, Intimacy, and the Flexible Self*, 203–28. New York: Oxford University Press.

Whyte, William Hollingsworth. 1956. *The Organization Man*. New York: Simon and Schuster.

Williams, Christine L. 2018. "The Gender of Layoffs in the Oil and Gas Industry." In *Research in the Sociology of Work: Precarious Work*, Vol. 31, edited by Arne L. Kalleber and Steven. P. Vallas, 215–41. Bingley, UK: Emerald Publishing.

Williams, Deadric T. 2019. "A Call to Focus on Racial Domination and Oppression: A Response to 'Racial and Ethnic Inequality in Poverty and Affluence, 1959–2015.'" *Population Research and Policy Review* 38(5): 655–63.

Williams, Joan. 2000. *Unbending Gender: Why Family and Work Conflict and What to Do about It.* New York: Oxford University Press.

Wilson, George, and Vincent Roscigno. 2015. "End of an Era? Managerial Losses of African American and Latinos in the Public Sector." *Social Science Research* 54:36–49.

Wing, Nick, and Arthur Delaney. 2017. "Tom Corbett, Pennsylvania Governor: Drug Users Boosting Unemployment Rate (UPDATE)." *HuffPost*, December 6.

Wingfield, Adia Harvey. 2009. "Racializing the Glass Escalator: Reconsidering Men's Experiences with Women's Work." *Gender & Society* 23(1): 5–26

———. 2013. *No More Invisible Man: Race and Gender in Men's Work.* Philadelphia: Temple University Press.

———. 2019. *Flatlining: Race, Work, and Health Care in the New Economy.* Oakland: University of California Press.

Yang, Yang. 2008. "Social Inequalities in Happiness in the United States, 1972 to 2004: An Age-Period-Cohort Analysis." *American Sociological Review* 73(2): 204–26.

Young, Cristobal. 2012. "Losing a Job: The Nonpecuniary Cost of Unemployment in the United States." *Social Forces* 91(2): 609–34.

Zuelke, Andrea E., Tobias Luck, Matthias L. Schroeter, A. Veronica Witte, Andreas Hinz, Christoph Engel, Cornelia Enzenbach, Silke Zachariae, Markus Loeffler, Joachim Thiery et al. 2018. "The Association between Unemployment and Depression-Results from the Population-Based LIFE-Adult-Study." *Journal of Affective Disorders* 235:399–406.

INDEX

Page numbers in *italics* indicate tables, charts, and figures.
Book titles are listed under the author's name.

generalizability, 254,

Gerson, Kathleen, 130, 261n37, 280n16, 284n3, 284n4

Gerstel, Naomi, 143, 262n56, 263n5, 269n36, 273n2, 277n58

Glaser, Barney G., 254

good jobs and bad jobs, segmentation of labor market into, 31–32, 39–40, 89–90

Goodman, Ellen, 110

Gough, Margaret, 131, 255–56n3

Gould-Werth, Alix, 219, 259n18, 270n48

Great Depression, ix, 1, 4, 34, 102, 209, 218

Great Recession: accelerated job loss in, 209; gender and, 27, 204, 260n29; health insurance, loss of, 105, 108; immediate responses to job loss in, 70; insecurity and, 80, 81, 97; paths to job loss and, 39; twenty-first-century job loss, different nature of, 15, 23, 27, 30, 32, 259n20, 260n29

great risk shift/great cost shift, 107, 223

Greenhouse, Steven, 76

guilt gap: concept of, 10, 210, 212; health/health insurance and, 108–11, 195; healthy behaviors and, 122–24; household responsibilities and, 131, 141, 142–43, 144, 149, 205; motherhood ideals and, 214. See also self-sacrifice; health/health insurance, lack of guilt felt by men regarding; health/health insurance, self-sacrifice by/guilt of women regarding

Hacker, Jacob, 76, 107, 223

hard work, American belief in importance of, 226–27

Hays, Sharon, 131–32, 272n24, 282n21

health care jobs, for women, 278n26

health/health insurance, 104–25; ACA, 106, 111, 115, 119, 120, 204, 222, 223, 224; CHIP, 106–7, 111, 124, 216; class and, 105; COBRA coverage, 64, 116–19, 272n38; college education and, 20; debt related to, 96; employment, health coverage tied to, 104–8,

223; food and health, 121–24; gender and, 10, 11, 105, 108–25; guilt gap and, 108–11, 195; healthy behaviors, gender and eschewing/practicing, 121–24; lack of guilt felt by men regarding, 116–21, 125; Medicaid, 104, 107, 120, 125, 198, 216; mental health, impact of job loss on, 33, 67, 99, 100–102; one year after job loss, 182–83, 186, 188–90, 193, 195, 198, 203–6; participant sample distribution regarding, 271nn7–9, 272nn25–26, 272–73nn37–41, 273n43, 273n45, 273n50; policy recommendations regarding, 222–24; seeking/not seeking insurance, 105, 108; seeking/not seeking medical care, 105–6, 108; self-sacrifice by/guilt of women regarding, 108–16, 124–25; sleep habits and patterns, 123–24; stress-related health issues, job loss leading to, 24–25; unemployment episodes harming, 9; VA benefits, 120

Heckman, James, 87

Henly, Julia, 263n9, 277n65, 283n27

Hispanic. See race

Hochschild, Arlie: The Second Shift, 133; The Time Bind, 253

Hodges, Melissa, 278n26

homelessness/eviction, 7, 81, 217, 281n31

household responsibilities, 126–50; bargaining theory and, 130; childcare and middle-class families, 138–39, 175; childcare and working-class families, 141, 143, 147–48, 170–71, 175; "extensive mothering" norms and, 139, 276n48, 277n64; family assistance with, 132, 141, 148; feminist scholarship on, 261n35, 261n36, 261n37, 272n30, 276n45; "fun dad" role, males undertaking, 134, 135, 145, 147; guilt gap and, 131, 141, 142–43, 144, 149, 205; indoor chores, 133, 136, 137, 145; "intensive mothering" norms and, 131–32, 137, 277n64; looking for work and, 170–71, 175–81, 221–22; marital discord over, 205–6; men in female-dominated fields or

change versus job loss, 38–39, 41; life course approach to, 35–36; lockstep workers, 41, 42–45, 55, 203, 263–64n10; participants' experience of, 36–42; transitory work pathway, 41, 42, 45–48, 55–56, 264n12

Patterson, Sarah, 42

Perkins, Frances, 102, 218

Pew Research Center, 81, 129, 130, 192, 281n19

policy recommendations, 209–29; aims and goals of, 226–29; childcare credit expansion, 220–22; clarification of current unemployment policies, 215–17; health insurance provisions, 222–24; incentives to return to work, 224–26; inequality, job loss reproducing and generating, 210–15; recalculating unemployment benefits and payments, 217–20; regularity of job loss in today's economy and, 209–10; tolls of job loss for all unemployed, 210; wage gap, decreasing, 222

positive aspects of unemployment: children, ability to spend more time with, 85, 100; as opportunity, 101; as "time off," 8, 34, 101, 138, 157, 162–65, 169, 175–76, 225

poverty: health/health insurance and, 104, 106, 124; insecurity after job loss and, 82, 85, 90, 103; job searches affected by, 11; looking for work and, 168, 169, 170, 174, 178; minimum unemployment benefits and, 22–23; nonworking spouses, households with, 26, 82; one year after job loss, 196, 199, 207; policy recommendations and, 212, 217–18, 220, 222, 225–29

Pregnancy Discrimination Act, 47

privilege: advantages of class, gender and/or race, 6, 11, 19, 52, 132, 186, 193–94, 206, 210–11, entitlement felt by middle-class men, 11, 163, 175–76, 181; unawareness of own systemic advantages, 11, 258n22. See also class; gender; inequality; middle-class men; race

Pugh, Allison, 70, 208, 269n28, 279n33

race: chronic unemployment and, 52–53; class identification by, 19; discrimination 6, 60, 67–69, 252, 256n8, 257n10, 266n20, 266n21, 266n24; emotional toll of discriminatory firings, 60, 67–69; household responsibilities and, 132; insecurity, exposure to, 94, 96, 97, 269n40; interviewer bias/positionality and, 252; job-seeking networks, access to, 11, 193; limitations of study regarding, 6–7, 251; moral judgment of unemployment in America and, 227; rehiring differences and, 260n30; schedule control issues and, 283n32; self-sacrifice by women and, 113; unemployment insurance/benefits, access to, 9, 172, 227, 270n47, 283n31; wage gap and, 69; whiteness as a credential of, 52

Rao, Aliya, 33, 82, 128, 158, 255n3, 269n29, 284n12; *Crunch Time: How Married Couples Confront Unemployment*, 33, 283n2

Ray, Victor, 52

Reczek, Corinne, 273n54,

redistributive policies, American attitudes toward, 227–28

replaceability/expendability, feelings of, 60, 61–64

return to work. *See* looking for work

Ridgeway, Cecilia, 27, 260n25, 260n26, 279n46

risk aversion, gender, and unemployment, 54–55

Risman, Barbara, 260n24, 260n26

Rivera, Lauren, 11

Roehling, Patricia, 41, 42, 263–64n10

Roosevelt, Franklin Delano (FDR), 102, 218

Ruppanner, Leah, 274n19

Sassler, Sharon, 140, 144

savings, availability of: insecurity and, 89–91, 93–97, 269n40; looking for work and, 172–75; one year after job loss, 187, 191, 195, 196–97, 203

working-class men (*continued*)
  response to job loss by, 60, 65, 66, 100–101; insecurity, exposure to, 83, 86, 89, 103, 174, 178; labor force attachment, and, 32; lack of guilt, 176; looking for work, 10, 157, 162, 165–68, 219; stigma about job loss, 32; one year after job loss, 185, 189, 196, 199–201; unemployment benefits on, impact of generosity of, 32. *See also* household responsibilities; marriage and family
working-class women: guilt over job loss, 109, 127; health/health insurance/healthy behaviors and, 111–12, 122, 123–24; household

responsibilities and, 126–28, 129, 139–44 148, 149, 175, 178–79, 180, 213; immediate response to job loss by, 60, 64, 101; insecurity, exposure to, 83–86, 103, 107, 174, 213; labor force attachment, and, 30, 100, 134–35, 177; looking for work, 11, 157, 158, 161, 168–71, 180; motherhood beliefs, cultural norms about, 29, 113; one year after job loss, 184, 185, 194–95, 196–99, 213; severances, lack of, 72, 74–75, 212; as transitory workers, 41, 46–47; work opportunities, 31. *See also* guilt gap; household responsibilities; marriage and family; single parents

INDEX OF PARTICIPANTS

A NOTE ON THE TYPE

This book has been composed in Arno, an Old-style serif typeface in the classic Venetian tradition, designed by Robert Slimbach at Adobe.